Admiral
of the
New Empire

Dewey as Admiral of the Navy, in full dress and wearing the Tiffany sword.
(Official U.S. Navy Photo)

Admiral
of the
New Empire

The Life and Career of George Dewey

RONALD SPECTOR

LOUISIANA STATE UNIVERSITY PRESS
BATON ROUGE

ISBN 0–8071–0078–1
Library of Congress Catalog Card Number 73–908070
Copyright © 1974 by Louisiana State University Press
All rights reserved
Manufactured in the United States of America

Designed by Albert Crochet. Composed in Harris Intertype CRT Times Roman, and printed
and bound by Graphic Composition, Incorporated, Athens, Georgia.

*To my parents and
to Dianne.*

Contents

Illustrations

Preface

Thirty years ago, in what is probably the most notable American naval biography, Elting Morison examined the career of Admiral William S. Sims. He found Sims and the institution he represented thoroughly admirable. Today, after the experience of Vietnam, few historians would be quite so willing to view the military in such a favorable light. Yet American historical writing about the navy, with some recent notable exceptions, remains largely uncritical and even laudatory about its subject. In a recent study of the naval officer corps, Professor Peter Karsten observes that "there are no biographies or composite biographies written about American naval officers in a critical or even detached tone."* This book is one attempt at such a biography. In it I have tried to provide a critical, although not, I hope, an unsympathetic, look at one of the more neglected figures in naval history.

Aside from popular books on the admiral written immediately after his victory at Manila Bay there have been only two scholarly studies of Dewey: Laurin Hall Healy and Luis Kutner, *The Admiral* (Chicago, 1944); and Richard S. West, Jr., *Admirals of American Empire: The Combined Story of George Dewey, Alfred Thayer Mahan, Winfield Scott Schley, and William Thomas Sampson* (Indianapolis, 1948). Written almost thirty years ago, and without benefit of access to the Navy Department records or the Dewey family correspondence (although Healy and Kutner were furnished some items by the admiral's son), these books are necessarily incomplete.

* Peter Karsten, *The Naval Aristocracy: The Golden Age of Annapolis and the Emergence of Modern American Navalism* (New York, 1972), 427.

Neither devotes more than a few pages to Dewey's long tenure as admiral of the navy from 1900 to 1917.

Given the inadequacies of the older studies of Dewey, is a new one really necessary? Even the admiral's most worshipful admirers would never have maintained that Dewey was a fascinating personality. Indeed, as a man, rather than a naval hero, he was quite unremarkable. Set against his more colorful contemporaries like Alfred Thayer Mahan, Theodore Roosevelt, Stephen B. Luce, John Hay, William S. Sims, and Leonard Wood, he appears a pale figure indeed. Before his meteoric rise to fame in 1898, he had devised no new weapons, planned no great campaigns, written no important pieces, explored no uncharted seas, and contributed no new strategic insights to the navy. He was, in short, an ordinary naval officer.

Precisely because he was so ordinary, Dewey's attitudes and beliefs may well have been far more representative of the naval officer corps than those of the "stars" like Mahan or Sims. But Dewey's career is of interest not only because of what it tells us about the naval officer corps but also, and more importantly, because of what it tells us about American naval policy after 1900. Most studies of Dewey's life would lead one to believe that his career reached a conclusion with his victories at Manila in 1898 and his tumultuous welcome home in 1899. In fact, Dewey remained on active duty for the next eighteen years as president of the General Board of the Navy, head of the Joint Army-Navy Board, and elder statesman of the sea service. Despite his long experience, his immense prestige, and his real ability as an administrator and strategist, Dewey was clearly out of his depth in these roles. He brought to his position the outlook, attitudes, and habits acquired during a long career in the late nineteenth-century navy. These habits of thought and action proved increasingly inappropriate to the rapidly changing political and military conditions of the early twentieth century.

Another man might have transcended the limitations of his background; conversely, he might have broken under the strain. Dewey did neither. He worked hard and conscientiously and, according to his lights, did the best he could. He attempted, with progressively less success, to steer a middle course between the militant younger officers who demanded a radical reform of the organization and operation of the navy and the defenders of the status quo who refused to recognize any shortcomings in the service. The achievements of the American naval establishment, as well as its failures, were not entirely of his making, but he was nevertheless heavily involved in both.

A study of Dewey's career presents certain practical problems. There is first of all a surprising dearth of sources. The Vermont Historical Society collection of Dewey papers is helpful for Dewey's early life but does not go much beyond the Civil War. The main group of Dewey papers is the large, and largely useless, collection in the Library of Congress. As a national idol the admiral naturally sent and received a great many letters after 1898, but these are seldom concerned with matters of substance. There are relatively few letters of any kind in the collection which pertain to Dewey's life before his appointment as commodore of the Asiatic Squadron in 1897. Dewey's *Autobiography* is helpful in this regard, but it is far from a completely candid or reliable document. The book was largely written for the admiral by the journalist Frederick Palmer, who relied heavily on previously published stories for his accounts of Dewey's early years. Dewey was, in any case, an extremely reticent, not to say secretive, person and seldom allowed his correspondence, either public or private, to give him away. Few of his contemporaries have left any record of their impression of the admiral, and what few descriptions exist are largely stylized tributes to a naval hero.

Although there is a paucity of material on Dewey's personal life and his pre–1898 career, there is an overabundance of material on Dewey's official life as admiral of the navy. The records of the Navy Department contain a vast number of papers signed by Dewey, but this gives rise to another problem: how to determine which papers were actually prepared by Dewey or by his direction and which papers were merely passed along for his signature. Fortunately, there is a means of partially overcoming this problem. The letters which Dewey wrote to his son, George Goodwin Dewey (which have only recently become available) often contain frank discussions by the admiral of the issues of the day and important episodes in his career. These letters are supplemented by those of the second Mrs. Dewey, Mildred McLean Hazen, who often discussed important incidents in the admiral's career with her stepson. In addition, Mrs. Dewey kept a diary, preserved in the Library of Congress, in which she often recorded her husband's opinions and conversations. Using these as a guide, supplemented by a few letters to friends in the main collection, I have tried to give major attention to those issues and events with which Dewey appears to have been personally concerned.

The intense popular interest in Dewey at the turn of the century predictably produced a large number of "Dewey stories" and anecdotes. Many of these have been uncritically repeated by historians down to the present day. In the work that follows I have endeavored to include only incidents and conversations which were recorded by a participant soon after the event took place or can be independently documented or have been recorded by more than one source. This has meant omitting some colorful but dubious anecdotes such as the story of Dewey's rescuing a drowning shipmate at the Battle of Port Hudson or making anti-German remarks to the German-bred mayor of Chicago.**

** The Port Hudson incident is in most of the 1899 era popular biographies cited in the bibliography. The story of Dewey's alleged anti-German (and anti-Semitic and anti-Italian) remarks is told in Carter H. Harrison, *Growing Up with Chicago* (Chicago, 1944), 157.

Acknowledgments

A great many people assisted in various ways in the preparation of this book. Kenneth Hagan and Allan Millett took time from their own busy schedules to give the entire manuscript a close and thorough reading. Peter Karsten kindly allowed me to make use of his *The Naval Aristocracy* while it was still in manuscript and also offered numerous suggestions. William Cooper, Gary Crump, Harold Langely, and Karl Roider all read parts of the book in various stages of completion.

Rear Admiral John D. Hayes and Captain Paul R. Schratz first initiated me into the mysteries of naval affairs when I was a graduate student, and they have continued to be of help since then. Like many other historians, I have also benefited from the advice and assistance of Doris Maguire, formerly of the United States Naval Academy Library.

I owe a special debt of thanks to Chief of the Operational Archives Division of the Office of Naval History Dean C. Allard, and to his staff, particularly Kathy Lloyd and May Seaton. I am also grateful to Aloha P. South of the Old Military Records Division, National Archives; William Cunliffe of the Modern Military Records Division; Sandra Wrangel of the Diplomatic Records Branch; and Charles Cooney and Mary Wolfskill of the Manuscript Division of the Library of Congress.

Charles Morrisey and his capable staff at the Vermont Historical Society made my research in Montpelier most rewarding, as did Anthony Nicholosi, Archivist of the United States Naval War College and Richard Sommers of the United States Army Military History Research Collection. I have also benefited from the advice of Leroy F. Eure, former librarian of the Naval War College.

Jane Kleiner of the Louisiana State University Library was most helpful in securing for me the loan of many strange and outlandish books "the like of which hath never been seen before in East Baton Rouge Parish . . . nor ever shall be again. . . ."

Helene Masson and Mary Ronan Clarke displayed amazing resourcefulness in transforming my illegible scrawl into typescript. Charles East and Leslie Phillabaum, of the LSU Press, were both helpful in bringing the manuscript to publication. Mr. Philip K. Lundeberg provided invaluable aid in locating suitable photographs.

Any resemblances to style which this book may possess result from my association with two master writers, Gaddis Smith, my dissertation adviser at Yale University, and Charles MacDonald, Chief of the Current History Branch, United States Army Center of Military History.

Finally, my Washington colleagues, Jeffrey J. Clarke and Warner Starke, who share my office, have offered loud and persistent suggestions as to what I could do with Admiral Dewey.

The views and conclusions expressed below are entirely my own and do not reflect the views of any of the abovementioned individuals or of the United States government.

Admiral
of the
New Empire

<><><><><><><><><><><><><><><><><><><><><><><><><><><><><><><><><><><><><><><><>

CHAPTER I

Obscurity

War was almost an anticlimax. After the shock of the *Maine* disaster, the electrifying newspaper headlines, the heated arguments in the House and Senate, the mob rally in Virginia which burned President McKinley in effigy,[1] the chilling speech by Senator Redfield Proctor of Vermont describing the horrors he had seen in Cuba—after all these things the joint resolution passed by Congress on April 20, 1898, calling for Cuban independence and empowering the president to use the armed forces of the United States to attain this end seemed rather weak medicine.

All eyes were on Cuba where the navy had begun a blockade of the island's ports. In the United States the people responded with enthusiasm to the call for volunteers. William Jennings Bryan and Theodore Roosevelt had both undertaken to raise a regiment while "Buffalo Bill" Cody explained to readers of the New York *World* that he could drive the Spaniards from Cuba with thirty thousand Indian braves. In Denver, Mrs. Martha Shute announced that she planned to raise a regiment made up entirely of women.[2]

April 24, the first Sunday of the war, was a quiet day in Washington. In the ornate State War and Navy Building the offices were nearly deserted save for a few clerks and duty officers. Both Secretary of the Navy John D. Long and Secretary of State William R. Day were absent, but Rear Admiral Arendt S. Crowninshield, chief of the Bureau of Navigation, the navy's most important bureau, was at his post in the navy wing. Down the hall from the admiral,

1. H. Wayne Morgan, *William McKinley and His America* (Syracuse, 1963), 367.
2. Charles H. Brown, *The Correspondents' War* (New York, 1967), 159.

1

in the cypher room, Lieutenant H. H. Whittesley, the duty officer, and Samuel C. Hudwell, the duty clerk, were thumbing through the morning papers when a messenger entered with a coded telegram. It was from the commander-in-chief of the Asiatic Squadron at Hong Kong. He had been informed by the British governor-general that a state of war existed between the United States and Spain, and, in accordance with the rules of neutrality, had been requested to leave the port within twenty-four hours.

As soon as the message was decoded, Lieutenant Whittesley took it to Admiral Crowninshield. Crowninshield glanced at the telegram and immediately departed for the White House to see President McKinley. As he left, he remarked to Whittesley that "now there was no other place for them to go but Manila."[3] Secretary Long and Secretary of State William R. Day, who had been reached by telephone, joined Crowninshield at the White House. A meeting with the president was held at the conclusion of which the admiral was ordered to prepare a suitable telegram instructing the Asiatic Squadron to attack the Spanish forces at Manila. Crowninshield scribbled some notes on a piece of paper and handed them to the president, who made a few changes and then told Crowninshield to have the message put in cypher.

Later in the day, Long took the completed telegram back to the White House and returned with the president's signature. A few minutes later, the telegram was tapped out over the open wires to the Asiatic Squadron twelve thousand miles away: "War has commenced between the United States and Spain. Proceed at once to the Philippines. Commence operations against the Spanish squadron. You must capture or destroy. Use utmost endeavors. Signed, Long."[4] That was all. The success of the American war effort in the Pacific depended now entirely on the Asiatic Squadron of four

3. H. H. Whittesley to John D. Long, August 22, 1901, in Record Group 45, Area 10 file, National Archives (hereinafter cited as RG 45, Area 10 file).

4. The three principal sources on the writing of this famous telegram are all in general agreement as to what took place on April 24. These sources are Whittesley to Long, August 22, 1901, in RG 45, Area 10 file; Samuel C. Hudwell (the duty clerk) to Captain H. A. Baldridge, August 27, 1940, in RG 45, Miscellaneous Correspondence; and John D. Long to Agnes Long, October 9, 1898, Long Papers, cited in John A. S. Grenville and George B. Young, *Politics, Strategy, and American Diplomacy* (New Haven, 1967), 270.

small cruisers and two gunboats and on the professional skill and nerve of its commander, Commodore George Dewey.

The man whose victory would shortly elevate him to the status of instant folk hero among his fellow countrymen was already over sixty years old and had spent nearly forty years in the United States Navy. In many ways he was a typical naval officer; no more talented and certainly no better known than many of his fellows. The anxieties, attitudes, and aspirations which characterized most of his colleagues were also characteristic of him. During the next two decades, however, he would occupy a position of prestige and influence in public affairs unequaled by any other naval officer before or since. The habits of thought and action acquired during his long career rendered him quite unsuited to the role of naval statesman he would shortly be called upon to fulfill. A genial and obliging person who disliked controversy, he had the knack of giving people the impression that he agreed with them, whatever their point of view. He had the tendency, common among such men, of trying to reconcile the irreconcilable, and many of his "compromises" in controversial matters served only to baffle and infuriate all concerned. Intensely loyal to his friends and colleagues, he would come to their defense even if it meant compromising his own views and convictions.

Like many career naval officers he was concerned above all with the maintenance of his professional and personal reputation or "honor," as nineteenth-century writers usually referred to it. The obligation to guard one's "honor," strongly impressed upon the naval officer from his first days at Annapolis, presented a special problem to Dewey as admiral of the navy. As one of the leading naval heroes of his day, his "honor," or prestige, was correspondingly very great. Anything which might cause that prestige to be called into question—an incorrect judgment in naval matters, an unpopular or controversial stand on naval policy—had to be avoided at all costs. How to maintain his reputation ("honor"), and still function effectively as the navy's advocate in unpopular as well as popular questions, was a problem Dewey never solved.[5] This, then,

5. For a discussion of the concept of "honor" and its role in the nineteenth-century navy see Peter Karsten, *The Naval Aristocracy: The Golden Age of Annapolis and the Emergence*

was the man whose victory in an obscure corner of the world was to thrust him into the very vortex of public affairs in the confused and turbulent years between the turn of the century and the First World War.

George Dewey was born in Montpelier, Vermont, on the day after Christmas, 1837. Although his biographers after 1898 delighted in tracing his descent from such worthies as Charlemagne and Alexander the Great, his immediate ancestors occupied a somewhat humbler station in life. His father, Julius Yemans Dewey, was a graduate of the medical school of the University of Vermont and a prominent local physician. He was a founder and later president of the National Life Insurance Company, a very profitable enterprise in which George's two older brothers, Charles and Edward, later served as president and vice president, respectively.

Dewey, his two brothers, and a younger sister, Mary, spent their early years in a moderate-sized white frame house which fronted on the Vermont State House. When Dewey was five years old his mother died of tuberculosis, leaving Dr. Dewey a widower with four young children. He later remarried. Dewey remembered little of his mother, but his relations with his father appear to have been extraordinarily close. In his autobiography, Dewey recalled: "To my father's influence in my early training, I owe primarily all that I have accomplished. . . . From him I inherited a vigorous constitution and an active temperament. . . . He was one of those natural leaders to whom men turn for unbiased advice. His ideas of right and wrong were very fixed."[6]

After Dewey became a national idol, old residents of Montpelier, at the urging of eager newspapermen, found little difficulty in "remembering" many colorful and prophetic incidents from Dewey's early years. Gradually, the stories grew with the telling, until today it is impossible to separate fact from fiction.[7] By all accounts, however, young Dewey was a mischievous, high-spirited

of Modern American Navalism (New York, 1972), 37–41.
    6. *The Autobiography of George Dewey* (New York, 1913), 4.
    7. Dewey repeats many of these tales in his *Autobiography*.

boy. Mrs. Emily J. C. Henry, a childhood acquaintance, recalled that, as a girl, she had once been sitting in the parlor of the Dewey home talking with George's sister, Mary, and other girls, when "the parlor door was suddenly thrown open and 12-year-old George suddenly burst in armed with a large watermelon. 'Catch it,' he cried, tossing it towards us." The watermelon hit the floor, shattering into a thousand pieces, on the Dewey's new carpet. "Help yourselves, girls," called Dewey as he made a hurried retreat.[8] There seems to have been a succession of such incidents and, in 1852, when George was fifteen, his father, possibly in an effort to curb the boy's high spirits, enrolled him in Norwich University, a military school on the Connecticut River across from Hanover, New Hampshire. He remained there two years, adding greatly to his reputation as a practical jokester, and in 1854, received an appointment to the naval academy at Annapolis.

Dewey's appointment to Annapolis came about in a curious way. He had originally hoped to attend the military academy but there was no vacancy for West Point from Vermont. It happened, however, that the young man who was to have been appointed to Annapolis from Dewey's district decided to withdraw. Dewey's father thereupon persuaded Senator Solomon Foote to name George in his place.[9]

The naval academy which George Dewey entered in the fall of 1854 was still a very young institution, having been founded by Secretary of the Navy George Bancroft in 1845; but it had already acquired many of the characteristics it was to retain throughout most of the nineteenth century. The conventional four-year course had just been introduced in 1851 and the cadet corps was quite small, averaging about one hundred "acting midshipmen." Normally only about half the class, and sometimes considerably less than half, remained to receive their commissions at the end of four years. The remainder resigned, failed academically, or were dismissed for disciplinary reasons. In Dewey's class, only fifteen of the sixty men who entered as "plebes," or fourth classmen, remained to graduate.

8. Emily J. C. Henry in Chicago *Journal*, May 7, 1898.
9. Dewey, *Autobiography*, 12–13.

Despite the nostalgia which their Annapolis years later evoked in Dewey and many of his contemporaries, it is clear from their letters and reminiscences that the naval academy of their day was a particularly unpleasant place in which to spend one's youth. "Acting midshipmen," or "naval cadets" as they were sometimes called, were housed in pairs in tiny 15-foot square rooms which were devoid of furniture except for a small iron bed and a bureau "of the simplest kind."[10] Their day began at 6:15 A.M. with an inspection of rooms followed by formation and roll call. Classes began at 8:00 A.M. and continued intermittently until 4:00 P.M. after which there was usually infantry drill or practice with "the great guns" and field artillery pieces. The evening hours were spent at compulsory study until taps at about 9:15 P.M.[11]

Rigid discipline prevailed. Each class of midshipmen was organized into gun crews and ordinarily ate and took instruction together. The crews marched to classes and to meals; they stood, sat, and ate on command; "loud talking is not permitted and breaches of good breeding and decorum are noticed and reported."[12] For minor infractions, the cadets were assigned demerits which varied in number according to the seriousness of their offense. During Dewey's first year at the academy, he managed to accumulate 113 demerits; 200 meant dismissal.

Far from lowering Dewey in the eyes of his classmates, the high spirits and love of practical jokes which earned him many of his demerits actually raised him in their esteem. As one midshipman of the 1860 class explained to his father, "a moderate lot of demerits don't do the least harm but show you are not quite subdued. As a general thing those who run a whole year without them are the outcasts of the institution who are friendless as well as spiritless."[13] If this was true, "Shang" Dewey,[14] at the end of his first year, must have been a very popular boy indeed.

10. Edward C. Marshall, *History of the United States Naval Academy* (New York, 1862), 52.
11. *Ibid.*
12. *Ibid.*
13. Quotation in Karsten, *Naval Aristocracy*, 38.
14. The origins of this nickname are obscure, as are most naval academy nicknames. Dewey, in his *Autobiography*, was unable to recall how he had acquired it.

Far more dreaded by the naval cadets than the demerit system was the notorious "hazing" of the new midshipmen by the upperclassmen. In Dewey's day, this included such practices as making men stand on their heads for hours on end and, in at least one case, an actual tar and feathering.[15] In his autobiography, Dewey recalled that "hazing was rife" but justified it as a way of "whipping raw youths, whose egotism may have been overdeveloped by fond parents, into the habit of comradeship and spirit of corps."[16] In addition to hazing, fighting and dueling appear to have been endemic in the nineteenth-century academy. Dewey appears to have engaged in his share of what he later referred to as "fistic arbitration of grievances." In the course of one such encounter, Dewey later recalled: "I did not lose a second and, springing around the table, I went for him and beat him under the table until we were separated. That was a pretty serious infraction of discipline at mess."[17]

All in all, it was a rather monotonous and confining life which Dewey and his classmates led at the academy. The cadets were not permitted weekends off, athletics were unknown, and the only amusement was a Saturday night stag "hop" in the basement of the old recitation hall. The subjects studied—mathematics, logic, physics, ordnance, navigation, and astronomy—had little intrinsic interest for the kind of active young men who were attracted to the academy in the 1850s.[18] In any case, a great deal of emphasis appears to have been placed on rote memorization which was dull and time-consuming. "The rule was just one endless grind of acquiring knowledge."[19] Consequently, Dewey must have felt considerable pleasure and relief when, on June 18, 1858, he and his fourteen remaining classmates received their diplomas and their commissions as acting midshipmen. By considerable application

15. Karsten, *Naval Aristocracy*, 38.
16. Dewey, *Autobiography*, 18.
17. *Ibid.*, 19.
18. Ironically, the departments such as gunnery, tactics, and steam navigation, which might have attracted the practical-minded, had not kept pace with developments in their fields. They succeeded only in imparting a great deal of obsolete information to the midshipmen. See Karsten, *Naval Aristocracy*, 44–47.
19. Dewey, *Autobiography*, 17.

and effort, Dewey had been able to rise to fifth in his class, an achievement which he attributed to his talent for mathematics and languages.

Following his graduation Dewey was ordered to report immediately to the U.S.S. *Wabash*, a new steam frigate which was to be flagship of the Mediterranean Squadron. Dewey lamented "these cruel orders sending me off to sea without a chance to say goodbye." Barely twenty-one years old and facing the prospect of an 18-month cruise, young George suffered bouts of acute homesickness. "Night after night I have walked the decks till midnight thinking of home and loved ones there and wondering when, if ever, I will be at that fireside again." He soon cheered up, however, and reported to his father that "I have found the service all that I could wish. My ship is a paradise and all her officers gentlemen." Dewey and his four classmates in the *Wabash* had applied together for the same ship and formed a congenial group. "I think we suit each other better than any other five that could be put together" wrote Dewey.[20] One of the five was Henry A. Howison who had graduated one number ahead of Dewey in the class of 1858. Forty years later he was to be Dewey's rival in a more serious competition.

The *Wabash* left Hampton Roads on July 22, 1858, and returned to Brooklyn Navy Yard seventeen months later. Her cruise was quite unremarkable, but during the course of it, Dewey developed an affection for the Mediterranean and its ports, an affection he was to retain all his life. He also had his first experience of the great world of European politics and of the elaborate protocol and ceremony which surround a flagship on foreign station. Exchanging salutes with foreign warships, attending balls and dinners, inspections by the sultan of Turkey and Grand Duke Constantine of Russia—these were heady experiences for a 21-year-old midshipman from a small town in Vermont. So enthralled was Dewey with the spectacle of European political pageantry that he even began to collect photographs and clippings of European statesmen and royalty which he mounted in an album in much the same way that

20. Dewey to Julius Y. Dewey, June 13, July 8, August 11, June 19, 1858, in Dewey Family Correspondence, Vermont Historical Society, Montpelier, Vermont.

youths of a later generation would preserve the pictures of baseball players or movie stars.

To his family in Vermont, Dewey sent colorful, if somewhat naive, descriptions of his experience in foreign climes. Constantinople, where the domes of the mosques are "all like that of our State House" was "a large dirty city filled with dirty Turks, dirtier Greeks, prowling Jews and dogs without number." Rhodes was "miserable" and Cyprus "worse." At Beirut "we had hundreds and hundreds of wild Arabs on board us. . . . They certainly have never seen anything like her [the *Wabash*] before and without a doubt we have rendered the greatest service to our American missionaries."[21]

Like most serious young men of his day, Dewey was of a religious turn of mind and missionaries did not inspire in him the same scorn as in some of his more experienced fellow officers. At the naval academy he had voluntarily conducted Bible classes for local children and in the *Wabash* he was a regular attender at Sunday services where he served as leader of the ship's choir. Throughout his life he carried a small book containing his favorite Bible texts which he read every day.[22]

As an ambitious young midshipman, however, Dewey naturally had other things on his mind besides religion. He was furious when he learned, early in 1859, that Congress had arbitrarily restored to the "active list" twenty-six officers who had been selected by the Navy Department for retirement. "It puts me back some four or five years at least," he explained to his father, "and restores men to active duty who are not worthy to command a dirt cart. . . . But Congress does not wish to know anything of their *moral* character. They only know that these men have brought enough *political influence* to bear at the *right* point! [italics in original]"[23] Dewey's religious faith was to remain strong throughout his life, but his views of the uses of political influence were to mellow considerably.

21. Dewey to Julius Y. Dewey, October 24, 1858, in Dewey Family Correspondence.
22. Sydney K. Evans, "Religion in Leadership," United States Naval Institute *Proceedings*, LIII (June, 1927), 643 (hereinafter cited as USNIP); Dewey to Julius Y. Dewey, August 11, 1858, in Dewey Family Correspondence; E. David Cronin (ed.), *The Cabinet Diaries of Josephus Daniels* (Lincoln, Nebr., 1963), 299.
23. Dewey to Julius Y. Dewey, January 16, 1859, in Dewey Family Correspondence.

After two more short cruises, Dewey returned to the academy in January, 1861, to sit for his lieutenant's examination. He passed out third in his class and received his commission in April, 1861. He was on leave in Montpelier when word of the surrender of Fort Sumter reached Vermont. A few days later, he was on his way to war.

The ship in which Dewey was to serve for the next two years was the old steam frigate *Mississippi*. A veteran of Commodore Perry's expedition to Japan in 1854, she had been considered, at that time, a marvel of mechanical progress; but now, with her enormous side-wheel paddles, she was already obsolescent beside the newer screw-propelled warships of the Union navy and a mere antique beside the new ironclad steamers of the European powers. Dewey joined the *Mississippi* at Boston on May 10, 1861, and a few days later she was on her way south to join the Union blockaders in the Gulf of Mexico. For several weeks after her arrival, the *Mississippi* remained at Key West, Florida, as temporary flagship of the blockading squadron until she was relieved by the frigate *Colorado*. In July, she took up station off Mobile Bay and later off the Mississippi delta as a rather ineffective addition to the blockade squadron.

But greater enterprises were afoot. Around the end of 1861, Mr. Gustavus Vasa Fox, the assistant secretary of the navy, and Secretary Gideon Welles succeeded in persuading President Lincoln and his advisers to agree to an attack on New Orleans from the mouth of the Mississippi River. The loss of this most important commercial city of the South would be a severe blow to the Confederate cause, as well as a psychological victory for the North. A reverse, however, coming at a time when northern arms were meeting with little success on land, might have a disastrous affect on the morale of the Union.

The commander chosen for this undertaking was Captain David Glasgow Farragut. Farragut was over sixty years old when he was given command of the West Gulf Squadron, but "time had not staled nor custom withered" his keen mind or his dynamic personality. "The Department and the country will require of you success," Secretary of the Navy Welles wrote to him in his letter of appointment; and Flag Officer Farragut was not a man to settle for less.[24]

The defenses of New Orleans were formidable. At a bend in the river several miles below the city were two large forts, Fort Jackson on the left bank and Fort St. Philip a little further up the river, on the right. Below Fort Jackson, the Confederates had constructed a barrier composed of eight old schooners connected by chains and anchored across the breadth of the river. Before the forts could be passed, the chain barrier would have to be broken.

It was questionable whether Farragut would be able to get his fleet into the river at all. To silence the forts, he would need the aid of his big frigates and steam sloops-of-war like the *Mississippi* and his own flagship, the *Hartford*. These ships were never designed to fight in a river. They were large and unwieldy and could not operate in shallow water.

Several miles below the forts, the Mississippi River, before emptying into the Gulf of Mexico, divides into four streams resembling, as one author has observed, the four claws of a chicken.[25] At the westernmost channel, Southwest Pass, the bar at the entrance was only nineteen feet deep. At the other passes it was still shallower. Most of Farragut's big ships drew far more than nineteen feet of water; they would have to be lightened and towed across the bar. Undeterred by these difficulties, Farragut arrived off Ship Island, in the Gulf of Mexico, on February 18, 1862, and began his preparations for the passage of the forts.

At about this time, the *Mississippi* received a new commander, Captain Melancthon Smith, an officer of the old school, an eccentric and a temperance enthusiast. All six of the officers in the *Mississippi* who were senior to Dewey had by this time been transferred to other ships and Dewey, although only twenty-five years old, was now the executive officer. The *Mississippi*, with a crew of

24. Gideon Welles to David G. Farragut, January 20, 1862, in *Official Records of the Union and Confederate Navies in the War of the Rebellion* (30 vols.; Washington, 1894–1927), Ser. I, Vol. XVIII, p. 8, hereinafter cited as *Official Records, Navies.* Unless otherwise indicated, all citations are to Series I.
25. Richard S. West, Jr., *The Second Admiral: A Life of David Dixon Porter* (New York, 1937), 38.

350 men, would have had about a dozen lieutenants in peacetime. Now, however, young Dewey, two ensigns, and the captain were the only line officers in the ship. Despite their differences in temperament, Smith and his new executive got along well together and, when Farragut proposed assigning a more experienced officer to the *Mississippi* as executive, Captain Smith dissuaded him.[26]

For Dewey, this was undoubtedly one of the most rewarding periods of his career. The pages of his autobiography, usually so stilted, fairly glow with enthusiasm when he speaks of his experiences aboard the *Mississippi*. In Farragut, Dewey found a hero. "Farragut has always been my ideal of the Naval Officer, urbane, decisive, indomitable," he recalled many years later. "Valuable as the training at Annapolis was, it was poor schooling beside that of serving under Farragut in time of war."[27]

On March 18, 1862, the *Mississippi* and the other ships of Farragut's fleet began the laborious task of crossing the bar at the entrance to Southwest Pass. It required four days to drag the *Hartford* and her sister ship, the *Brooklyn*, over the bar, careening them on their sides. The *Mississippi*, however, could not be careened. She would have to be pulled straight across the bar. Farragut ordered that everything movable be taken out of her. Her guns, ammunition, and spare riggings were all transferred to lighters and she retained only enough coal to make the passage across the bar. Then four small steamers ran cables to her and began tugging her slowly over the soft mud while her paddle wheels churned futilely. It took eleven days to drag her into the deep water. Finally, on April 8, Farragut was able to report to the Navy Department that all of his big ships were in the river.[28]

Brigadier General J. O. Barnard, chief engineer of the Army of the Potomac and builder of Fort St. Philip, had advised the secretary of the navy that an attempt to pass the forts and capture the city with the forts still intact was far too dangerous to be undertaken. Either the fleet would have to capture the forts before attacking the city or it would have to wait until troops were available

26. Dewey, *Autobiography*, 51.
27. *Ibid.*, 51–52.
28. Farragut to Welles, March 16, March 18, April 8, 1862, in *Official Records, Navies*, XVIII, 67, 71, and 109.

to attack New Orleans from the land side. "To pass the fort with a fleet and appear before New Orleans is merely a raid, no capture. New Orleans and the river cannot be held until communications are perfectly established."[29] Nevertheless, this is what Farragut proposed to do. He made his decision in the knowledge that his fleet was dangerously short of ammunition and that, once past the forts, his communications with his bases would be very uncertain.

Farragut's decision to proceed boldly with the attack on New Orleans made a profound impression on young Lieutenant Dewey. As he later noted: "Whenever I have ever been in a difficult situation . . . I have asked myself 'what would Farragut do?' . . . I confess I was thinking of him the night we entered Manila Bay and with the conviction that I was doing precisely what he would have done."[30]

On the night of April 20, two Union gunboats, the *Itasca* and *Pinola*, under cover of a heavy bombardment, slipped in among the anchored schooners which formed part of the Confederate barrier, and cut a broad hole through a portion of the chain. Four days later, Farragut was ready to begin the attack. At 2:00 A.M. on the morning of April 24, the *Hartford* signaled the fleet to get underway. The ships were in two columns. The right-hand column, led by the *Cayuga*, was to engage Fort St. Philip. The left hand, led by the flagship *Hartford*, was to engage Fort Jackson.[31] The *Mississippi* was in the right-hand column behind the *Cayuga* and the big steam sloop *Pensacola*. Captain Smith, whose night vision was poor, decided to allow Dewey to maneuver the ship while he directed her guns' crews.

The *Cayuga* passed the fort without being seen but as the *Pensacola* proceeded slowly past, the Confederate batteries opened fire. Captain Morris of the *Pensacola*, hoping to silence the batteries, stopped his ship and fired a full broadside at the forts. When the Confederates began firing again a few moments later, Morris again stopped and fired into the forts.[32] To Dewey, trying to keep station behind the *Pensacola*, this constant starting and stopping was mad-

29. Barnard to Welles, January 28, 1862, *ibid.*, 77.
30. Dewey, *Autobiography*, 50.
31. Farragut to Welles, May 6, 1862, *Official Records, Navies*, XVIII, 198.
32. Henry W. Morris to Farragut, April 28, 1862, *ibid.*, 202.

dening. Twice the *Mississippi* had to stop and reverse her engines to avoid colliding with the *Pensacola*. All of this time, the ships were under continuous fire from the forts.[33]

Observing the scene from the vantage point of the *Mississippi*'s foretop was an illustrator for *Harper's Weekly*. As the man watched the battle, he noticed what appeared to be a giant, lead-gray cigar floating half-submerged in the water and drifting toward the *Mississippi*. It was the Confederate ironclad ram *Manassas*. The *Manassas*, a part of the Confederate fleet defending New Orleans, had originally been a tugboat. When the war began, she had been rebuilt into an egg-shaped ram armed with a single Parrot gun, with only her side and back above the water line. "Here is a queer looking customer on our port bow!" shouted the correspondent to Dewey. The lieutenant glanced at the *Manassas* and ordered the helm hard-a-starboard. Slowly the *Mississippi*'s stern came around to the right, but the more maneuverable ram had already sheared off, away from the Union cruiser. Turning hard to port again, she struck the *Mississippi* a glancing blow just aft of her paddle wheel, causing little damage, and then continued down the river. The *Mississippi* by this time was drawing out of range of the forts and gradually came abreast of the other ships of the Union squadron off the quarantine station.[34]

Meanwhile, Captain A. F. Warley, commander of the *Manassas*, had been having his own troubles. Passing down the river to attack the Union ships below the forts, he came under fire from Fort Jackson. The *Manassas*'s iron plates could not protect her against the heavy guns of the Confederates, and Warley, unable to signal the forts, had no choice but to turn back upriver. Just as dawn was breaking, the lookouts in the Union fleet observed the *Manassas* rounding the bend near the quarantine station. Steaming past the *Mississippi*, Farragut leaned far out of the rigging of the *Hartford* and called to Captain Smith: "Run down that ram." Slowly the *Mississippi* again came around, making a 180-degree turn in the narrow river. The ship shuddered slightly as she worked up to full speed and tore down the river straight toward the *Manassas*. One

33. Dewey, *Autobiography*, 63–64.
34. *Ibid*.

glance at the 1,600-ton *Mississippi* charging down on his vessel "like a steam roller upon a turtle," was enough for Captain Warley. He headed the *Manassas* toward shore, cut the delivery lines, and ordered the crew over the side. Then he drove her onto the shore just as the *Mississippi*, in passing, fired a broadside which penetrated her stern and set the ship on fire. A boarding party from the *Mississippi* completed the work of destruction, and the *Manassas*, now a flaming wreck, drifted free of the bank and floated downriver past the forts to blow up in sight of the Union ships at the head of the passes.[35] The crew of the *Mississippi* could now make out the burning hulks of the rest of the Confederate fleet along the banks of the river. The next morning, the Union ships got underway and anchored off New Orleans. The largest city of the South was in the hands of the enemy.

For Dewey, the months after the battle were an anticlimax. The *Mississippi* was anchored off New Orleans as a guard ship; "our existence was pretty monotonous for naval officers in the midst of a great war. We envied the men on the other ships of the blockade or up the river with Farragut."[36] Nevertheless, there were compensations. "I begin to like New Orleans," Dewey wrote in July, 1862, "and were it not for the people here, should like it *very* much. As it is, it is far preferable to blockading. We have one or two steamers from the North a week, plenty of ice and fresh food, and some pleasant rides and walks on shore."[37]

Although he had small sympathy for "rebels," General Ben Butler's corrupt and arbitrary reign as military governor of New Orleans filled Dewey with disgust. "These people all go home rich it is true," he wrote, after Butler and his gang had been relieved by General Nathaniel Banks, "but there is hardly one whose name is without blots and blemishes. They came out as I have often said not to fight but to make money."[38]

From his quiet duty in New Orleans, Dewey watched the course

---

35. "Extract from Papers of Lieutenant W. F. Warley, C.S. Navy," *Official Records, Navies*, XVIII, 338–43; West, *The Second Admiral*, 32; Dewey, *Autobiography*, 70–71.
36. Dewey, *Autobiography*, 84.
37. Dewey to Julius Y. Dewey, July 15, 1862, in Dewey Family Correspondence.
38. Dewey to Julius Y. Dewey, December 20, 1862, *ibid*.

of the war with increasing anguish. "Let's have no more milk and water work," he wrote after McClellan's defeat in the Peninsular Campaign. "Now is the time to arm and cut loose the slaves. Offer ten dollars for the head of a *guerrilla* (another name for *coward*) and *put this rebellion down* [italics in original]." But the news from the East continued to be bad. After the Second Battle of Bull Run and the Union disaster at Fredericksburg, Dewey wrote to his father, "It seems as if God has forsaken the cause of the Union. . . . I know I am wicked in thinking so, but how else can we account for our late numerous reverses? We have more and as brave men, more money, more everything, and still we are coming out second best. There is something rotten in Denmark."[39] When the *Mississippi* was ordered north, in the spring of 1863, to join Farragut below Port Hudson, Dewey was more than ready.

In order to reduce the flow of supplies to Vicksburg, the last remaining Confederate stronghold on the Mississippi, Farragut had determined to try to pass as many ships as possible by the Confederate batteries near Port Hudson, in Louisiana, where the Red River meets the Mississippi. He intended to use them to link up with the Union forces at Vicksburg and then to interdict the flow of supplies reaching the Confederates via the Red River from Freeport and the West.

The night of March 14, 1863, was chosen for the attack and at 10:00 P.M. the fleet got underway. Each of the big ships—the *Hartford*, *Richmond*, and *Monongahela*—had a steam gunboat lashed alongside to aid them in making headway against the swift current and to pull them clear if they should go aground. Only the *Mississippi* was to make the ascent alone. Just off Port Hudson the Mississippi River makes a sharp, horseshoe bend to the left. At intervals below the bank, on the right side of the river, the Confederates had constructed seven batteries. As the *Hartford* drew abreast of the first battery, the southerners opened fire. The *Hartford* managed to run the gauntlet of enemy fire but the *Richmond*, the next ship in line, was hit by a shell which severed her steam pipe. With her engines rapidly losing steam pressure, the *Richmond* was unable to

39. Dewey to Julius Y. Dewey, July 15, 1862, January 1, 1863, *ibid.*

make any headway in the strong current and turned back down the river.[40]

In the *Mississippi*, the fourth in line behind the *Monongahela*, Dewey again had the conn. Straining into the smoke and darkness, he could barely see the outlines of the *Monongahela* some distance ahead. The rest of the squadron was invisible. Suddenly a large ship loomed up out of the darkness. The ship was heading rapidly down toward the *Mississippi*. Just as the *Mississippi*'s gunners were about to fire on her, she was recognized as the disabled *Richmond*.

At half-past midnight, the *Mississippi* came abreast of the last Confederate batteries and into the most dangerous part of the river just below the horseshoe. Crouched in a rowboat lashed to the *Mississippi*'s bow was a civilian river pilot. Farragut had engaged a pilot for each of the ships to guide them past the forts and around the horseshoe bend. Now the *Mississippi*'s pilot, straining into the gloom, thought he made out the turn directly ahead and ordered: "Starboard the helm; full speed ahead!" At full speed, the *Mississippi* swung to the left—and ran hard onto a mudbank. Captain Smith ordered the engines reversed and steam raised to the maximum pressure, but the ship refused to budge. For thirty-five minutes, the *Mississippi*'s paddle wheels slashed futilely at the soft mud while the Confederates, who had now found the range, poured in a hail of shell.[41] The *Mississippi* was now on fire forward and, around 1:00 A.M., Captain Smith finally gave the order to "Abandon Ship."

Still puffing calmly on his cigar, Smith ordered the sick and wounded into one of the three boats which had not been shot away. Only a small portion of the *Mississippi*'s crew could be crowded into the remaining two boats and these were ordered to make for the nearest bank and then to return immediately. They were so slow in returning, however, that on the second trip, Dewey jumped into one of the boats, determined to make sure that they returned a second time. As the boat touched shore, Dewey ordered four men to remain for the return trip and the rest to take cover behind the

---

40. Farragut to Welles, March 16, 1863, *Official Records, Navies*, XIX, 665; James R. Alden to Welles, March 15, 1863, *ibid.*, 673.
41. Melancthon Smith to Gideon Welles, March 19, 1865, *ibid.*, 680.

levee. "They obeyed one part of my command with alacrity. That is, all but one scrambled over the levee in a free-for-all rush." By threats, pleas, and finally at gunpoint, Dewey managed to man the boats and return to the *Mississippi*. During this episode, the young officer experienced acute anxiety that his actions might be misinterpreted. "It is everywhere the rule that the last man to leave [a ship] should be her captain; and I, as Executive, should be next to last. What if a shot should strike the boat? What if a rifle bullet should get me? All the world would say I had been guilty of about as craven an act as can be placed at the door of any officer." It gives some insight into Dewey's character that, forty years later, after having borne some of the heaviest responsibilities ever placed on an American naval officer, he could describe this episode, which might have sullied his personal reputation, as "the most anxious moment of my career."[42]

In the end, both Dewey and Captain Smith, with all but 64 of the *Mississippi*'s crew of 233, safely reached the Union forces. "I need say nothing now except that she was bravely fought to the very last," wrote Dewey to his father. "I lost everything except what I stood in."[43]

The passage of Port Hudson was a very limited success. Only the *Hartford* and her consort, the *Albatross*, managed to pass the forts that night and enter the upper river. Farragut, undismayed, remarked that the Union losses were regrettable but that one "could not make an omelette without breaking eggs." This was too much for Captain Smith. "He thinks we're an omelette,"[44] he groaned.

After a few weeks ashore in New Orleans, Dewey was ordered to duty as executive officer of the *Monongahela*, which was now serving as Farragut's flagship. It was in the *Monongahela*, in July, 1863, that he had closest call of his career, when a Confederate shell exploded on the ship's quarter deck killing the captain and four other officers but leaving Dewey unscathed. During the next several weeks Dewey exercised de facto command of the *Monon-*

42. Dewey, *Autobiography*, 97.
43. Philip Y. Nicholson, "George Dewey and the Transformation of American Foreign Policy" (Ph.D. dissertation, University of New Mexico, 1971), 59.
44. Dewey, *Autobiography*, 98.

gahela, winning official praise for his "coolness, skill and judgment."[45]

Dewey ended the war a lieutenant commander. At twenty-eight, he had served as executive officer of no less than six ships and participated in four major campaigns as well as numerous spells of patrol and blockade duty. He had also, while stationed in Portsmouth, New Hampshire, met Susan Boardman Goodwin, the daughter of the governor, who was later to become his wife. Their courtship was not a smooth one, however. For one thing, Dewey's commanding officer, Commander A. C. Rhind, appears to have been one of his rivals for Susie's hand.[46] For another, Dewey spent much of his time in Portsmouth engaged in litigation arising out of his having struck a navy yard worker over the head with a speaking trumpet. He apparently felt little remorse over the incident and the resulting $5.00 fine which he was ordered to pay by the court, but he devoted a great deal of time to contesting the assessment of $8.50 in court costs.

The end of the war found Dewey far from Portsmouth serving as the executive officer of the sloop-of-war *Kearsage*, assigned to the European station. The *Kearsage* was known far and wide for her famous victory over the Confederate raider *Alabama* and Dewey was proud of his assignment, but he fretted at his enforced absence from Susie. "I have not heard from Portsmouth for some time and am consequently somewhat uneasy," he confided to his father. "I am *sure* many letters have been lost or I should be very miserable. . . . I am quite worried about my little Susie and do not know what to make of this long silence."[47]

In March, 1866, when Dewey was transferred to the *Canandaigua*, he worried about the effect of the news on Susie. "I am anxious to know how she looks upon this *new* ship. I am already a year out now and to be ordered to a newly commissioned ship and thus put in for another year will seem rather hard. I must tell her of all the money I am going to save. Perhaps that will help matters."[48]

45. *Official Records, Navies*, XX, 334.
46. William M. Clemens, *The Life of Admiral Dewey* (New York, 1899).
47. Dewey to Julius Y. Dewey, October 29, 1865, in Dewey Family Correspondence.
48. Dewey to Julius Y. Dewey, March 16, 1866, *ibid.*

Whatever Susie may have thought of his prolonged absence, the story ended happily when she and Dewey were married in the Episcopal Church of Portsmouth on October 27, 1867. After a brief leave, Dewey took his bride to Annapolis, where he had been assigned as an instructor and officer-in-charge of fourth classmen.

At Annapolis the new superintendent, Admiral David Dixon Porter, was engaged in transforming the naval academy into one of the foremost military schools in the world.[49] Porter revamped the curriculum to allow more time for courses in the sciences and engineering and embarked on a massive building program which included a modern laboratory, a gymnasium, dormitories, and a new brick building to house the newly created Department of Steam Engineering.

Along with many other young couples, the Deweys enjoyed (or endured) the admiral's seemingly endless round of teas, hops, and dinner parties which earned the institution the nickname of "Porter's Dancing Academy." In this congenial and stimulating environment, Dewey and his wife enjoyed three happy years. At the end of that time, Dewey was detached from the academy and ordered to take command of the third-class sloop-of-war *Narragansett*.

Dewey took command of his ship at Portsmouth and brought her into New York Navy Yard for extensive repairs. The ship remained at her moorings for the next three months while her captain vainly awaited orders to sail. Finally, in January, 1871, Dewey was ordered to take command of the store ship *Supply*, which the navy had provided to carry food and medicines donated by Americans to French victims of the fighting in the Franco-Prussian War.

The *Supply* was a sailing ship, old and slow. By the time she reached Cherbourg, the French had surrendered and Paris was in the hands of the Commune. Dewey took his cargo to London to be disposed of and returned to the United States. Upon his arrival he was assigned to the torpedo station at Newport, Rhode Island.

Dewey undoubtedly felt pleased to have a billet ashore since Susie was expecting a child. Shortly before Christmas, 1872, she

49. West, *The Second Admiral*, 303–14.

gave birth to a son, George Goodwin Dewey. Susie, however, failed to recover from the birth of her son and died five days later. Although he never spoke of it, there can be no doubt that the death of Dewey's wife affected him deeply. "He is so crushed," his mother-in-law observed in a letter to a friend shortly after Susie's death.[50] Many years later, as Dewey was leaving San Francisco to take command of the Asiatic Squadron, a well-wisher remarked that he was fortunate in not having to leave a wife behind. "The old man jerked his head toward the officer, pulled a gold watch from his vest pocket, opened its case and displayed a tiny picture inside. 'My wife goes with me always,' the commodore answered quietly."[51]

The years between the age of thirty and sixty are usually the years of a man's greatest professional achievement. For Dewey, however, and for many of his contemporaries like Winfield Scott Schley, Charles S. Sperry, William T. Sampson, Alfred T. Mahan, and others who were to win fame in the Spanish-American War, the years between 1865 and the late 1890s were years of frustration, tedium, and stagnation. In his autobiography, Dewey devotes only one chapter to his thirty-two years of service between 1865 and 1896. These were years of marking time, a hiatus between the excitement and adventure of youth and the fame and responsibility which finally came to him in old age.

In order to understand the peacetime navy in which Dewey spent so many of his working years, it is important to understand two factors which ultimately had a profound impact upon it. The first was the rapid and continuous series of innovations in all phases of naval technology which had begun around 1850 and seemed likely, by the mid-1870s, to transform the whole nature of naval warfare. So rapid was the progress in the development of ordnance, armor, torpedoes, and propelling machinery that, in the 1870s and 1880s, a ship might be obsolete before it was launched. In 1881, Lord Clarence Paget, the parliamentary secretary of the Admiralty, proudly informed the House of Commons that the newest British

50. Mrs. Ichabod Goodwin to Mrs. William H. Parsons, January 24, 1873, in George Goodwin Dewey Papers, Office of Naval History, Washington, D.C.
51. Laurin H. Healy and Luis S. Kutner, *The Admiral* (Chicago, 1944), 4.

battleship "will be armed with the latest type of gun—whatever that may be next year."[52]

The following year, Lord Thomas Bassey, third lord of the Admiralty, published the first volume of his gigantic tome entitled *The British Navy*. In the second half of the first volume, he dutifully described all of the various types of battleships in use in modern navies: central battery ships, turret ships, bow battery ships, barbette ships, mastless turret ships, belt and battery ships, monitors and even saucer-shaped ships in the Russian fleet. "The fashion in building ships-of-war," Prime Minister William E. Gladstone observed, "is as fickle as that of ladies' hats."[53]

Throughout the two decades after the Civil War, the United States Navy remained almost completely untouched by these revolutionary changes. In 1885, the navy was still a collection of wooden or iron-plated cruisers similar to the ships that had fought at New Orleans with Farragut in 1862.[54] In addition, there were a dozen or so over-age monitors of the Civil War vintage which had been repaired and repaired again, until nothing was left of the original ships but their names. Admiral David Dixon Porter likened the ships of the American navy to a Chinese fort on which dragons had been painted to frighten the enemy. "What more painful to one who loved his country," exclaimed Commander Frank G. McNair in 1874, "than to see a fleet armed with smooth-bore guns, requiring close quarters for their development, moving at the rate of 4½ knots!"[55]

Naval officers serving on foreign station were acutely aware of the inferiority of their ships to those of even second-rate powers like Italy, Brazil, and Chile. When Dewey was given command of the old steam sloop *Pensacola* in 1885, he complained that "there was not a fourth-rate British cruiser of modern build that could not easily have kept out of range of her battery, torn her to pieces and set her on fire."[56] A French officer visiting an American man-of-

52. Bernard Brodie, *Seapower in the Machine Age* (Princeton, 1940), 214.
53. Arthur Marder, *The Anatomy of British Seapower* (Hamden, 1964), 1.
54. Many of these ships, like the *Pensacola* and *Richmond*, were still in commission.
55. Frank G. McNair, "Our Fleet Maneuvers in the Bay of Florida and the Navy of the Future," USNIP, I (1874) 162–76.
56. Dewey, *Autobiography*, 158.

war in the 1880s reportedly pointed to her guns and exclaimed nostalgically: "Ah! Capitaine, les vieux canons!"[57]

The second all-pervading fact of life for the officers of the 1865–1898 period was that the navy had an incredible surplus of officers. In 1877, there were over fifty-nine for every ship and by 1882, there was one officer for every four enlisted men. Some men who had been lieutenants in 1869 were still lieutenants in 1881, and many of them had passed fifty years of age.[58]

This surplus of officers made promotion maddeningly slow. The pre–Civil War seniority system, designed to protect the navy from political influences, was still in effect and provided for promotions on a strictly linear basis. If a man lived long enough and avoided spectacular displays of incompetence, he would in his turn, ascend unto admiral; but by that time he would probably have passed the age of sixty. The fortunate survivor usually could spend but a year of two as admiral before reaching the mandatory retirement age of sixty-two.

Under these conditions, the more ambitious and energetic officers felt completely frustrated. Many left the service and those who remained adopted various expedients to alleviate their condition. They lobbied for a more flexible personnel system; they talked, argued, pleaded, and wrote about the need for a more modern navy; and, finally, they attempted to enhance their own professional competence by mastering a technical specialty. Young officers like William Folger, Seaton Schroeder, and Joseph Strauss became experts in the field of ordnance; while others like Bradley Fiske and Frank Sprague pioneered in electricity. In 1882, a group of progressive officers founded the Office of Naval Intelligence which assigned many young officers as attachés. They were thereby given a chance to examine European naval progress at first hand. Other officers had their professional awakening at the Naval War College which Rear Admiral Stephen B. Luce had founded in 1884 and which was to be the scene of Mahan's famous lectures on the

57. Alfred T. Mahan, *From Sail to Steam: Recollections of Naval Life* (New York, 1968), 197.
58. Charles O. Paullin, "A Half Century of Naval Administration," USNIP, XXXIX (September, 1915); Karsten, *Naval Aristocracy*, 50.

influence of seapower upon history. The United States Naval Institute and its *Proceedings*, founded in 1873, served as a forum in which these progressive younger officers, and some older ones as well, could air their ideas and opinions.

These developments formed the backdrop to Dewey's post–Civil War career in the navy. In many ways, however, Dewey was more fortunate than most of his fellow officers. A lieutenant commander at the close of the Civil War, he had the advantage of being a jump or two ahead on the promotion ladder. By the late 1890s he was a commodore, while many men who had graduated from the academy just four or five years later were still lieutenants. He also had the not-inconsiderable advantage of a substantial private income. His share of his father's holdings in the National Life Insurance Company, prudently invested and managed by his brothers, made Dewey a man of some means, particularly by navy standards. In the midst of the 1893 depression, his brother could inform him that most of his investments were still paying dividends and that he was currently worth $68,400, no mean sum in a day when an ensign received a yearly salary of $1,700. In that same year, Dewey was able to give his son George $860 simply to buy clothes for college.[59]

Nevertheless, Dewey shared the frustrations felt by many officers at the antiquated state of the navy. "In those days," he recalled, "naval officers had reason for regretting their choice of a profession in which they had to see officers of other nations enjoying the use of material for keeping up with professional progress which they themselves wholly lacked."[60] He was also in sympathy with most of the progressive programs and causes and was one of a large group of officers who attempted to intervene on behalf of Mahan in 1893 to prevent the budding historian from being ordered to sea.[61] In general, however, his contribution to the great nineteenth-century movement within the service to rebuild and professionalize the navy was inconspicuous. He contributed no articles to the Naval Institute *Proceedings*, never attended the War

59. Charles Dewey to Dewey, February 2, 1891, June 6, 1893, in Dewey Papers, Library of Congress.
60. Dewey, *Autobiography*, 158.
61. Dennis Hart Mahan, Jr., to Alfred T. Mahan, May 3, 1893, cited in Karsten, *Naval Aristocracy*, 344.

College, and was too senior to be an attaché. As for the efforts of the younger officers to lobby for a more flexible personnel system, Dewey loftily dismissed them with the statement: "It has been a rule with me never to join any group of officers in a common effort for bettering their position at the expense of other officers, not to say at the expense of the efficiency of the service."[62] To the end of his life, he remained a fighter and an organizer rather than an innovator or a theorist.

After the death of his wife, Dewey was detached from the torpedo station at his own request and given command of the *Narragansett* again. The ship had now been assigned to survey the Pacific Coast of Mexico and Lower California. This tedious duty in the blazing heat and virtual isolation of the Gulf of California was relieved only by occasional visits to the port of La Paz to refuel and collate data. Here Dewey struck up a friendship with an American mining engineer named Brook who was the manager of a silver mine at Triumfo, about forty miles from La Paz. The mines at Triumfo were owned and managed by Americans who employed several hundred Mexican laborers to work them.

During one of the *Narragansett*'s visits to La Paz, two of the Mexican laborers were killed by Brook over what he later described as a "question of honor." The outraged employees laid siege to Brook and the other foreign supervisors in their compound. Brook dispatched an urgent request for help to the *Narragansett*. Without any hesitation, Dewey sent his executive officer, Lieutenant George C. Reiter, to call on the district governor, who was also a brigadier general, and to demand that the governor send some of his troops to protect the Americans. "He was to state further to the governor that, in the event of failure to act promptly in compliance with my request, I should take possession of the city and the customs house."[63] As Reiter delivered his message, the astonished governor could observe through his window the *Narragansett* moving into position to bombard the town. Early the next morning, a company of Mexican soldiers left La Paz on a rapid forced march to the mine.

Some months later, word of these extraordinary events reached

62. Dewey, *Autobiography*, 167.
63. *Ibid.*, 148.

Washington in a newspaper article. The Navy Department dispatched a copy of the article to Dewey, together with a request for a report on the events described. In his reply, Dewey explained that he had "not considered it of sufficient importance to be made the subject of a report."[64] Dewey's dangerous habit of "not bothering" the Navy Department with unimportant matters and of handling things himself was to have momentous and tragic consequences, but, for the moment, the Navy Department approved his actions and the newspapers lauded his initiative.

In July, 1875, Dewey returned to the United States and served two years in Boston as a lighthouse inspector for the Second Lighthouse District. In 1878, he was appointed naval secretary to the Lighthouse Board in Washington, D.C. The activities of the board, during Dewey's four-year tour, appear to have centered mainly around debating the question of whether to substitute lard oil for mineral oil in the lamps. "The duty is not very arduous," wrote Dewey to his brother Charles, "so I suppose it ought to please me but it doesn't. I want for more occupation."[65] Duty with the Lighthouse Board did afford the commander an opportunity to discover the delights of the national capital. "Washington social life," he recalled, "with its rounds of dinners and receptions, was a new and enjoyable experience for me." During his four years in Washington, he developed a marked preference for life in the capital, but his health was poor and he was glad to accept command of the *Juniata*, an old steam sloop which was under orders for the Orient.

The *Juniata* proceeded leisurely toward Suez, but at Malta, Dewey was hospitalized with an abscess of the liver, complicated by a severe case of typhoid. He remained in the British hospital for over a year, and at times his doctors doubted that he would live. In the spring of 1882, he finally left the hospital but was still too weak to resume his duties. For two years he traveled from one health spa to another in an effort to regain his health. Finally, in 1884, he felt strong enough to accept command of the newly completed U.S.S. *Dolphin.*

The *Dolphin* was one of the four modern steel warships—the

64. *Ibid.*
65. Dewey to Charles Dewey, February 23, 1878, in Dewey Family Correspondence.

others were the *Atlanta, Boston,* and *Chicago*—which Congress had finally authorized in 1882 as the first step in providing modern warships for the navy. As the first modern warship to be built in American yards in almost twenty years, the *Dolphin,* not surprisingly, turned out to be badly built; it was too slow and far too expensive. On her trials, she failed to make her designed speed, her propellor shaft broke in two, and the navy refused to accept her. While the government and the *Dolphin*'s builders wrangled, Dewey, now a captain, gladly accepted command of another ship, the steam sloop *Pensacola.* This was the same ship which the *Mississippi* had followed past the batteries of Fort Jackson twenty-two years before. The *Pensacola* was assigned to the European Station in which she served as flagship of Rear Admiral Samuel F. Franklin.

Once again there was the usual round of balls, reviews, and naval ceremonies which had so impressed Dewey as a midshipman. By 1889, however, as the *Pensacola*'s four-year cruise drew to an end, he may have grown a bit tired of it all. In any case, he was thoroughly tired of wallowing around in "old tubs" like the *Pensacola,* and he probably thought wistfully of the good life he had known in Washington in the seventies. When his friend Winfield Scott Schley, who was serving as chief of the Bureau of Equipment and Recruiting, reminded him that his post would soon be vacant, Dewey saw his chance.[66]

In his autobiography, Dewey declared that prior to 1897, "it had been a rule with me never to try to bring political influence to bear on the Navy Department in my favor." This sentence, like so much else in Dewey's published statements and writings, is the product of either a faulty or over-selective memory. As soon as Dewey learned of the vacancy in the bureau, he proceeded to solicit all the political help he and his family could muster to secure that position for himself. His brothers Charles and Edward wrote to the two Vermont senators, George F. Edmunds and Redfield Proctor, on his behalf; and Charles also personally called upon Charles Veazy, a close friend and former law partner of Senator Proctor. The senator promised to intercede in Dewey's behalf.[67] Dewey himself

66. Winfield Scott Schley, *Forty-five Years Under the Flag* (New York, 1904), 192.
67. Charles Dewey to Dewey, March 9, March 23, 1889; Edward Dewey to Dewey,

was not idle. The man who in 1859 had deplored the use of political influence in the Navy Department now wrote personally to his senators and to former Secretary of the Navy William E. Chandler, now a United States Senator, who promised to talk with the secretary of the navy about the appointment. He also wrote to Eugene Hale, the powerful chairman of the Senate Naval Affairs Committee who replied that he would "be glad to say a word in your favor."[68]

One problem which threatened to complicate Dewey's campaign was the fact that 1888 had been an election year and Senator Proctor had just been named secretary of war. Many of Dewey's backers feared that the president and Secretary of the Navy Benjamin F. Tracy might be unwilling to give Vermont yet another political plum. On May 15, 1889, with the question of Schley's successor still unsettled, Rear Admiral John D. Walker, chief of the Bureau of Navigation, advised Dewey to "come here and see your friends. Take my advice without asking for reasons and say nothing to nobody."[69] Dewey's personal calls on his "friends" in Washington appear to have been decisive. In July of 1889, he succeeded Schley as chief of the Bureau of Equipment.

The new chief took office at a time when the pace of the American naval revival was quickening. In 1884, the *Dolphin* and her three larger sisters had been the only modern warships in the navy. Five years later, at the end of Grover Cleveland's first administration, the navy had thirty-eight modern men-of-war with a total displacement of over 100,000 tons either completed or under construction.[70] Benjamin Tracy was an expansionist and a convinced advocate of sea power. Not content with merely expanding the navy's cruiser force, Tracy succeeded in securing congressional approval for the first American battleships, the *Indiana, Oregon,*

March 18, 1889; George F. Edmunds to Dewey, April 4, 1889, all in Dewey Papers.

68. William E. Chandler to Dewey, March 18, 1889; and Eugene Hale to Dewey, March 19, 1889, *ibid.*

69. Walker to Dewey, May 15, 1889, *ibid.*

70. Harold M. and Margaret Sprout, *The Rise of American Naval Power* (Princeton, 1939), 188–89.

and *Massachusetts,* all of which were to see action in the Spanish-American War.[71]

The new ships which were now coming out of the builders' yards in increasing numbers were far more expensive to operate and maintain than the old relics of the Civil War era like the *Pensacola* and the *Juniata.* In his annual reports, Dewey's predecessor had argued cogently for a larger appropriation for the Bureau of Equipment which had the responsibility of providing anchors, rigging, cables, and other fittings for the new ships and of keeping them supplied with coal. The ships of the old navy, although equipped with steam power, had primarily relied on sails for their motive power. Captain Caspar F. Goodrich later recalled that "to burn coal was so grievous an offense in the eyes of the authorities that, for years, the captain was obliged to enter in the log, in red ink, his reasons for getting up steam."[72] The fast new cruisers of the "new navy," although often equipped with auxiliary sails, were basically steam men-of-war. Their large power plants required a much greater amount of coal.

The shortage of coal had now become so acute that vessels had had to be taken out of commission or "kept in service only by the most rigid, and in some instances, unprofitable parsimony."[73] Since most of the bureau's available funds had had to be used for the purchase of coal, very little had been available for supplying the ships in commission with the necessary fittings and supplies. Ships returning from long cruises could not be properly refitted; they had to be supplied with obsolete equipment or laid up altogether. In his

71. For recent accounts of Tracy's administration, see Walter R. Herrick, Jr., *The American Naval Revolution* (Baton Rouge, 1966); B. F. Cooling, *Benjamin Franklin Tracy: Father of the Modern American Fighting Navy* (Hamden, Conn., 1973).

72. Caspar F. Goodrich, *Rope Yarns from the Old Navy* (New York, 1931), 65. This directive was not as silly as it might appear. Since the United States had no overseas coaling stations it was believed that ships on foreign cruises ought to save their coal for emergencies or for maneuvering in battle. For good discussions of "Old Navy" policies see Lance Buhl, "The Smooth Water Navy: Naval Politics and Strategy in the United States, 1865–1876" (Ph.D. dissertation, Harvard, 1968); and Kenneth M. Hagan, *American Gunboat Diplomacy and the Old Navy, 1877–1889* (Westport, Conn., 1973).

73. *Report of the Secretary of the Navy, 1889,* "Appendix 10, Bureau of Equipment and Recruiting" (Washington, D.C., 1889), 284.

annual reports for 1889 and 1890, Dewey urged Congress to substantially increase the bureau's appropriation so that it could purchase the necessary coal. In 1890, he succeeded in obtaining an increase of almost $200,000 in the coal allotment. Consequently, when, during the Chilean Crisis of 1892, the ships of the South Atlantic Squadron were required to do a great deal of steaming at high speed, Dewey was able to provide the necessary coal.

Dewey's years at the head of the bureau also saw the introduction of such devices as electric searchlights and signaling apparatus in all the ships of the new navy, as well as the introduction of a modern engine room telegraph system which enabled officers on the ship's bridge to signal small variations in speed to the engine room and observe the ship's engine revolutions by means of automatic indicators on the bridge telegraph. The first telephones had been installed on an experimental basis in the U.S.S. *Philadelphia* in 1890. By 1892 all of the new vessels of the navy were being equipped with internal telephone systems.[74]

By the end of his three years as head of the Bureau of Equipment, Dewey had established a reputation as an energetic administrator and a friend of innovation. To suggest, however, as some of his more eulogistic biographers were to do, that his leadership of the bureau was so brilliant and spectacular as to make him a marked man in the navy, is absurd. The commodore had done a creditable job in rather routine assignments; as an administrator, he had been no more and perhaps somewhat less impressive than his brother officers like John G. Walker in navigation, or Sampson in ordnance, or even his own predecessor Schley.

In Washington, the commodore's life settled into a comfortable, well-ordered routine. His rooms at 1730 H Street, N.W., were kept spotlessly clean by his housekeeper Rhoda Wilder and his manservant George Cox. Mrs. Wilder later recalled that Dewey was "as neat as a pin. He never left a match on the floor, a scrap of paper or any of his clothing scattered about. He even hung up his nightshirt in its proper place."[75]

74. Ibid.; *Report of the Secretary of the Navy, 1891* (Washington, D.C., 1891), 146.
75. Murat Halstead, *Life and Achievements of Admiral Dewey: From Montpelier to Manila* (Chicago, 1899), 161.

Dewey's day began every morning at 6:00 A.M. when he arose, bathed, and read the papers. At precisely 8:00 A.M. George Cox brought him his breakfast and returned to remove the dishes at 8:30. To be even a few minutes late at either task was to incur the commodore's extreme displeasure. The breakfasts themselves never varied: fruit, boiled eggs, and corn muffins with orange marmalade. Dewey generally took lunch and dinner at the Metropolitan Club where he was a member of the governing board and an enthusiastic chess player. The Metropolitan Club, in the 1890s, was a gathering place for many well-known and well-heeled members of the Washington social set. Here Dewey rubbed elbows with diplomats, cabinet members, senators, and other high-ranking officers of the army and navy.

As a handsome, well-to-do widower, Dewey fitted well into the Washington social scene. "There were few more popular men than Commodore Dewey," Rear Admiral Franklin later recalled. "People seek him out; and whenever he is on shore, he is kept busy with his social engagements."[76] He was an extremely smart dresser, and this, combined with his still-trim physique and his flowing mustache, gave him a rather striking apearance. He kept a blooded mare which he rode twice a day for exercise. At fifty-five he was still lean and hard, tipping the scales at the same 155 pounds he had weighed ten years before.

The commodore prided himself on his youthful appearance. His son George Goodwin recalled that once during 1893 he had come aboard ship to find his father escorting two attractive young women on a guided tour. "This is my younger brother George," said Dewey, indicating George Goodwin who was then a sophomore in college.[77]

The end of Dewey's four years as chief of the Bureau of Equipment did not cause any change in his comfortable Washington life. In 1893, he was appointed president of the Lighthouse Board, on which he had previously served as "naval member" in the 1880s. After two years, he was assigned as president of the Board of

76. Adelbert Dewey, *The Life and Letters of Admiral Dewey* (New York, 1899), 114.
77. Healy and Kutner, *The Admiral*, 126.

Inspection and Survey, which had the responsibility for inspecting and passing final judgment on the new warships. This duty gave Dewey an opportunity to familiarize himself with the ships of the new navy.

In the spring of 1897 it became known in Washington that the post of commander-in-chief of the Asiatic Squadron would soon fall vacant. This was just the sort of isolated, semi-independent command which Dewey, who had been promoted to commodore in May, 1896, desired. Early in June he wrote to the Bureau of Navigation to apply for the post.[78]

Other naval officers also had their eyes on the Far East in that spring of 1896. One floor down from Dewey the energetic head of the Office of Naval Intelligence (ONI), Lieutenant Commander Richard Wainwright, had been watching with special attention the events unfolding on the nearby island of Cuba, where the Spanish government was, unsuccessfully it seemed, attempting to put down an insurrection against its rule. To Wainwright it appeared not unreasonable to assume that the United States might become involved in diplomatic complications with Spain arising out of this unsettled state of affairs and that from these complications war might result.

Wainwright believed that the United States ought to be prepared with a plan for this contingency. Sometime during the winter or early spring of 1896 he directed one of the officers of his staff, Lieutenant William W. Kimball, to prepare a plan of war with Spain. By the first of June, 1896, Kimball had completed his plan and submitted it, through Wainwright, to the secretary of the navy. Whether the plan was the work of Kimball alone or the product of consultation with others cannot now be determined, but it exhibited a simplemindedness about world politics and about the efficacy of naval power not untypical of many naval officers of the time.

Kimball assumed that the "real cause" of any war with Spain would be "friction upon the Cuban question" and that the object of such a war would be "to liberate Cuba, collect a war indemnity from Spain, and to settle the particular question which was the

78. Chief, Bureau of Navigation, to Dewey, June 19, 1896, in Dewey Papers.

immediate occasion for the war."[79] The "most economic means" for attaining these ends, Kimball believed, was for the United States to "utilize its superior sea power" to conduct a "purely naval war of blockades, bombardments, harassments, raids on exposed colonies, and naval actions." He argued that this scheme would result in the fewest casualties and the least financial expenditure, offered the quickest way of injuring Spain, and, in any case, would be the only possible method of proceeding if the war should break out during the rainy season in Cuba. The plan would also permit "the establishment of a Cuban Republic through the efforts of its own citizens instead of through conquests and occupations through an organized army of invasion from the U.S."

To obtain the second object of the war, an indemnity, which Kimball believed the United States would surely demand from Spain, the lieutenant suggested that the American Asiatic Squadron, made up of half a dozen light cruisers and gunboats, "should capture and reduce Manila," the capital of the Spanish Philippines, "at the earliest possible date." "With Manila in our hands," Kimball observed, "it would be an easy matter to control the trade of Ilo-Ilo and Cebu. . . . The ease with which the revenues of the island could at once be attained and the fact that these revenues might be held until a war indemnity were satisfactorily arranged indicate that Manila should be a serious objective." Kimball also believed that the American possession of the Philippines would serve to deter Spain against fitting out cruisers or privateers to prey on American commerce. "Our Government could assure Spain that Manila would have to pay for every merchantman captured."

Wainwright and Kimball were not alone in their conviction that the United States ought to prepare for a war with Spain. During the blistering depression summer of 1896, while the attention of most Americans was focused on the great presidential nominating conventions, the attention of a small group of influential naval officers was focused upon Cuba and Spain. Rear Admiral Stephen B. Luce, a former commander of the North Atlantic Squadron and the founder of the Naval War College, wrote to the then-president

---

79. W. W. Kimball, "War with Spain, 1896; General Considerations of the War, the Results Desired, and Consequent Kinds of Operations to Be Undertaken," RG 38.

of the college, Captain Henry C. Taylor: "To me it is utterly inconceivable that the government has not long ago matured plans for a joint military and naval campaign, having for its end the occupation of Cuba."[80] In fact, the Naval War College, like ONI, an impoverished but vigorous institution, was in the process of doing just that. During the summer of 1896, Taylor and the officers of the college began a war plan for Spain which was substantially completed by the following winter. "I hope," Taylor wrote to Luce, "some day you will find that your suggestion about Cuba has borne good fruit."[81]

The War College plan was strikingly different from the plan produced by the Office of Naval Intelligence. Since 1894, the War College had been engaged in planning for a war with the traditional American rival, Great Britain. Memories of the recent crisis with the British over the matter of the Venezuelan boundary were still fresh. Captain Taylor, who had been charged with naval planning during the crisis, decided it was prudent to assume that England might join Spain in war against the United States. This single crucial consideration resulted in a plan quite unlike that of Lieutenant Kimball. Since Spain allied with England would possess overwhelming naval superiority, the plan envisioned a defensive campaign by the American navy in the Gulf of Mexico. The War College did agree that the war ought to be regarded as "purely a naval problem" and conceded that in the event Spain had to fight the United States alone it would be advisable to "direct our attention towards . . . coasts not necessarily our own."[82]

Secretary of the Navy Hillary A. Herbert, perhaps confused by the multiplicity of plans, created a special board composed of the chief intelligence officer, the chiefs of the Bureaus of Navigation and Ordnance, the commander-in-chief of the North Atlantic Squadron, and the president of the Naval War College, to consider the problem of war with Spain. In December, 1896, the board

---

80. Stephen B. Luce to Henry C. Taylor, July 10, 1896, in Luce Papers, Library of Congress.
81. Taylor to Luce, August 5, 1896, Records of the U.S. Naval War College, Naval History Collection, U.S. Naval War College Library, Newport, Rhode Island.
82. "Solution to the Problem, 1896," Records of the Naval War College.

produced still a third plan in which it was assumed that Spain alone would fight the United States. The new plan called for the Asiatic Squadron to reinforce the American vessels already in European waters, and to join with them in an attack on the Canary Islands. The board believed that these ships, reinforced by some of the armored ships of the North Atlantic Squadron, could capture the Canary Islands and use them as a base of operations against the enemy's naval forces in Spanish waters.[83] Henry C. Taylor registered a vigorous dissent against this scheme for a major naval effort "in a region 3,500 miles from our home bases" and recommended that "all the naval forces at the disposal of the government be concentrated upon Cuba."[84]

On June 27, 1897, President William McKinley's new secretary of the navy, John D. Long, reconvened the board, which was now composed of a new group of officers in the respective billets. Only Commander Wainwright, the chief intelligence officer, had served on the previous board. Among many other measures, the new board recommended that the Asiatic Squadron, instead of coming west, should "go down and show itself in the neighborhood of the Philippines" and possibly attack Manila ". . . for the purpose of further engaging the attention of the Spanish Navy [away from the main theater of operations] and more particularly to improve our position when the time comes for negotiations with a view to peace."

This was how matters stood in the summer of 1897 as the United States and Spain slowly drifted toward war. McKinley and Long viewed events with increasing anxiety and gloom, but not so Long's eager young assistant Theodore Roosevelt. Roosevelt was a believer in the inevitability, not to say desirability, of war with Spain. A frequent visitor to the Naval War College and a correspondent of Luce, Taylor, and Kimball, he took up the idea of an attack on the Philippines with enthusiasm. Throughout the summer and fall of 1897 he endeavored with some success to "sell" the plan to his chief and to the president. "I gave him a paper," Roosevelt wrote of one of his meetings with the president, "showing . . . what I thought

83. "Plan of Operations Against Spain," RG 38.
84. *Ibid.*

ought to be done if things looked menacing about Spain. If we get [Commodore John G.] Walker with our main fleet on the Cuban coast within 48 hours after war is declared . . . and if we put four big, fast, heavily armed cruisers under, say, Evans, as a flying squadron to harass the coast of Spain . . . I doubt the war would last six weeks. . . . Meanwhile, our Asiatic squadron should blockade and, if possible, take Manila." In November Roosevelt reported to Kimball that Long also seemed well disposed toward the plan.[85]

With the president and navy secretary at least half persuaded, it remained to select the commander for the Manila enterprise. The leading contenders were Dewey and Commodore John A. Howell, who many years before had been Dewey's messmate in the *Wabash*. Sometime during the summer of 1897 Roosevelt appears to have reached the conclusion that Dewey, not Howell, must be the man to lead the attack. As Roosevelt records, "Here was a man who could be relied upon to prepare in advance and to act fearlessly and on his own responsibility when the emergency arose."[86]

The origins of Roosevelt's enthusiasm for Dewey are somewhat obscure. The two were, of course, well acquainted through their association in the Navy Department and at the Metropolitan Club, and Roosevelt was often Dewey's riding companion in his frequent rides in Rock Creek Park.[87] The young assistant secretary appears to have valued Dewey's opinion on technical matters, but there is no evidence that Dewey knew of, or shared, the exuberant expansionism of Roosevelt and his circle.[88]

Roosevelt's aversion to Howell may in fact have been a more decisive consideration than his admiration for Dewey. The assistant secretary had been displeased by Howell's performance as a member of the Navy Department's Armor Board and had com-

85. Roosevelt to Henry Cabot Lodge, September 21, 1897, and Roosevelt to William W. Kimball, November 19, 1897, both in Elting E. Morison (ed.), *The Letters of Theodore Roosevelt* (8 vols.; Cambridge, 1951–54), I, 690, 716–17.
86. *Theodore Roosevelt: An Autobiography* (New York, 1915), 211.
87. John M. Ellicott, "Contacts with the Hero of Manila Bay," USNIP, LXXVI (January, 1950).
88. Morison (ed.), *Letters of Roosevelt*, I, 673.

plained to Long about the commodore's indecisiveness and fear of responsibility.[89]

It is not surprising then that when Roosevelt discovered a letter to Secretary Long from Senator William E. Chandler supporting Howell's application for command of the Asiatic Squadron he quickly moved to head it off. "Before you commit yourself to Howell I wish very much you would let me have a chance to talk to you," he wrote to Chandler. "I have seen a good deal of him [Howell]. . . . He is an honorable man and a man of great inventive capacity but I have rarely met one who strikes me as less fit for a responsible position. . . . I hardly know of a man of high rank in the Navy whom I would be more reluctant to see entrusted with a squadron or fleet. . . . He is irresolute and he is extremely afraid of responsibility. . . . You and I feel alike not only on foreign policy but on the kind of man who should carry out that foreign policy and if we do take vigorous action . . . we must have it taken by men with whom there is no chance of failure."[90]

According to Dewey's and Roosevelt's recollections, the young assistant secretary, after writing to Chandler, called Dewey into his office and urged him to make use of his long acquaintance with Senator Redfield Proctor to secure the Far Eastern command for himself. Proctor, a longtime friend of the Deweys, appealed to Long and to President McKinley to have Dewey appointed to the Asiatic Squadron. This is substantially the version given by Roosevelt and Dewey in their autobiographies, and by Dewey's son, George Goodwin, to his biographers in 1940. Long, however, in his memoirs published in 1903, denied that he had ever been opposed to Dewey's appointment or that any political pressure was brought to bear on Dewey's behalf.[91] Long's memoirs appeared in 1903 when Dewey still enjoyed immense prestige, and Long understandably may not have wished to be remembered as having opposed the choice of the "Hero of Manila Bay."

In any case, the contention that no political influence was used

89. Roosevelt to Long, September 20, 1897, *ibid.*, 683.
90. Roosevelt to Chandler, September 27, 1897, *ibid.*, 691.
91. John D. Long, *The New American Navy* (2 vols.; New York, 1903), I, 177.

is almost certainly incorrect. On October 16, Senator Proctor reported to Dewey that he had seen the president and that his interview had been "every bit as satisfactory and even more positive than my interview with the secretary. I said to him that he could do me a great personal favor and at the same time do the right and best thing for the service. He made a note in my presence to show the secretary. But I have no doubt the secretary would have reached the same conclusion."[92]

Whether or not Long would have reached the same conclusion, he was greatly annoyed at the way Dewey had secured his appointment. He intensely disliked officers "who in roundabout ways and by securing interposition of senators, representatives and 'friends' besieged the department and endeavored to manipulate their assignments." It was probably for this reason that Dewey was denied the customary courtesy rank of acting rear-admiral which was accorded to commanders on the Far Eastern Squadron in order to put them on a basis of equality with the commanders of European squadrons there. As the first commodore to command the Asiatic Squadron since Perry, Dewey would be inferior in matters of protocol to almost all of his foreign counterparts. Dewey was indignant over this "little pin-pricking slight." Both he and Roosevelt defended his conduct in the matter of the appointment by describing it as an act of self-defense against the politicking of Commodore Howell. Yet Dewey, as we have seen, was far from the political innocent described in Roosevelt's memoirs. He had not hesitated to employ wire-pulling in order to become chief of the Bureau of Equipment, and it is unlikely that he felt any qualms in 1897 once he had set his heart on having the Asiatic Squadron.

On October 21, 1897, Dewey was detached from duty as president of the Board of Inspection and Survey and ordered to proceed to Japan to relieve Acting Rear-Admiral Frederick G. McNair as commander-in-chief of the Asiatic Squadron. In the event of war with Spain, which now appeared more and more likely, Dewey would have one of the most desirable commands with sole responsibility for dealing with the enemy forces in his theater.

92. Redfield Proctor to Dewey, October 16, 1897, in Dewey Papers.

In the worshipful biographical sketches of Dewey which appeared in large number after 1898, it was frequently asserted that he had been chosen for his command because, of all the officers of his rank, he was preeminently suited for it. As Roosevelt wrote in *McClure's Magazine*: "In the summer of 1897 there were in Washington captains and commanders who later won honor for themselves in the war with Spain. . . . All these men were a unit in their faith in Commodore Dewey, in their desire to serve under him should the need arise and in their unquestioning belief that he was the man to meet an emergency in a way that would do credit to the flag."[93] Perhaps a more accurate description of the commodore's standing in Washington was that given by an officer of the Metropolitan Club who observed that "the men who met him at the club no more realized the fire in him than his neighbors saw a general in Ulysses S. Grant."[94] There was, in fact, nothing in Dewey's record up to 1897 to suggest that he was in any way extraordinary. He had had no sea duty in eight years and only four years at sea in the last twenty years. His Civil War record was good but no better that of many other officers, including Commodore Howell. His role in the development of the new navy had been distinctly minor. He belonged neither to the group of brilliant scientifically inclined officers like Sampson and Bradley A. Fiske nor to the circle of serious strategists like Mahan, Luce, and Henry C. Taylor. In the final analysis, Dewey owed his appointment to efforts of influencial political friends like Senator Proctor and Theodore Roosevelt and to nothing else.

93. Healy and Kutner, *The Admiral*, 131.
94. Frederick Palmer, *George Dewey, USN* (New York, 1900), 48.

CHAPTER II

"It Will Be Short Work for Us"

On New Year's Day, 1898, Commodore George Dewey was rowed out to his new flagship, the cruiser *Olympia*, lying at anchor in the roadstead of Nagasaki. Standing in the stern sheets, Dewey could see the *Olympia* riding easily at her moorings, her white and buff paint gleaming in the morning sun. Although rated as a "protected" or light cruiser, the five-year-old *Olympia* was really a sort of pocket-battleship. Her two turrets, each containing two eight-inch rifles, were set in armored barbettes four inches thick. Her four-inch armored deck protected two triple-expansion engines capable of driving the ship at the then phenomenal speed of twenty-two knots. On her gun deck she carried ten five-inch quick-firing guns, and her sides and fighting tops bristled with smaller quick-firing cannons and four Gatling machine guns. At 5,870 tons, she was nearly as large as the battleship *Maine* which was at that moment preparing to leave her base at Port Royal, South Carolina, for a visit to Havana.

The other ships of Dewey's command were scattered up and down the China coast performing their time-honored functions. The cruiser *Boston* was at Chemulpo, Korea, observing the uneasy rivalry between Russia and Japan for control of the hapless imperial government and ready to land her marines on a moment's notice to protect the American embassy at Seoul. The gunboat *Petrel* was on her way to Canton to stand by during the Chinese New Year celebrations since it was believed that the Chinese were especially inclined to antiforeign outrages during that season. Further north, the antiquated gunboat *Monocacy*, a "double-ender" of

Civil War vintage, armed with smooth bores, patrolled the mouth of the Yangtze River at Shanghai. The cruiser *Raleigh*, transferred to the Far East from the Mediterranean Squadron, was approaching Aden while the gunboat *Machias* was in the Indian Ocean on her way back to the United States.

These little cruisers and gunboats were the sole representatives of American military power in the Far East. Beside the great fleets of Russia, Britain, and Japan they were an inconsiderable quantity. But few Americans knew, and even fewer cared, about the momentous moves and countermoves, the careful jockeying for position, that was taking place between the European powers in China. In November of 1897 Germany, using as a pretext the murder of two German missionaries, had forced the Chinese government to grant it a ninety-nine year lease of Kiaochow Bay on the Shantung Peninsula. The Russians, who had already received permission to build a spur line of the trans-Siberian railroad across Manchuria to Vladivostok, sent a naval squadron to Port Arthur in December. The French and British, meanwhile, began to search for ways to enlarge their own spheres of influence while the Japanese eyed the Russian moves in Manchuria and Korea with suspicion. Rear Admiral Frederick G. McNair, Dewey's phlegmatic predecessor, refused to become alarmed by these developments. In a long, written review of the Far Eastern situation which he prepared for Dewey's benefit, McNair noted that the German seizure of Kiaochow would "require careful watching" but refused to credit "rumors" about the seizure of other territory in China by the great powers.[1]

During his first weeks on the station, Dewey watched the situation with intense interest. "Affairs are very unsettled here," he wrote to his son in January. "The Germans, English and Russians and Japanese are playing a big game of bluff since it remains to be seen who will take the pot."[2] He wrote frequently to the commanding officer of the *Monocacy* at Nanking asking to be kept informed about political developments in the Shanghai area.[3]

1. McNair to Dewey, RG 45, Area 10 file.
2. Dewey to George Goodwin Dewey, January 4, 1898, in George Goodwin Dewey Papers.
3. Asiatic Squadron Station Letters, February 19, March 10, March 25, 1898, in Dewey

Like many other Americans in the Far East at the turn of the century; Dewey thought of China as a vast potential market for American goods. "We have very great interests here [in Japan] and in China," Dewey explained in a letter to his son. "Our trade with both Japan and China is very large."[4] He also took a less sanguine view of events in the Far East than had Admiral McNair. Commenting on the arrival of a Russian naval squadron at Port Arthur, he observed: "Things look decidedly squally out here and I should not be surprised to see a general war at any time."

For the United States, however, the immediate danger in 1898 was not war over China but war with Spain. Ever since Dewey had received word of his appointment, this contingency had been uppermost in his mind. While still in Washington, he had become concerned over the lack of ammunition for the Asiatic Squadron. All of his ships were far below even their peacetime allowance of ammunition, and the next new supply was scheduled to be sent out in the cruiser *Charleston* which was then in dry dock and not likely to be in service for six months or more. With Roosevelt's help, Dewey persuaded the Navy Department to send some of the ammunition supply in the gunboat *Concord* which was scheduled to join the Asiatic Squadron in February. The rest of the allotment was shipped to Honolulu in the old sloop-of-war *Mohican* and then transferred to the cruiser *Baltimore*, scheduled to reinforce Dewey in March. The *Baltimore* arrived just forty-eight hours before the news of the war with Spain reached the Far East, and even with her added supply, Dewey's ships went into action with their ammunition bunkers almost half empty.[5]

On January 15, the *Olympia*, now flying Dewey's pennant, headed north and east through the Straits of Tsushima and into Yokohama harbor. On February 1 the commodore boarded the morning train to Tokyo for an audience with the emperor. "What a contrast," he later noted, "was my reception to that of the other

Papers.
    4. Dewey to George Goodwin Dewey, February 4, 1898, in George Goodwin Dewey Papers.
    5. Nathan S. Sargent, "Admiral Dewey and the Manila Campaign" (MS in Dewey Papers), 2.

American commodore who had cast anchor in the Gulf of Yeddo forty years previously. One commodore was regarded with an apprehensive consternation, while the other was welcomed with all the amenities of modern times."[6] A few days later, the *Concord* steamed into Yokohama harbor with her precious cargo of ammunition, a portion of which was immediately transferred to the *Olympia*. Then, on February 11, the two ships headed south for the British Crown Colony of Hong Kong.

Along with other official papers, Admiral McNair probably handed over to Dewey the Navy Department's plan for an attack on the Philippines with which Dewey was already generally familiar from his conversations with Roosevelt. On January 28 he was advised by the Navy Department to retain all men whose enlistments had expired until further notice. Yet now it suddenly appeared there might be no war after all. The liberal Sagasta government which took office in Spain in the fall of 1897 announced a comprehensive scheme of reforms for Cuba with a promise of virtual autonomy, ended the notorious "reconcentration" policy, and recalled General Valeriano Weyler to Spain. In his annual message to Congress, President McKinley adopted a wait-and-see attitude and spoke hopefully of the Cuban reforms. Then on February 15 the *Maine* blew up in Havana harbor with the loss of more than 250 of her crew. McKinley appointed a naval court of inquiry to investigate the destruction of the *Maine* but many Americans had already made up their minds. "THE MAINE WAS DESTROYED BY TREACHERY," proclaimed the Hearst Press.

In Hong Kong Dewey received a telegram from Long: "*Maine* destroyed at Havana February 15 by accident. Half-mast all colors until further notice."[7] Upon receipt of Long's telegram, Dewey ordered his officers to cancel all social engagements out of respect for the dead of the *Maine*. On February 25 the commodore received a telegram from Roosevelt, then acting secretary of the navy: "Order the Squadron except *Monocacy* to Hong Kong. Keep full of coal. In event of declaration of war, Spain, your duty will be to see that the Spanish Squadron does not leave the Asiatic Coast and

6. Dewey, *Autobiography*, 177.
7. Long to Dewey, February 17, 1898, in Dewey Papers.

then offensive operations in Philippine Islands. Keep *Olympia* until further orders."[8] On the afternoon of the twenty-sixth, cables were dispatched to the *Boston* and *Concord*, already on their way from Chemulpo, to expedite their arrival at Hong Kong. The *Raleigh* had arrived one week before; with the arrival of the *Concord* on March 4, the entire Asiatic Squadron, with the exception of the *Baltimore* and the antiquated *Monocacy*, was in Hong Kong harbor. Dewey had already dispatched a coded telegram to Oscar F. Williams, the American consul at Manila, requesting information on the Philippines.

Far from being "terra incognita to Americans" as the commodore later claimed in his autobiography, the Philippines had been continuously visited by American seamen and merchants since the end of the eighteenth century. The American trade with the Philippines was, in fact, at least as old as the American trade with China. For a time during the early years of the nineteenth century, the United States had been the chief market for Filipino exports as well as a leading supplier of her imports. The volume of Filipino-American trade had, of course, greatly declined by the 1890s; but American firms still did business with Manila, and two American scientific expeditions had visited the islands in the 1890s.

Since 1896 the Filipinos had been in more or less continuous revolt against Spain. In December, 1897, the leaders of the insurgent "provisional government" and their president, Emiliano Aguinaldo, had signed a truce with Governor-General Fernando Primo de Rivera. The truce was a sort of package deal whereby the Spaniards promised to institute certain reforms and the Filipino revolutionaries promised to surrender their arms to the Spanish. Aguinaldo and his associates were to enter voluntary exile in Hong Kong and receive a payment of 800,000 pesos from the Spanish government. Aguinaldo, at least, planned to use the money to further the aims of the revolution.

---

8. Roosevelt to Dewey, February 25, 1898, *ibid.* This telegram has been widely misinterpreted. Although Long had not authorized the sending of the telegram or, indeed, any of Roosevelt's actions during "his day" as acting secretary, the sending of the cable was in line with the department's long-standing plans and preparations for war with Spain. Long neither disapproved the telegram nor made any attempt to rescind it.

In any event, the promised reforms failed to materialize. Aguinaldo and his friends remained in Hong Kong but in Luzon, Cebu, and Panay the revolt broke out anew. By the time Dewey sent his cable to Williams, the consul was reporting to the State Department that "conditions here and in Cuba are practically alike. War exists and battles are of an almost daily occurence. . . . A republic is organized here as in Cuba. Insurgents are being armed and drilled and are rapidly increasing in number and efficiency and all agree that a general uprising will come as soon as the present governor-general embarks for Spain."[9]

Dewey later complained that the navy's latest official information on the Philippines dated from 1876. In fact, however, the Navy Department had maintained an attaché in Madrid since 1897 and through this officer, the Bureau of Navigation was able to furnish Dewey's aide, Captain Benjamin Lamberton, with a list of Spanish war vessels in Philippine waters.[10] For up-to-date "hard" intelligence, however, Dewey depended primarily on Consul Williams. Dewey wrote to Williams that he was considering "sending one of the smaller vessels of my Squadron to communicate with you and exchange salutes, if you think advisable. I beg also that you inform me what Spanish war vessels are present . . . and what, if any, changes there have been in the land defenses of that port in recent years."[11]

To Consul Williams, who had been in Manila less than a month and who was without military experience, this was a large order. As the sole official representative of the American government, he was closely watched, his mail was frequently opened and read. "Two or more spies watch me constantly and my clerk is the son of a Spanish colonel," Williams wrote to Lieutenant H. H. Caldwell, Dewey's flag secretary. "At times, I suspect the key to my consulate and its safe are in the possession of persons who have no right to them and that my office has been visited." Nevertheless through employing agents of his own and through his excellent connections with the Spanish officials, Williams was able to obtain

9. Leon Wolfe, *Little Brown Brother* (New York, 1961), 84.
10. Bureau of Navigation to Lamberton [February, ?], 1898, in Dewey Papers.
11. Dewey to Oscar F. Williams, February 17, 1898, *ibid.*

the necessary information. On March 1, he reported that "any two U.S. ships could enter the port, silence the forts and capture the city." He urged Dewey to make a visit personally in his flagship and predicted that this would "delight the authorities here and greatly help our relations with Spain."[12] But by this time, Dewey was bound by Roosevelt's orders to remain at Hong Kong.

Ten days later, Williams submitted a more detailed report on the Spanish defenses. He reported that the forts of Old Manila were "too antiquated to merit consideration in modern war," and that the fort at the entrance to the Pasig River was "but a toy; one shot would wreck it." The forts facing on the bay, however, were better armed, had some modern heavy guns, and were kept fully manned. He also noted that the Spanish warships were all well provisioned and had their full crews on board. However, the "bay and its channels are both free from mines and torpedoes."[13] On March 14 he again advised: "I am not an expert but I believe Manila to be very weak. . . . I think commercial and church interests would demand surrender to you if only you throw a few shot and shell into the walled city." The Spanish batteries, he added, were believed to be short of ammunition.[14] As late as April 5, Williams reported that the approaches to Manila had still not been mined because the insulated wire to arm the mines had not yet arrived from Europe.[15]

The consul also reported on the progress of the insurrection. "Pacification here is a foolish unfounded claim," he wrote to Caldwell on March 12. "The rebels are stronger than ever and as domestic clouds darken in Spain they have more confidence than ever." Entire native regiments were going over to the rebels with their arms. The Spanish troops were few and widely scattered and "fifty per cent hors de combat."[16]

Then Williams touched on a theme that was to become increas-

12. Williams to H. H. Caldwell, March 10, March 12, 1898, *ibid.*
13. Williams to Caldwell, March 10, 1898, *ibid.* To avoid suspicion, Williams sent his messages to Dewey as personal letters to Caldwell rather than official dispatches to the commodore.
14. Williams to Caldwell, March 14, 1898, *ibid.*
15. Williams to Caldwell, March 12, 1898, *ibid.*
16. Williams to Caldwell, April 5, 1898, March 10, 26, 1898; April 8, 1898, *ibid.*

ingly familiar to Americans during the next few months. Commenting on the bloodshed and suffering attendant on the insurrection and the impotence of the Spanish officials, Williams declared: "Daily the cry arises, 'If the U.S. or Great Britain would only take these islands, how happy we would be. Why cannot the U.S. take us? Our islands are the gems of the ocean. The United States now takes half our export. They need an eastern home for their fleet such as the British have in Hong Kong.' "[17] The insurgents "would gladly aid our fleet and submit to our flag," Williams reported. "If I could command you and your fleet, I would capture every Spanish merchant and battleship and annex the islands before next Sunday." All of the arguments for annexation which were soon to echo through the halls of Congress had thus already been set out by an unknown American consul in an obscure backwater of the Pacific.

As hostilities grew closer and Spanish-American tensions increased, Williams found his position in Manila increasingly uncomfortable. Threats were made against his life and he was harassed by the constant surveillance of Spanish spies and officials. Since April 15, telegrams had been sent to Williams advising him to leave Manila and come to Hong Kong, yet he courageously remained at his post reporting information on last-minute developments to Dewey. Finally, on April 23, the British consul in Manila cabled that Williams had departed for Hong Kong on the steamer *Esmeralda.*

At Hong Kong, as war appeared more imminent, Dewey continued his preparations. All vessels of the squadron were overhauled and dry-docked; and on April 19 they received their warpaint—a dull, uniform gray applied over the dazzling white and buff of their peacetime rig. The *Monocacy* was docked at Shanghai and a part of her crew was used to reinforce the fighting ships. The new Treasury Department revenue cutter *McCulloch*, at Hong Kong for a shakedown cruise, was also pressed into service. With the permission of the Navy Department, Dewey also purchased the British collier *Nanshan*, together with a shipload of good Welsh coal and

17. *Ibid.*

the steamer *Zafiro* which was to serve as a supply vessel. Although Long had advised Dewey to arm these ships as auxiliary cruisers, the commodore decided to register them as unarmed American merchant vessels. In this way they would not be barred from neutral ports in time of war.

Once war was declared, Dewey's fighting ships would be barred from entering any of the ports of the Far East to obtain coal and supplies. On April 4, Minister Solon J. Buck in Tokyo confirmed that the Japanese government would not allow American warships to use its ports to obtain coal and supplies except on their voyages home to the United States. China, however, was too weak to enforce strict neutrality, and Dewey planned to move his squadron to Mirs Bay, a secluded bay thirty miles from Hong Kong, where supplies and coal could be stored for the use of the squadron. This decision to openly disregard the neutrality of China in case of war was made without consulting, or even informing, the Navy Department or anyone in Washington. When the captain of the *Monocacy* protested that there might be international complications, Dewey replied that "international complications where China is concerned are a secondary consideration."[18] As it turned out, the American squadron had no need to make use of its improvised base at Mirs Bay; but had it done so, the resulting ramifications, in the tense international atmosphere prevailing in the Far East at that time, are not hard to imagine. Once again Dewey had demonstrated his predilection for involving himself in situations fraught with dangerous political consequences without the slightest notion of what he was about or of the need for guidance from Washington.

As war approached, Dewey's anxieties about his ammunition supply increased. The *Baltimore*, which carried the bulk of the squadron's ammunition, had left Honolulu the third week in March but still had not arrived. On April 22, Long telegraphed that the Atlantic Squadron was blockading Cuba. "War may be declared at any moment. I will inform you." That same afternoon, the *Baltimore* was reported off Kowloon. By evening, she was steaming into Hong Kong harbor. Almost before the ship dropped anchor,

18. Asiatic Squadron Station Letters, April 9, 1898, *ibid.*

lighters were alongside to transfer her precious cargo of eight- and five-inch shells to the ships of the squadron. In less than forty-eight hours, the *Baltimore* was docked, scraped, coaled, and painted dull gray. Just as she emerged from dry dock, Dewey received a message from General Wilson Black, the governor of Hong Kong, requesting him to leave the harbor: "God knows, my dear commodore," the governor scrawled beneath his signature, "it breaks my heart to send you this notification."

As the American squadron prepared to depart Hong Kong, the bets were running heavily against its success in penetrating Manila Bay in the face of a hostile fleet supported by formidable shore installations. "A fine set of fellows," one Briton is supposed to have remarked, "but unhappily we shall never see them again." Two years later, in a letter to a newspaper reporter, Dewey recounted the fearful odds which his fleet faced in the Spanish Philippines. "The enemy's force was unquestionably superior to ours. Once you were inside the bay the fleet had guns to its front and rear. It would have been possible for those guns, properly served, to disable all our ships. The defenses of Manila can't be fairly estimated without considering these guns and the mines in the bay and the channels."[19] In 1898, however, Dewey was less pessimistic. In March of that year he assured the Navy Department that "with the squadron now under my command, the Spanish vessels could be taken and the defenses reduced in one day."[20] On the same day he wrote to his son: "My squadron is all ready for war and would make short work of the defenses of Manila." Again on April 7: "Our squadron will be far superior to the Spanish. I think it will be short work for us."[21] As for the mines which were supposed to form such a formidable barrier, the commodore dismissed them as "a specious bluff."[22] In conferences with his commanders, Dewey frequently expressed the belief that the depth of water and the swift current in the approaches to Manila Bay would make mining operations

19. Dewey to L. A. Pradt, December 30, 1899, *ibid.*
20. Dewey to Long, March 31, 1898, *ibid.*
21. Dewey to George Goodwin Dewey, March 31, 1898, in George Goodwin Dewey Papers.
22. Sargent, "Admiral Dewey and the Manila Campaign," 18.

impossible except with the aid of experts. In addition, the mines themselves would deteriorate rapidly in tropical waters and would have to be replaced frequently.[23]

Dewey's judgment may have been influenced somewhat by Farragut's "damn the torpedoes" attitude, but the commodore was probably more strongly influenced by his own experiences in the eastern Mediterranean in 1882. In that year, Arabi Pasha and his followers had mined the Suez Canal against the passage of British and French ships. An Italian admiral, declaring that the Egyptians were incompetent to mine anything properly, had boldly steamed through the canal in his man-of-war and reopened it to international traffic. Dewey's opinion of the competence of the Spaniards was not much higher.

The commodore's estimate proved to be correct. When the American squadron left Hong Kong, the Spanish were still vainly awaiting the arrival from Spain of the proper wire for their mines. Nor was Dewey being overconfident when he declared that his ships would "make short work of the Spanish squadron." Aside from the *McCulloch*, the Americans had six modern warships with an aggregate displacement of 19,098 tons. The Spanish force in the Philippines consisted of some thirty odd vessels, only seven of which actually took part in the battle. The largest Spanish ship, the *Reina Christina*, flagship of Admiral Patricio Montojo, displaced 3,520 tons and carried six 6.2-inch guns. His second largest ship, the old wooden cruiser *Castilla*, was armed with four old 5.9-inch guns. None of the other Spanish ships carried larger than 4.7-inch guns. They had nothing to match the 8-inch guns in the *Olympia*, *Baltimore*, and *Boston*. The American ships also mounted twenty-three 6-inch guns and twenty 5-inch guns to the Spanish twenty 4.7-inch. The total tonnage of the Spanish squadron was 11,689, about half that of the Americans. Most important, the Spanish fleet lacked trained seamen gunners.

Nor were the Spanish defenses of Manila Bay a formidable obstacle. Manila Bay is shaped like a large pear. The ten-mile-wide entrance is located at the stem of the pear and is divided into two channels by two small islands, Corregidor and Caballo. The two-

23. *Ibid.*

mile channel between Corregidor and the north shore is known as Boca Chica or the little mouth, while the southern passage between Caballo and the south shore is known as Boca Grande. Half way between Caballo and the south shore is a tiny rock known as El Fraile, or "the friar." Thirty miles from the entrance to the bay, the city of Manila occupies a frontage of about two miles along the bay. Six and a half miles south and southwest, a small narrow peninsula called Sangley Point forms a shallow bay known as Canacao, which was to be the anchorage of the Spanish fleet during the battle. Where the peninsula met the mainland was the Spanish arsenal of Cavite.

The most formidable Spanish batteries were those of the city of Manila, which comprised four modern 9.4-inch guns, four 5.5-inch guns, two 5.9-inch guns, and two 4.7-inch guns, with about two dozen obsolete muzzle-loaders of various calibers, all of which fronted on the bay. At Sangley Point were two 5.9-inch breech-loading rifles (which could not be laid for ranges under two thousand yards) and at Canacao one 4.7-inch gun. To guard the Boca Grande channel, the Spanish had nine antique muzzle-loaders which had too low a rate of fire to stop a modern cruiser. In addition, there were three 4.7-inch rifles on El Fraile and three 5.9-inch rifles on Caballo. These were the only modern guns defending the approaches to Manila. Against a fast modern squadron passing through the wide channel under cover of darkness, their effectiveness would be almost nil.

At 9:00 A.M. on April 25, the American squadron steamed out of Hong Kong harbor towards Mirs Bay. As they passed the British hospital ship anchored in the roadstead, the English sailors lined the rails and cheered the American warships. Almost simultaneously the code clerk in the Navy Department was hurriedly putting Long's final telegram into cipher. The message to "proceed at once to the Philippine Islands" reached Dewey that same night around midnight. (The *Olympia*'s excited gunners came near to sinking the little tug *Fame* carrying the telegram, which they mistook for a Spanish torpedo boat.)[24] The commodore replied that he would leave for Manila as soon as Consul Williams arrived with the

---

24. "Wayne" (real name unknown, a gunner in the *Olympia*) to brother, July 31, 1898, in USS *Olympia* Collection, U.S. Army Military History Research Collection, Carlisle, Pa.

last-minute news. The following morning, the *Fame* chugged into
Mirs Bay with the consul aboard. At 11:00 A.M. Dewey signaled all
commanders to come aboard the flagship where Williams gave
them a final briefing. At 2:00 P.M., the squadron steamed out of
Mirs Bay in two columns and turned south and west towards
Luzon.

The American plan to attack Manila, one of the worst-kept
military secrets in Washington, was known to the Spanish government at least as early as January, 1898, when the naval attaché in
Washington advised Madrid that, in the event of war, the Americans would strike first at the Philippines.[25] The Spaniards in Manila
now awaited the arrival of Dewey's squadron with a mixture of
anxiety and resignation. For at least thirty years the Spanish government had considered the problem of defending the Philippines
against an attack by a hostile fleet. In 1891, a naval commission
headed by Capitan del Frigata Don Julio del Rio had pointed out
that "it is impossible to prevent a squadron from entering Manila
Bay unless it is opposed by another squadron of at least equal
strength; shore batteries can be successively destroyed and torpedos drift away." Del Rio recommended that the Spanish squadron
be based on Subig Bay which he proposed to turn into a fortified
harbor. Subig seemed to be naturally adapted for purposes of
defense. The main channel was only a mile wide, and a fleet inside
the bay could be deployed in such a way as to envelop an attacking
squadron with its fire. A Spanish force at Subig would put the
attackers in a dilemma since they could not afford to attack Manila
with the enemy squadron still intact. If they did so they would be
vulnerable to an attack from the rear and to having their lines of
supply and retreat cut by the squadron at Subig. If the invader
chose to divide his fleet, sending part of it to attack Manila and part
of it to look for the enemy, he would be liable to defeat in detail
and would not have sufficient force to dominate the batteries of
Manila. "If the voice of reason is heard," concluded Captain Del
Rio, "we await the enemy at Subig. If certain material interests
prevail, we await him off Manila."

25. D. Victor M. Concas y Palau, *Causa Intruida por la Destruccion de la Escuadra de
Filipinas y Entreca del Arsenal de Cavite* (Madrid, 1899), 27.

As might have been predicted, the "voice of reason" did not prevail. Seven years later, in the spring of 1898, the base at Subig was still in the planning stages and the Spanish officers showed an understandable reluctance to leave the pleasures of Manila for the near isolation of Subig Bay. In the 1890s there were more than two hundred naval officers in the Philippines, and their interests were rather more social and financial than military. It can have been but scant comfort to Captain Del Rio (who was to lose his ship in the Battle of Manila Bay) that he had accurately forecast the course of events some seven years before. "The enemy admiral, if he finds Subig empty, will then stand in for Manila. Where is our squadron? If it is at Cavite he attacks the arsenal and our squadron which is almost motionless suffers helplessly until its annihilation is complete."[26]

The sinking of the *Maine* on March 15, 1898, finally jolted the Spaniards in the Philippines into action. At a meeting with the governor-general, it was agreed that the fleet should go to Subig Bay. The narrow eastern channel at the entrance to the bay was closed by sinking old hulks in the seaway. The western entrance was to be protected by shore batteries. The small number of mines which were available were planted in a line just inside the bay entrance. Beyond this line of mines, supported by the shore batteries, the Spanish squadron would await the arrival of the American fleet.

A few days after the governor-general's conference, a mixed commission departed for Subig to determine the best sites for mounting the four 5.9-inch guns allocated for the defense of the western channel. At the same time, additional steps were taken for the defense of Manila Bay. With the help of working parties from the gunboats *General Lezo* and *Don Antonio de Ulloa*, half a dozen modern breech-loading rifles were emplaced in El Fraile and Caballo so as to command the Boca Grande channel. By the end of the month all work on these installations had been completed and the batteries were ready to fire. Meanwhile, from Subig came discouraging news. The inspector of ordnance reported that the ce-

26. A copy of the commission's report may be found in the Dewey Papers.

ment work for the gun emplacements had not been finished. The engineer reported that the cement for the work had been delayed by the navy. The navy denied this and blamed the Ordnance Department. No one seemed to know exactly when the work would be completed.

On April 19, the minister of marine telegraphed Montojo, advising him to close the ports of the island with mines. Montojo shot back a one-line reply: "Your Excellency is aware I have no mines. I will do all I can." The minister replied that seventy mines "were on the way." They never arrived. In desperation, the warheads from a few of the torpedos carried by the ships of Montojo's squadron were removed and planted in the channel; but the lack of insulated wire made these of doubtful effectiveness. This, then, was the extent of the great mine danger which later received so much attention from the American press.

On April 25, to the accompaniment of much clanking and banging, the ships of Montojo's squadron began making preparations to get underway, some of them for the first time in years. By 1:00 P.M., all ships had steam up and the squadron steamed slowly out of Manila and turned north toward Subig. Beside Montojo's flagship, the *Reina Christina*, there were the old wooden cruiser *Castilla*, the small cruisers *Don Juan de Austria*, *Isla de Cuba*, and *Isla de Luzon*, and the dispatch boat *Marques del Duero*. The *Castilla* was so leaky that her propeller bearings had to be stopped with cement, thus making it impossible to use her engines. The transport *Manila* had to be summoned to tow her.

Arriving at Subig, Montojo discovered that the guns which were to have been mounted at the western entrance to the bay had not yet been installed and that it would take at least a month and a half to complete the work! One day later Montojo received a telegram from the Spanish consul at Hong Kong informing him that Dewey had sailed for the Philippines and was reported bound for Subig. On the twenty-eighth Montojo called a council of war. Except for Captain Del Rio, all the captains were agreed that the squadron ought to return to Manila. Subig was undefended and the water was so deep that the crews of sunken ships could probably not be saved.

Had Montojo chosen to scatter his ships among the many small islands, bays, and inlets south of Manila he might have caused the Americans endless trouble. Dewey would have been forced to either hunt down each of the Spanish men-of-war (a nearly impossible task with his small squadron), or face the threat of sudden attack and raids on his supply lines by the undefeated Spanish squadron. But Governor-General Basilio Augustin refused to countenance any such plan fearing that the Americans might bombard Manila.[27]

On April 28 Montojo's squadron again got underway and anchored in Manila Bay that same evening. In order to save the city of Manila from bombardment, Montojo decided to take position in the shallow water of Canacao Bay opposite Cavite arsenal. He thus deprived himself of the chance of support from the guns of Manila, including the four 9.4-inch guns of the Lunetta batteries, the only modern heavy guns the Spaniards possessed. Montojo and the governor-general were much criticized by contemporaries for their decision to spare the city at the expense of the squadron. French E. Chadwick and the British writer, H. H. Wilson, probably the foremost authorities on the battle in their day, both condemned Montojo for his failure to take position under the batteries. "Damage to Manila," observed Chadwick, "would not, from a national point-of-view, be commensurate with the loss of the Archipelago." "The general or admiral must in war steel his heart," admonished Wilson, "and neglect no advantage." Yet, after more than half a century of generals and admirals who were able to "steel their hearts and neglect no advantage," Admiral Montojo seems a rather sympathetic figure, whatever his military merits.[28]

Six hundred miles to the northwest, the American squadron steamed toward Manila at a speed of eight knots. The weather was clear and the sea glassy calm. The crews engaged in constant drills, and all of the remaining wood fittings were thrown overboard from most of the warships. In the *McCulloch* overzealous messboys threw all but a half dozen of the mess tables overboard, and the

27. Concas y Palau, *Causa Intruida*, 36.
28. French E. Chadwick, *Relations Between the United States and Spain: The Spanish-American War* (New York, 1911), 71.

crew was obliged to take meals on the deck until well after the battle.[29] Only aboard the *Olympia* did the woodwork remain in place. "The commodore knew best what we were going up against," recalled one sailor, "and we didn't tear out anything, just covered it [woodwork] with canvas and splinter nets." There was some grumbling among the crew about the danger of fire, but Dewey, who had seen many battles, was not about to be panicked into sacrificing all of his creature comforts.[30]

On the first day of the voyage the crew of the *Olympia* was mustered on the fantail where a bombastic declaration by the Spanish governor-general was read aloud to them. Then Consul Williams made a speech in which he recounted the many indignities he had suffered in Manila; how his life had been threatened, his country maligned and his flag insulted. "When he got through every mother's son of us cheered and cursed the Spaniards."[31] Lieutenant Carlos G. Calkins later recalled that the main anxiety of the Americans was that the Spanish fleet might not be in Subig or Manila, and many of the sailors expected to meet the Spanish squadron on the voyage to Luzon.[32] Dewey, however, remained confident that the enemy was in Subig or at Manila. At 2:45 A.M. on the thirtieth of April the *Olympia*'s lookouts could make out Cape Boliano on the island of Luzon, and at 4:00 A.M. the *Boston* and *Concord* were detached and sent ahead to reconnoiter Subig Bay. "You cannot imagine the suspense we are in," noted Seaman Charles W. Julian in his diary.

At 3:30 P.M. the scouts returned with their report. Subig Bay was empty! On the bridge of the *Olympia*, Dewey thoughtfully stroked his moustache as he read the signals from the *Boston*. "Now we have them!" he exclaimed. The squadron turned south for Manila Bay. At 5:30 the *Olympia* signaled for all captains to come aboard the flagship. It was already growing dark as the ships' cutters glided up to *Olympia*'s ladder and the captains and commanders with their

29. "Recollections of Mr. Archie M. Forbis" (first class boy, USS *McCulloch*), U.S. Army Military History Research Collection.
30. "Wayne" to brother, July 31, 1898, in USS *Olympia* Collection.
31. Diary of Charles W. Julian, in RG 45.
32. Carlos G. Calkins, "Historical and Professional Notes on the Naval Campaign of Manila Bay," USNIP, XXV (June, 1899).

aides clambered aboard. Dewey was waiting for them in his cabin. The meeting was brief. The commodore announced that he had decided to enter Manila Bay that evening. The ships would pass through the channel in single file with the *Olympia* leading. Lieutenant William Winder, Dewey's nephew, suggested that one of the supply ships lead the column to set off any mines that might be in the channel. "Billy, I have waited sixty years for this opportunity," Dewey replied. "Mines or no mines, I am leading the squadron in myself."[33]

It was now completely dark. The sea remained calm as the squadron headed south towards Boca Grande. All lights were extinguished except for a small one over the stern of each ship. "There was nothing to see except for the dim outlines of a few ships and the vague outlines of a coast two or three miles distant and there was nothing to hear except the sound of the engine and the swish of the water along the sides."[34]

At 9:45 the crews went to quarters. No hammocks were slung, and the gun crews slept on the decks beside their guns.[35] Around midnight, the squadron entered the Boca Grande Channel. The *Olympia* passed within half a mile of El Fraile but no shots were fired as she passed into Manila Bay. A few minutes later, a gun on El Fraile fired a single five-inch shell at the *Concord* and *Boston*. The *Raleigh*, *Boston*, and *Concord* all opened fire on the rock aiming at the flashes of the enemy's gun. Even the *McCulloch* banged away with her six pounder. After three more rounds, the Spanish batteries fell silent. On shore, signal fires and rockets blazed and from time to time a bugle sounded. But it was all too late. The American squadron was inside Manila Bay.

Dewey continued at slow speed so as not to reach the city before daylight. At 3:00 A.M. the lights of Manila were visible from the *Olympia*. Around 3:20 the word was passed to "stand easy." The men were permitted to lie down at their stations but sleep was difficult. "The decks were sprinkled with sand, and it would get

33. Healy and Kutner, *The Admiral*, 175.
34. Bradley A. Fiske, *Wartime in Manila* (Boston, 1913), 34.
35. Log of USS *Olympia*, Office of the Chief of Naval History; "Report of Commanding Officer, USS *Petrel*," in Dewey Papers.

into eyes, ears and nose, scratch the skin and occasionally someone would stroll over your recumbent form, as leisurely as if on parade."[36]

In the *Petrel*, Lieutenant Bradley Fiske was among the few men who were able to sleep. Around five o'clock Fiske was awakened by a messenger: " 'The captain wishes to see you on the bridge.' 'What about?' I said sleepily. "I don't know,' he said, 'but it is ten minutes to five and they have begun to shoot at us.' " Dawn was breaking as Fiske climbed onto the main deck of the *Petrel*. Far away on the right he could barely make out the Spanish ships off Cavite. The Lunetta and the other batteries before Manila had begun a desultory fire which continued throughout the battle but failed to do any damage. From the *Olympia*, Dewey ordered the squadron to turn three points to the right. The ships were now in column, four hundred yards apart, about three miles from the shore, and steaming parallel to it. As the squadron turned south, the batteries at Cavite and the Spanish ships opened fire. There was no reply from the American ships.

Dewey, wearing his white uniform and a golf cap, stood calmly on the bridge observing the Spanish fleet through his telescope. Beside him, Lieutenant Calkins, the *Olympia*'s navigator, called the range as the squadron moved slowly toward Cavite. The American ships closed up to two hundred yards. There was a great ripping boom as a Spanish shell passed overhead and landed several hundred yards away. Still the American ships did not reply. At last, when the range was about 5,500 yards, Dewey leaned over the rail of the pilothouse and called to Captain Charles V. Gridley in the conning tower: "You may fire when you are ready, Gridley." A few moments later, a sheet of orange flame roared from one of the *Olympia*'s forward eight-inch guns.

The *Petrel* and the *Baltimore* opened fire almost at the same time, and in a few minutes all the ships were covered with thick clouds of drifting smoke. At about five thousand yards, Dewey turned his column to starboard again to bring his ships parallel to the Spanish squadron and unmask his port batteries. All of the Spanish war-

36. Louis S. Young, *Life and Heroic Deeds of Admiral Dewey* (Springfield, Mass., 1899), 72. (Young was editor of the *Olympia*'s newspaper.)

ships could now be seen clearly from the *Olympia*. The *Don Antonio de Ulloa*, an old gunboat which had been unable to make the trip to Subig was moored with springs on her cables so that she would turn easily. Some distance away, the old *Castilla*, her porous sides protected by lighters filled with sand, was moored in a similar manner. The other five Spanish men-of-war were underway and "steamed about in an aimless fashion often masking their comrades' fire."[37]

Dewey and his captains had spent long hours debating the proper formation for the American squadron. Some officers suggested a line as the best formation since this would close the range most rapidly and facilitate ramming. Dewey, however, decided to rely on his superior gun power and adopted a column formation; this would allow his ships to bring the maximum number of guns to bear. Now he led his ships in column from east to west across the length of the Spanish squadron toward Sangley Point and then back again from west to east. The three leading cruisers, the *Olympia*, *Baltimore*, and *Raleigh*, concentrated their fire on the *Reina Christina* which was soon enveloped in a hail of falling shells and spray from near misses.

The *Christina*'s foremast disappeared in a shower of splinters as a shell exploded in the pilothouse, wounding the helmsman and the gun crews of the forward rapid-firing guns. On the next salvo a shell put the ship's steering gear out of commission. Another shell exploded in the hospital, covering the room with blood. Most of the wounded and the medical personnel were killed instantly. At the same time, the ship's rear magazine was hit and had to be flooded to prevent the ammunition from exploding. By 7:30 the *Christina* was a helpless wreck—her masts and smoke stacks shot away, her rudder out of control, and half of her crew out of action. Yet her remaining officers and men continued to blaze away with their few undamaged guns until, at 7:40, Admiral Montojo ordered the crew to abandon ship and shifted his flag to the *Isla de Cuba*.[38] The old

---

37. Chadwick, *Relations Between the United States and Spain*, 177.
38. Patricio Montojo, "Official Report, Battle of Cavite," in *Report of the Secretary of the Navy, 1899; Supplement to the Report of the Chief of the Bureau of Navigation* (Washington, 1899), 91–92.

Castilla was hit by no less than forty shells. Her wooden superstructure was repeatedly set on fire and by 10:00 A.M. she was a mass of flame, her smokestack shot away and all her guns out of action.[39]

In the *Olympia* Dewey led his ships back and forth across the front of the enemy, steadily shortening the range as the leadsman found the water to be sufficiently deep. The first pass was made at 5,000 yards, the next three at 3,000 yards, and the final pass from east to west was made at a range of only 1,800 yards.[40] As the American ships were beginning their second pass, a yellow steam launch flying a big Spanish ensign emerged from the cove behind Sangley Point and headed for the *Olympia*. "There could be but one interpretation of this movement; this was a torpedo boat and she had to be treated as such."[41] All of the *Olympia*'s rapid-fire guns were turned on the launch which was soon hidden in smoke and flying spray. Then the eight-inch guns opened up on her and even the Marines blazed away at her with their rifles. The launch, however, remained afloat, although out of control, and eventually drifted under the guns of Sangley Point, where the *Olympia*'s gunners continued to take potshots at her. The launch was in fact an unarmed Filipino market boat which had taken this inopportune time to make her run to Manila. Yet the "torpedo boat" took her place in the folklore of Manila Bay along with the Spanish "mines." The newspaperman, Joseph L. Stickney, who served as Dewey's volunteer aide, later recalled that he had sunk the launch practically single-handed.

In the *Baltimore* the gunners were as harassed by mechanical failures in their own weapons as they were by the fire of the enemy. The five-inch guns gave the most trouble with the guns frequently jamming, firing pins bending, and extractors breaking. These parts had to be repaired or replaced while at the same time keeping up the ship's fire at the Spanish.[42]

39. John M. Ellicott, "Effect of Gunfire at the Battle of Manila Bay," USNIP, XXVI (March, 1900), 7; Montojo, "Official Report, Battle of Cavite," 92.
40. "Report of Commanding Officer, USS *Petrel*," in Dewey Papers.
41. Calkins, "Historical and Professional Notes on the Naval Campaign of Manila Bay," 11.
42. "Report of Commanding Officer, USS *Baltimore*," in Dewey Papers.

From the *Olympia*, it was very hard to tell what damage if any was being done to the enemy fleet. After two hours of steady bombardment, all of the Spanish gunboats were still underway and their fire had not seemed to slacken. Even the burning *Castilla* continued to return the American fire. At one point the *Christina* attempted to ram the *Olympia*, but a hail of fire from the American ships changed her mind and she retreated back toward Cavite arsenal. In the gun turrets and the engine room spaces of the *Olympia*, the heat was intense; and the crew, not having eaten since the night before, was beginning to feel the strain.

At the beginning of the fifth run, Captain Gridley, his white uniform blackened by soot and smoke, climbed up from the conning tower to the platform over the pilothouse where the commodore was directing the battle. Shouting to make himself understood above the immense racket, Gridley reported that only fifteen rounds of ammunition remained for each of the *Olympia*'s five-inch guns. Dewey immediately signaled the squadron to haul off toward the center of the bay. The situation appeared very serious indeed. The Spanish squadron was still apparently intact after two hours of battle and the Americans were running short of ammunition. "I do not exaggerate in the least," recalled Stickney, "that as we hauled off into the bay, the gloom on the bridge of the *Olympia* was thicker than a London fog in November." At 8:40 the captains were called aboard the *Olympia* to report. The crews, meanwhile, had been told that the squadron had hauled off "for breakfast." "For God's sake Captain," cried one sailor to Captain Lamberton, "don't let us stop now! To hell with breakfast!"[43]

Dewey's officers soon discovered that the shortage of ammunition was the result of a miscount and that none of the ships had suffered any serious damage. A 4.7-inch shell, which failed to explode, had wounded half a dozen men in the *Baltimore*. The other ships reported no casualties at all. From the *Olympia* the crew could now see the Spanish ships, many of them on fire, withdrawing behind Cavite arsenal. Only the *Don Antonio de Ulloa*, her colors still flapping defiantly, remained in Manila Bay.

43. Joseph L. Stickney, "With Dewey at Manila," *Harpers*, XLCII (February, 1899), 15.

At 10:50 A.M., Dewey signaled his ships to get underway again. The *Baltimore*, which had been sent on ahead to check on a merchant steamer coming up the bay, was ordered to lead. When she reached a point directly opposite the batteries on Sangley Point, the *Baltimore* stopped her engines and opened a withering fire on the Spanish earthworks. In a few minutes every Spanish gun on Canacao Bay was out of action. The rest of the squadron concentrated on the *Ulloa* which was nearly blown out of the water. At a signal from Dewey, the little *Petrel* peeled off from the line and circled around the arsenal to get at the Spanish ships in the shallow water behind Cavite. The larger American cruisers began firing over the arsenal at the ships beyond.

In the Spanish squadron, the retirement of the American ships had caused surprise bordering on amazement. Their return caused consternation and a feeling of utter hopelessness.[44] Rounding Cavite, the *Petrel* could see the *Isla de Cuba*, *Don Juan de Austria*, and *Isla de Luzon* aground and partly filled with water. The *Christina* and *Castilla* were burning fiercely in the outer harbor. After a few rounds had passed through the arsenal, the Spaniards hoisted a white flag.

A whaleboat from the *Petrel* set fire to the remaining ships. They continued to burn throughout the day. Late that night, the fires reached the *Austria*'s magazines and she blew up in a spectacular display of fireworks as if celebrating the end of the battle. By 12:50 P.M. not a single Spanish warship remained in action. The Spaniards had lost seven men-of-war and over four hundred men had been killed or wounded. The shore batteries at Manila, the only ones still in action, continued their futile sniping until Dewey sent a message to the governor-general through a British merchant captain threatening to bombard the city unless the firing ceased immediately. The guns fell silent. They did not fire again until the day Manila fell.

In his message to the governor-general, Dewey had offered to leave the Manila-Hong Kong cable intact if he were allowed to use it to communicate with his government. When the governor-gener-

---

44. Concas y Palau, *Causa Intruida*, 89.

al refused, Dewey ordered the *Zafiro* to drag for the cable and cut it. Manila was now isolated and Dewey was more than ever on his own.

"Looking After Things Myself"

In the United States the first news of the battle was a telegram from the Spanish governor-general to Madrid which was reprinted in American newspapers. This telegram, sent during the lull in the action following Dewey's brief withdrawal, stated that the Spanish fleet "had obliged the enemy, with heavy loss, to maneuver repeatedly."[1] Other dispatches from Europe reported that the Spanish fleet had been badly damaged but that American losses had been heavy. At one point it was believed that five of Dewey's ships had been sunk.[2] The next day the New-York *Herald* published a dispatch from its special correspondent in Manila which reported the complete destruction of the Spanish fleet. But it was not until May 7 that Dewey's official report—two short telegrams carried by the *McCulloch* to Hong Kong—reached the United States.

The news of Dewey's victory, after days of anxious speculation, produced almost hysterical rejoicing in the United States. The New York *Journal* held a celebration in Dewey's honor in Madison Union Square, complete with band, fireworks, and more than 100,000 guests. "All the children born on the first of May are being named 'Dewey' by their parents," wrote a friend to the commodore. "They are selling Dewey hats, Dewey cigarettes, Dewey canes. There are Dewey spoons, Dewey candlesticks, Dewey paper weights. . . ."[3] From old friends and acquaintances, from distant relatives and men who had served with Dewey in the Civil War,

1. Chadwick, *Relations Between the United States and Spain*, I, 210–11.
2. *Ibid.*
3. Thomas O. Selfridge to Dewey, May 7, 1898, in Dewey Papers.

and from complete strangers, hundreds of congratulatory letters and telegrams poured into the Hong Kong cable office addressed to Dewey. An eleven-year-old girl in Boston sent him a ten dollar bill "to show you how much the people of Massachusetts think of you." "Every American is in your debt," cabled old friend Theodore Roosevelt.[4]

Lieutenant Fiske, on a visit to the *Olympia*, found Dewey surrounded by three large baskets, the size of wastepaper cans. "Those baskets are full of letters to me," sighed the commodore. "I have already read several dozen and every mail brings in more. I can't possibly answer them and neither can my staff because if we did, we could not do anything else."[5] The "Hero of Manila Bay" received hundreds of requests for autographs and souvenirs. So many people requested gold buttons from Dewey's coat that his uniforms were soon stripped bare and he had to resort to borrowing from his aides.[6]

In the United States newspapers and magazines soon blossomed forth with Dewey songs and poems in which enthusiasm and patriotic fervor more than compensated for any lack of talent. One offering, whose author chose to remain anonymous, was entitled "The Hero of Manila":

> Dewey! Dewey! Dewey!
> Is the hero of the Day
> And the Maine has been remembered
> In the good old-fashioned way—
> The way of Hull and Perry,
> Decatur and the rest
> When old Europe felt the clutches
> Of the Eagle of the West;
> That's how Dewey smashed the Spaniard
> In Manila's crooked bay,
> And the Maine has been remembered
> In the good old-fashioned way.

Another bard, O. H. Cole of Minnesota, composed a song to be

4. Roosevelt to Dewey, May 7, 1898; and Alice J. Mortimer to Dewey, July 16, 1898, *ibid.*
5. Fiske, *Wartime in Manila,* 84.
6. *Ibid.*

sung to the tune of "Yankee Doodle." The title, of course, was "Yankee Dewey."

> Yankee Dewey went to sea
> Sailing in a cruiser,
> He took along for company,
> Of men and guns a few, sir.
>
> He sailed to the Philippines,
> With orders for to snatch them,
> And thrash the Spaniards right and left,
> Wherever he could catch them.
>
> And Yankee Dewey did it too
> He did it so complete, sir
> That not a blooming ship is left,
> Of all that Spanish fleet, sir.

Even Finley Peter Dunne's "Mr. Dooley" was caught up in the Dewey mania. Mr. Dooley, in fact, discovered that the commodore was actually his cousin.

> "Sure," said Mr. Dooley, "Dewey or Dooley 'tis all the same. We dhrop a letter here an' there, except the haitches,—we never drop thim—but we're th' same breed iv fightin' men. . . . 'Surrinder,' he says. 'Niver,' says th' Dago. 'Well,' says Cousin George, 'I'll just have to push ye ar-round,' he says. An' he tosses a few slugs at the Spanyards. Th' Spanish admiral shoots at him with a bow an' arrow an' goes over an' writes a cable. 'This mornin' we was attackted,' he says. 'An,' he says, 'we fought the inimy with great courage,' he says. 'Our victory is complete,' he says. 'We have lost everything we had,' he says. 'Th' treacherous foe,' he says, 'afther destroyin' us, sought refuge behind a mudscow,' he says. . . . 'I cannot write no more,' he says, 'as me coattails are afire,' he says, 'an I am bravely but rapidly leapin' from wan vessel to another, followed be me valiant crew with a fire engine,' he says. 'If I can save me coattails,' he says, 'they'll be no kick comin,' he says. 'Long live Spain, long live mesilf.' "[7]

As late as September, Senator Proctor wrote the commodore that "the Dewey craze has not yet begun to fade. Your picture is everywhere, usually decorated with flags. There is a movement in many states to make May 1 'Dewey Day.' "[8] The pupils of the

7. Finley Peter Dunn, *Mr. Dooley in Peace and War* (Boston, 1899), 17.
8. Redfield Proctor to Dewey, September, 1898, in Dewey Papers.

Collegiate School of Philadelphia selected Dewey as one of the "three greatest men of all time" along with William the Silent and George Washington,[9] while the chef at Dewey's old Metropolitan Club announced the introduction of a new dish: *Poulet Sauté a la Dewey.*

Not a little of the admiral's continued popularity at home was because of his strict censorship of what was reported about his activities by the newspaper correspondents in Manila Bay. As he wrote to his son, "All of their bulletins must go through my hands and be read by me before going forward."[10]

On May 16 Congress passed an act increasing the number of rear admirals from six to seven in order to create a vacancy for Dewey, and passed a resolution of thanks to the commodore and to the men of the Asiatic Squadron. In July, Senator Henry Cabot Lodge, in a fever of hero worship, introduced a resolution that bronze medals be presented to all the men who had served in the battle. The admiral himself was to be presented with a jeweled sword designed by Tiffany's of New York. The resolution passed without debate and the Tiffany sword, in a twenty-two carat gold hilt studded with diamonds, was presented to the admiral by President McKinley himself. Unfortunately, it proved too heavy to wear except at White House receptions. The apogee of hero worship was reached in March, 1899, when, by act of Congress, Dewey was appointed to the rank of Admiral of the Navy with the provision that he might remain on active duty until his death, or if he chose to retire, might still draw his full salary of $14,500 a year.

Dewey himself was not one to belittle his achievements. "The Battle of Manila Bay," he wrote in a letter to his son, "is one of the most remarkable naval battles of the ages." He went on to suggest that young George's boss "should show his appreciation by promoting you."[11] In the manner characteristic of the nineteenth century naval officer, Dewey had already begun to worry about his reputation lasting and to express anxiety that others might surpass him. "This appreciation of the American people is gratifying," he

---

9. Peter Thomas to Dewey, August 26, 1898, *ibid.*
10. Dewey to George Goodwin Dewey, June 16, 1898, in George Goodwin Dewey Papers.
11. *Ibid.*

told a reporter, "but I sometimes wonder if it will last." There must follow other battles in the Atlantic and the glory of triumph in them may surpass that which has come to me."[12] For the rest of his career the admiral was to devote great efforts to insuring that his reputation and prestige were *not* eclipsed.

In any case, it was to be more than a year before the admiral could return home to enjoy the adulation of his countrymen. For the present, the Battle of Manila Bay had created more problems than it had solved. The Spanish squadron had been annihilated and American ships commanded the broad waters of Manila Bay,[13] but the city remained in Spanish hands. In a cable to Secretary Long, Dewey stated that his force could "take the city at any time, but have not sufficient men to hold." Long replied that troops were on the way and asked how many were required.[14] Until the troops could arrive, Dewey's ships had to maintain the blockade in the blazing heat of the Philippine summer. "The time dragged very drearily," recalled Bradley A. Fiske. "The weather was hot and enervating and almost our only recreation was sitting in the poop and talking about what was going to happen. Mosquitoes were a constant nuisance."[15]

Dewey was soon to have more than mosquitoes to contend with. The destruction of the Spanish fleet had opened a whole Pandora's box of new problems. The Spanish government began almost immediately to prepare reinforcements to relieve Manila and, with the future of the islands now so uncertain, other powers, particularly Germany and Japan, began to cast covetous eyes on the Philippines. Moreover, the Philippine insurgents, encouraged by the Spanish reverses, were intensifying their efforts and had already extended their control over large areas of Luzon.

The threat of powerful Spanish reinforcements was the most pressing problem. At the outbreak of the war, the Spanish navy, most of whose larger ships were either unfinished or hopelessly

12. John Barrett, *Admiral George Dewey: A Sketch of the Man* (New York, 1899), 19.
13. The batteries at the entrance to the bay surrendered peaceably to the Americans a few hours after the battle.
14. Dewey to Long, May 4, 1898, and Long to Dewey, May 7, 1898, both in RG 45, Area 10 file.
15. Fiske, *Wartime in Manila*, 61.

antiquated, was no match for the small but efficient navy of the United States. Shortly after the beginning of the war, Admiral Pasqual Cervera, with four of the best ships—the armored cruisers *Almirante Oquendo, Christobal Colon, Maria Teresa,* and *Viscaya*— and two destroyers, had sailed for the West Indies. After successfully eluding the American fleet, Cervera slipped into the harbor of Santiago de Cuba. The Americans finally discovered him there ten days later, safely at anchor behind the Spanish batteries.

Meanwhile, news of the disaster in the Philippines caused widespread consternation and dismay in Spain, and the government felt it was essential to make some effort to reinforce the islands. When Cervera's squadron sailed, he had left behind two large ships: the old battleship *Pelayo,* which had been built in France in 1885, and the armored cruiser *Carlos V,* which was under repair. On June 15, the minister of marine ordered Admiral Manuel de la Camara to proceed with these ships to the Far East. Camara's squadron, besides the *Pelayo* and *Carlos V,* consisted of the auxiliary cruisers *Patriota* and *Rapido,* two large, fast converted merchant steamers, and two armed transports with troops embarked. Although this was not a very formidable fleet it was, on paper at least, superior to Dewey's squadron which had no armored ships and nothing to match the big guns of the *Pelayo* and *Carlos V.*

In Paris, the alert young naval attaché, Lieutenant William S. Sims, watched these developments with interest. Sims and his colleague in London, Lieutenant John C. Colwell, operated a whole network of agents and informers throughout France and Spain. Sims's agents not only provided him with information, but enabled him to give out false information to the Spanish officials in Paris. By mid-May, Sims was convinced that Camara's destination was the Philippines. One of his agents, an intimate of the Spanish ambassador in Paris, reported that the squadron was fitting out at Cadiz but would not be ready to sail before the end of the month.[16] In Washington, the Naval War Board urgently advised the secretary that modern coast defense guns and mines be sent to Dewey at once and that the monitor *Monterey,* then on the West Coast, be

16. Sims to Office of Naval Intelligence, May 20, 1898, in RG 38, Records of the Office of Naval Intelligence.

ordered to the Philippines. At the same time, reports of a possible Spanish expedition to the Philippines reached Dewey, who asked, in a telegram to Long, to be kept informed of the movements of the Spanish squadron and, if possible, that a battleship or armored cruiser be sent to reinforce him. Long replied that the Spanish squadron had not yet sailed and that the monitor *Monterey* had been ordered to the Far East and might reach Dewey by the end of July.[17]

In Paris, Sims now played his trump card. He dispatched his best agent, an impoverished French baron and former naval officer, to Madrid, where he soon became an intimate of one of the Spanish cabinet ministers.[18] On June 16 Sims reported that Camara had sailed. The Naval War Board, now thoroughly alarmed, advised the secretary that two of the battleships of the North Atlantic Squadron, then blockading Cervera at Santiago, ought to be detached and sent to raid the Spanish Coast if Camara should actually pass the Suez Canal. In the meantime, this force, under the command of Commodore John C. Watson, was to remain in readiness with Commodore Sampson's fleet off Santiago.

On June 18 the department cabled Dewey that the Spanish fleet was off Ceuta headed east toward Suez and that the monitor *Monadnock* was also being sent to reinforce him. It was unlikely, however, that the slow *Monadnock* could reach Manila before Camara. The *Monterey* was being delayed by engine trouble at Hawaii, and the second and third contingents of the American army force, destined for the Philippines, were still at sea. General F. V. Greene, the commander of the second contingent, which arrived in the Philippines on July 17, calculated that if all these forces made their best speed, Camara would reach Manila on July 26, the third army contingent on July 28, the *Monterey* on August 4, and the *Monadnock* on August 14.

The Navy Department, through Sims and his agents, had meanwhile been carrying on a war of nerves with the Spanish government. Sims's men were amply supplied with alarming tales

17. Records of the Naval War Board, in RG 45; Dewey to Long, May 27, 1898, and Long to Dewey, May 29, 1898, in RG 45, Area 10 file.
18. Sims to ONI, May 28, 1898, in RG 38.

about what Watson's squadron would do to the Spanish coastal cities once Cervera had been destroyed. These reports produced widespread concern among the public but failed to persuade the Ministry of Marine to recall Camara.[19] On June 26 the department telegraphed that Camara was off Port Said. The next day, he was reported to have passed through the Suez Canal.

Although concerned about the progress of Camara, Dewey remained outwardly calm and confident. "We will have the *Monadnock* and *Monterey* here in early August, I hope, and then the Dons will be sorry they came," he wrote to his son George. "But I wish the *Monterey* were here *now!*"[20] Precisely what plan Dewey had evolved for meeting Camara remains a matter of conjecture. The Naval War Board had recommended that he withdraw eastward in order to rendezvous with the *Monterey* and the *Monadnock* and then return and attack Camara. According to General Greene, who met with the admiral soon after his arrival in the islands, this was precisely what Dewey planned to do. General T. M. Anderson, who would remain behind as commander of the army troops already ashore, was confident that his troops could hold out in the hills west of Cavite until the fleet's return, which Dewey believed would not be later than August 10.[21] Nathan Sargent, however, in his semiofficial account, suggests that Dewey planned to "leave Manila with his whole force and go to the southern archipelago" where he would "attack the Spaniards in the flank while they were hampered with transports and colliers."[22]

The question of a plan, however, became purely academic on the morning of July 3 when Admiral Cervera's squadron at Cuba suddenly emerged from Santiago harbor in a half-hearted attempt to escape the American blockaders. Within a few hours, the entire Spanish squadron had been annihilated by the American fleet under Admiral Sampson. This unexpected battle radically altered the strategic picture at sea. Less than a week after the battle, Commo-

19. Allen to Sims, June 9, 1898; Long to Sims, June 11, June 18, 1898, in RG 38.
20. Dewey to George Goodwin Dewey, July 18, 1898, in George Goodwin Dewey Papers.
21. Francis V. Greene, "The Capture of Manila," *Century Magazine*, LVII (March–April, 1899), cited in Chadwick, *Relations Between the United States and Spain*, II, 382.
22. Sargent, "Dewey and the Manila Campaign," 74.

dore Watson hoisted his broad pennant in the battleship *Oregon* as commander of the raiding squadron, now renamed the Eastern Squadron, and began taking on coal for his voyage to Spain.

But the navy's war of nerves and the crushing defeat at Santiago now began to have their effect. On July 9 Señor Mateo Sagasta rose in the Cortes to demand that Camara be recalled and to predict that the widespread popular fear of the American raiders might lead to an uprising if he were not. When the cabinet met, the minister of marine still argued for sending Camara on to attack Dewey or even San Francisco! But his colleagues demured.[23] Camara turned around in the Red Sea and headed back toward Spain with the only remaining force capable of reasserting Spanish sovereignty in the Philippines.

Next to the Battle of Manila Bay itself, probably the best-remembered thing about Admiral Dewey at Manila Bay is his misadventures with the Germans between May and August, 1898. Around these events a whole array of venerable legends has grown up, steadily embellished over the years, until today they are often repeated quite uncritically in many texts and popular histories.[24] At the time, and ever afterward, Dewey tended to look upon these events as part of a personal contest between himself and "the Dutch." In fact, only a few of the complicated diplomatic maneuvers among the great powers were precipitated by the imminent Spanish loss of the Philippines. The Spanish defeat at Manila Bay had created a sort of power vacuum in the Philippines which, in view of the precarious balance of power in East Asia and the ambitions of the great powers, could not remain unfilled.

The Germans were particularly interested in the situation in the Far East. They had entered the colonizing business later than their French and British rivals and were anxious to pick up any stray

23. Sims to ONI, July 14, 1898, in RG 38.
24. Perhaps the hardiest and most widely believed of these myths is the story that, during the American naval attack on the city of Manila, the British commander, Captain Edward Chichester, moved his squadron between the Americans and the Germans to prevent any acts of treachery on the part of the latter. This myth was effectively dealt with as long ago as 1958 when William R. Braisted showed that, while two of the British ships did steam in between the American and German squadrons, they were motivated solely by the desire to have a better view of operations. (*The United States Navy in the Pacific, 1897–1909* [Austin, 1958], 49.) Nevertheless the story still appears from time to time in American history texts.

pieces of territory. German naval officers urged their government to acquire coaling stations at strategic points in East Asia and the Pacific. A few days after Dewey's victory, Prince Heinrich of Prussia, the admiral commanding the Asiatic Squadron, informed his government that now that Spanish rule appeared to be at an end, "the natives would gladly place themselves under the protection of a European power, especially Germany." The prince's source for this extraordinary intelligence was a merchant from Manila who was, coincidentally, a German. A few days later, Consul Kruger in Manila cabled an even more remarkable report to Berlin. The Filipinos, it seemed, "do not think they are capable of establishing a republic and believe they would be best off as a kingdom. The throne would probably be offered to a German prince."

These dispatches were received with considerable excitement in Berlin, where the chancellor, Bernhard von Bülow, observed that "in the end, the control of the sea may depend upon who rules the Philippines, either directly or indirectly." The kaiser scribbled an enthusiastic "Ja!" in the margin. But von Bülow cautioned that it would be necessary to proceed with care. The offer of the throne was tempting, but there was the unhappy experience of Maximillian in Mexico to consider. In any case, the wishes of the natives could not weigh against the wishes of the great sea powers. England and the United States might come to an agreement about the Philippines whereby one or the other might annex the islands. Germany must therefore avoid any overt moves in the Philippines until she had reached an understanding with one or another of the great sea powers. In the meantime, it would be wise to send Vice Admiral Otto von Diederichs, who had just assumed command of the Asiatic Squadron, to the Philippines with his command to make an on-the-spot investigation of the situation and to determine the wishes of the natives.

A few days later, the kaiser informed von Bülow that the Philippines must not pass to any other power either wholly or in part without Germany's receiving some equitable political compensation. "His Majesty views the Philippines with the greatest interest," observed von Bülow to the German ambassador in London.[25]

25. All German correspondence from *Die Grosse Politik*, XV, 34–39; see also Lester B. Shippee, "Germany and the Spanish-American War," *American Historical Review*, XXX

On June 2 Admiral von Diederichs was ordered to "proceed to Manila in order to form personally an opinion on the Spanish situation, the wishes of the natives and foreign influences upon the political situation."[26] The admiral was never informed about the larger political implications of his mission, or of the plans of von Bülow and the kaiser for the Philippines.

The first German ship to arrive at Manila was the small cruiser *Irene* on May 6, 1898. She had been preceded by three other foreign men-of-war: the British gunboat *Linnett* and the heavy cruiser *Immortalite*, and the French cruiser *Bruix*. "The atmosphere of battle was still in the air and could be felt by all who looked upon the scene,"[27] recalled one of the *Irene*'s sailors. The *Irene* was followed by the small cruiser *Cormoran* two days later and then, on June 12, by the first-class cruiser *Kaiserin Augusta* with Admiral von Diederichs. During the following week, two more German ships appeared: the old battleship *Kaiser* and the cruiser *Prinzess Wilhelm*.

Dewey, fully occupied with the enforcement of the blockade and anxiously watching for the arrival of Camara's squadron, viewed the appearance of the Germans with a jaundiced eye. From his autobiography, it is clear that his experiences in China had left Dewey with a deep suspicion of the Germans, whom he viewed as the most aggressive and dangerous of the powers in the East. Of the numerous foreign navies whose warships had visited Hong Kong harbor while the Asiatic Squadron was assembling there, only the Germans seem to have irritated and antagonized Dewey. The Russians, French, and Japanese all had larger fleets in the China seas than the Germans, yet Dewey scarcely mentions them in his autobiography. Every sin of omission or commission on the part of the Germans, however, is described in detail.

The most annoying of these incidents in Hong Kong had occurred during a state dinner given by Prince Heinrich of Prussia,

---

(July, 1925).

26. Commanding admiral to von Diederichs, June 2, 1898, cited in Thomas A. Bailey, "Dewey and the Germans at Manila Bay," *American Historical Review*, XLV (October, 1939).

27. Ernest Heilman to Lt. Commander C. H. Roper, February 4, 1930, in RG 45.

younger brother of the kaiser. When toasts were drunk the American president's health was toasted last of all the heads of state, even though, according to protocol, Dewey—as squadron commander—ought to have taken precedence over some of the other foreign guests. The commodore took this as a deliberate slight directed at his country. He left the banquet at an unusually early hour, and from then on "American officers were conspicuous by their absence at entertainments given by, or for, the Germans." The American social boycott soon became a cause celebre in the small, close-knit circle of European Hong Kong. Eventually Prince Heinrich was obliged to make a personal apology for his mistake, which he attributed to his lack of experience in matters of protocol.[28]

After this, the commodore and the prince appear to have gotten along very well indeed. Dewey later described Prince Heinrich in his autobiography as a "vigorous and charming companion and a thorough sailor." Dewey became a frequent visitor aboard the German flagship *Deutschland*. But his long talks with Prince Heinrich seemed only to confirm Dewey's belief in the aggressive intentions of the Germans.

Whatever his views, Dewey may well have wished that he still had Prince Heinrich to deal with as he contemplated the German squadron, by this time stronger than his own, and commanded by the forceful and stubborn Admiral von Diederichs. The Spaniards, on the other hand, looked upon the arrival of von Diederichs' powerful force as a gesture of support for them, and German relations with the insurgents, about whom the kaiser's foreign office was so solicitous, took a definite turn for the worse. The Filipinos believed that the German squadron might well take sides against them.[29]

As the days wore on, Dewey became more and more apprehensive. By this time, there were nearly a dozen foreign men-of-war in Manila. The British, under Captain Edward Chichester, were friendly; the French and Japanese correct; but the Germans were becoming more and more of a nuisance. Their ships were constantly entering and leaving the bay, steaming about aimlessly, or

28. Dewey, *Autobiography*, 185.
29. von Diederichs to Admiralty, August 2, 1898, *Die Grosse Politik*, XX, 62.

shifting their anchorages at odd hours. The commander of the
British squadron reported that the Americans viewed the "myste-
rious" comings and goings of the Germans as a "gigantic game of
bluff."[30] Dewey insisted on the right to identify all ships entering
the harbor, especially at night, but the Germans frequently ignored his signals and attempts to communicate. The German flagship *Kaiser*, entering the bay at night, ignored the launch sent to
investigate her and continued on into the bay.

On July 6 the steamer *Darmstadt* arrived with relief crews for the
German ships. After the crews had been transferred, however, the
Darmstadt did not depart but remained at anchor with the German
squadron. Dewey feared that her fourteen hundred men might be
used as a landing force.[31] Lieutenant John M. Ellicott of the *Baltimore* noted that there "seemed to be some hook-up between the
Germans and Camara."[32] There were also rumors that the Germans were helping the Spanish to improvise torpedo boats in the
Pasig River.[33] Oskar King Davis, a correspondent for a New York
newspaper, was surprised when he called upon the admiral one
morning to find him discussing battle plans with Captain J. B.
Coghlan, "if we should have to fight the Germans."[34]

Events finally came to a head early in July. On the afternoon of
July 6 the small German cruiser *Irene* was cruising in Subig Bay
when her lookouts reported a Spanish launch approaching, flying
a white flag. The launch carried a message from the commander
at Isla Grande, the last Spanish stronghold on Subig Bay, which
was then under heavy attack by the Filipino insurgents. Fearing
that the place was about to fall, the Spanish commander implored
the Germans to evacuate his women and children. Commander
Obenheimer, the *Irene*'s captain, hesitated. He was under orders
not to interfere in any way with operations. On the other hand, he
could not well leave noncombatants to the mercy of the insurgents.
Everyone in Manila had heard stories about the treatment of Span-

30. Bailey, "Dewey and the Germans," 65.
31. Dewey, *Autobiography*, 257.
32. John M. Ellicott, "The Cold War Between Dewey and Diederichs in Manila Bay,"
USNIP, LXXXI (November, 1955), 123.
33. *Ibid.*
34. Oskar King Davis, *Released for Publication* (New York, 1925), 13.

iards who fell into their hands. There was no time to request instructions from Admiral von Diederichs. Reluctantly, Obenheimer ordered the *Irene* to proceed to Isla Grande.[35]

Early the next morning, two American warships, the *Raleigh* and the *Concord*, entered the bay on their way to bombard the Spanish outpost. Near the entrance to the bay they passed the *Irene*, headed back for Manila with her noncombatants aboard. The *Raleigh* had already cleared for action but "general quarters" had not yet sounded on the *Concord* and her topside watch stared idly at the German cruiser as she steamed by. A few minutes later the *Concord* also cleared for action and both ships opened fire on Isla Grande.[36] That was all. The *Irene* barely noted the arrival of the two American ships in her log.[37] Yet Dewey believed, or professed to believe, that the Germans had been interfering on behalf of the Spaniards and that only the arrival of the American ships had caused them to break off their activities and flee the bay. Dewey later declared that he had purposely sent two of his smaller ships to Subig so that the odds would be fairly even if the *Irene* wanted to fight.[38]

The same day, Dewey sent his flag lieutenant to the *Kaiser* with a stiff note summarizing the American complaints about the conduct of the Germans. They had consistently ignored his efforts to communicate. One German ship, entering the bay in the middle of the night, had failed to stop or identify itself until an American ship fired a shot across her bow. The Germans' night movements obliged the Americans to expose their positions to the Spanish by turning on their searchlights.

Admiral von Diederichs mildly replied that he had no intention of interfering with the American operations and promised that as far as possible, he would avoid all movements of his ships at night. He told the flag lieutenant that many of the incidents complained of had not been brought to his attention before and concluded by observing that "Admiral Dewey had conducted the blockade in the

35. Heilman to Lt. Commander C. H. Roper, February 4, 1930, in RG 45.
36. Bailey, "Dewey and the Germans," 65.
37. Braisted, *The United States Navy in the Pacific*, 38. Captain Coghlan of the *Raleigh* found no conclusive evidence that the Germans had been interfering with the insurgent operations.
38. Bailey, "Dewey and the Germans," 66.

mildest possible way and he did not want to embarrass him in the slightest."[39]

Three days later von Diederichs sent his own flag lieutenant to the *Olympia* with an explanation of the alledged German infractions. The lieutenant was also instructed to protest the boarding of the *Irene* on June 27 by the revenue cutter *McCulloch*. At this point, Dewey lost his temper. "Why, I shall stop each vessel whatever may be her colors," he raged at the astonished lieutenant. "And if she does not stop, I shall fire at her! And that means war, do you know Sir? And I tell you, if Germany wants war, all right, we are ready."[40] This melodramatic episode was reported with relish by Dewey's admirers who concluded that the admiral had, by his firm stand, frightened the Germans into mending their ways.[41] In fact, Admiral von Diederichs refused to attach any importance to Dewey's statements, "especially not to the threats" which he attributed merely to Dewey's losing his temper under the strain of his responsibilities.[42]

The real question at issue between the Germans and the Americans was a highly technical one. It involved the American insistence on establishing the identity of all ships in the blockade area. With the Spanish reinforcements expected at any time, this was a necessity. Dewey pointed out that a neutral flag was not sufficient to establish the identity of a strange man-of-war. The Spanish might hoist a neutral flag as a *ruse de guerre*. If the vessel were intercepted at night, as the German ships often were, the problem of establishing her identity would be even more difficult. Therefore, Dewey claimed the right to establish the identity of strange ships by signaling, hailing, and visiting.

The Germans acknowledged Dewey's right to stop ships and establish their identity, but they refused to concede the right to board their ships. Under international law, the right of visit and search was confined to merchantmen. Men-of-war could not be boarded without permission. The Germans believed that Dewey

39. *Ibid.*
40. *Ibid.*, 67.
41. Sargent, "Dewey and the Manila Campaign," 72.
42. *Die Grosse Politik*, XX, 63.

claimed the *droit de visite* with respect to men-of-war in the harbor. In a letter to von Diederichs, the day after his outburst, Dewey explained that as commander of the blockading force, he believed he had the right to stop any vessel entering or leaving the harbor and "to make such inquiry as was necessary to establish her identity." Von Diederichs responded by issuing orders to his commanders to resist, by force if necessary, any attempt to board their ships except at night. Even Captain Chichester agreed with von Diederichs that Dewey did not have the right to visit and search neutral men-of-war. Tensions eased somewhat on the fourteenth when Dewey explained that by "inquiries to establish identity" he did not necessarily mean visit and search. With this clarification, a tacit compromise was reached. The Americans avoided incidents with the Germans during the day and the Germans allowed their ships to be boarded after dark.

During all this time, Washington remained largely unaware of Dewey's difficulties with the Germans. In his autobiography, Dewey reports that when he was later questioned about this by the president, he replied that "it seemed best that I look after it myself at a time when you had worries of your own."[43] He noted that he had already had some experience of blockade in the Civil War and that "international law had been one of my favorite studies."

Dewey's decision not to "worry" the president with his difficulties left Washington wholly in the dark during the first few weeks of complicated maneuvering over the disposition of the Philippines. Little reliable information could be obtained from the American legation in Berlin. The ambassador, Andrew D. White, an admirer of all things German, was antiexpansionist in foreign policy matters. He viewed the German moves with small concern, observing that "the advancement of the German colonial system means the spreading of civilization."[44] Although alarmed from time to time by the strident anti-Americanism of the German press, White was never seriously worried about German intentions during the first weeks of the war.[45]

43. Dewey, *Autobiography*, 252.
44. Shippee, "Germany and the Spanish-American War," 270.
45. *Ibid.*, 267; Andrew D. White, *The Autobiography of Andrew D. White* (New York,

Under these circumstances, the first intimation of trouble with Germany which Washington received, aside from unsubstantiated newspaper accounts, was Dewey's telegram of July 13 reporting that the *Irene* had attempted to prevent the insurgents from taking Isla Grande.[46] The same day, Ambassador White reported the substance of a conversation he had had with Baron von Richtofen, the acting head of the German Foreign Office. Von Richtofen told the ambassador that Germany ought to be allowed to acquire Samoa and the Caroline Islands as compensation for the American annexation of Hawaii and that "one or two positions in the Philippine group and the Sulu Archipelago would be wanted."[47] White remained unperturbed by von Richtofen's remarks. He agreed that such a settlement would go far toward improving German-American relations, but explained that his government had not yet arrived at a definite decision on these matters and therefore he had no instructions on the colonial question one way or the other.

Commander Francis M. Barber, the American naval attaché in Berlin, took a much less sanguine view. Thoroughly alarmed by White's report of his "unofficial" conversation, he personally telegraphed the Navy Department to urge that Dewey's squadron be doubled as an unofficial reply to the Germans. Secretary Long sharply instructed Barber to confine himself to military matters and to leave political affairs to White. Nevertheless, the reports of White and Barber, supplemented by rather lurid tales from Sims's and Colwell's agents in Spain and by Dewey's telegram, had thoroughly alarmed the government. On July 22, the secretary of state instructed White to ascertain discreetly how long the Germans intended to keep their squadron at Manila. On the same day, Long telegraphed Barber to "ascertain quickly and quietly what armored vessels are preparing for sea in German ports, with state of preparation."[48]

Barber replied that Germany had six battleships and seven armored coast-defense ships, all in a high state of readiness, but that

1905), 168–70.
    46. Dewey to Secretary of the Navy, July 13, 1898, in RG 45, Area 10 file.
    47. Shippee, "Germany and the Spanish-American War," 269.
    48. Long to Barber, July 22, 1898, in RG 45, Area 10 file.

there appeared to be no night work or other unusual activity indicating preparations for war.[49] A few days later, White saw von Richtofen again. Expressing his personal opinion, White said that German-American tension might be eased if the German ships at Manila would come and go rather than remain constantly at Manila.

In Manila itself, the tension had lessened perceptibly. The *Irene* sailed on July 9 and Dewey had been reinforced by the cruiser *Charleston* and a contingent of American troops on June 30. Dewey and von Diederichs took to exchanging personal calls, and Dewey allowed the Germans to buy fresh meat from the British steamer *Culgoa*, which had been purchased for the Americans in Hong Kong. In a letter to Consul General Rounseville Wildman in Hong Kong, Dewey allowed that "the Germans are behaving better and I don't think there is the slightest intention on their part to interfere at present. What they may do later remains to be seen."[50] On July 4, perhaps to induce the department to expedite the arrival of his monitors, Dewey cabled: "Hope *Monterey* will be here before surrender to prevent possible interference by the Germans."[51]

This telegram, the first to suggest that the Germans might intervene, produced a flurry of excitement in Washington. Plans were pushed forward to reinforce Dewey with battleships from the Atlantic Squadron, but the "danger," such as it was, had already past. The German Foreign Office discovered that it could find no support among the great powers for its scheme to acquire a part of the islands or to neutralize them under great power protection. The British were openly opposed and informed Ambassador John Hay in London that they would prefer that the United States take the islands. The Japanese were unwilling to do anything that might offend the United States.[52] On August 2, von Diederichs informed his government that his stay at Manila had made him extremely skeptical of any insurgent inclination towards Germany. The Fili-

49. Barber to Long, July 23, 1898, in RG 38, Incoming Cables.
50. Edwin Wildman, "What Dewey Feared in Manila Bay," *Forum*, 59 (May, 1915), 528.
51. Dewey to Long, July 4, 1898, in RG 45, Area 10 File.
52. J. K. Eyre, "Japan and the American Annexation of the Philippines," *Pacific Historical Review*, XI (March, 1942), 55–73.

pinos repeatedly asked why such a large squadron had been sent to Manila when, during past outbreaks, one or two ships had sufficed. It was widely believed among them that the Germans had come to take sides with the Spanish against the insurrection.

Under these circumstances, the German government rapidly lost interest in the Philippines and concentrated on acquiring the Ladrones and the Carolines. On August 18, Ambassador White reported that von Diederichs with the battleship *Kaiser* had been ordered to represent Germany at the celebration of the coronation of the queen of the Netherlands in Batavia. In any case, Dewey's squadron, strengthened by the arrival of the *Monterey* and *Monadnock* on August 4 and 16, was now superior to the German fleet.

By the signing of the Spanish-American armistice on August 12, the Germans had ceased to figure seriously in Dewey's calculations. But his experience with von Diederichs left a bad taste in his mouth. When the French admiral called on board the *Olympia* to say goodbye, he congratulated Dewey, saying that "in all your conduct of affairs here, you have not made one mistake." Dewey is reported to have replied: "Oh, yes, I made one. I should have sunk that squadron over there." For years afterwards, Dewey was strongly—almost fanatically—anti-German. At times his conduct as president of the general board was to be strongly influenced by this almost paranoid suspicion of the Germans.

CHAPTER IV

"If the People Knew What You Favored"

> "If I was Mack, I'd lave it to George.
> I'd say: 'George,' I'd say, 'if
> ye're f'r hangin' on, hang on it is.
> If ye say, lave go, I dhrop thim.'
> Twas George won thim with' shells,
> an' th' question's up to him."
>
> [Finley Peter Dunne, *Mr. Dooley in Peace and War* (Boston, 1898), 47.]

Of all Dewey's activities at Manila, none was more important and, in the long run, more tragic than his relations with the insurgents. After his one-sided victory in the Battle of Manila Bay, the admiral enjoyed as great a degree of public adulation as any man since the Civil War. Americans were confident that he, better than any other man, understood the complicated developments in the islands which were reported in the newspapers during the spring and summer of 1898. As the Washington *Post* observed: "It is by no means certain that history will not glorify Dewey quite as much for his management of the stormy elements on the island as for his splendid naval achievement."[1] Had Dewey taken a firm stand on the question of annexation he might well have had a decisive influence on the course of the debate. "If the people knew what you favored," wrote his friend and sponsor Senator Redfield Proctor of Vermont, "they would all fall in with you so earnestly that both the President and Congress would have to agree."[2] As Albert Shaw recalled, "So

---

1. Washington *Post*, June 28, 1898.
2. Redfield Proctor to Dewey, November 19, 1898, in Dewey Papers.

unbounded was the confidence of the country in his good sense and knowledge of the questions at stake, that a good part of the country reserved judgment upon the question whether or not we were rightly in the Philippines . . . until the Admiral should speak."[3]

During 1898 and for a number of years thereafter, until the echoes of the great debate finally died, Dewey was confidently invoked as an authority by both sides. The imperialists lauded him as one of the first Americans to see the "advantages" of American possession of the Philippines, while the anti-imperialists declared that he had done all in his power, consistent with his duty as a senior naval officer, to warn the government of the folly of its course in the islands. In fact, the question of what Dewey favored is far more complex than these simplistic arguments suggest. Indeed, an examination of the admiral's beliefs and misconceptions throws considerable light on the whole confused and ambivalent attitude of Americans towards the Philippines in those crucial months after the victory at Manila Bay.

Before considering Dewey's views, it is well to keep in mind the fact that for several weeks after the Battle of Manila Bay Washington was cut off from all but the most cursory communication with Dewey because of the absence of telegraphic communications. Yet even had Dewey been in full communication with Washington, the information he could have supplied about the political situation in the Philippines was of very limited value. He was, in fact, nearly as uninformed about the volatile state of affairs in the islands as were his admirers back home. Having little direct contact with the Filipino people, he relied on heresay, rumors, and the advice of non-Filipino "experts." These frequently served to reinforce his own misconceptions.

Most of Dewey's information about the political situation in the Philippines came from two consular officials in Manila: the American Consul Oscar F. Williams and the Belgian Consul Edouard Andre. It will be recalled that Williams had assured Dewey that the Filipinos, who were then in revolt against the Spanish, would welcome an American attack on Manila and subsequent annexation to the United States.[4]

3. Quoted in Mark Sullivan, *Our Times* (4 vols.; New York, 1927), I, 337.
4. Williams to Dewey, March 10, March 12, 1898, in Dewey Papers.

Returning to the Philippines with Dewey's squadron, Williams continued to advise the admiral on the mood of the insurgents. Although the Filipinos rapidly set about establishing a provisional goverment, nothing Williams saw caused him to change his mind about the ultimate desire of the Filipinos to belong to the United States. Reporting on the Philippine Declaration of Independence and the establishment of a provisional government, Williams blandly observed that "a form of government was adopted but Aguinaldo and his friends all hope the Philippines will be held as a colony of the United States. . . . It has been my effort to maintain harmony with the insurgents in order to exercise influence hereafter when we reorganize the government."[5]

Dewey received much the same information from Edouard Andre, another self-styled expert on the Philippines. Andre had large business interests in Manila and elsewhere and was naturally anxious to have law and order restored in the islands by some "civilized" power rather than face the uncertainties of the provisional government. Andre was instrumental in arranging the almost-bloodless surrender of Manila to the American forces, and Dewey placed great confidence in his judgment and integrity.[6] Andre's advice was much the same as Williams': the Filipinos would welcome American rule. "The Indians," Andre advised Dewey, "do not desire independence. They know they are not strong enough; they trust the United States government, and they know that they will be treated rightly."[7] In August, Andre wrote to Dewey that he had received letters from "advanced natives" in all parts of the Philippines who "inform me that they are really anxious to recognize the authority of the American government and resume their normal pursuits. The idea of independence has very little influence with the natives who, as a rule, do not consider their country as a nation and have no idea whatsoever of nationality."[8] Similar assurances came from Rounseville Wildman, the American consul in Hong Kong. Wildman reported that "in spite of all statements to the contrary, I know they [insurgents] are fighting for annexation

5. Williams to Secretary of State, June 16, 1898, in RG 45, Area 10 file.
6. Dewey to Otis, October 19, 1898, in Dewey Papers.
7. Andre to Dewey, August 29, 1898, *ibid*
8. Andre to Dewey, August 24, 1898, *ibid.*

to the U.S. first and for independence second if the U.S. decides
to decline. . . . The most prominent leaders . . . say they would
not raise a finger unless I could assure them that the U.S. intended
to give them citizenship if they wished it."[9]

On the basis of this advice, Dewey could only conclude that the
insurgents were fighting not for independence but merely to throw
off the Spanish yoke and that if the United States should choose
to take the islands, the Filipinos would welcome the move. "At the
beginning I don't believe Aguinaldo had any idea of independence
at all. I think it was simply a case of success turning a man's head,"
Dewey told the New York *Evening Post* in 1901.[10] Before a senate
committee he reaffirmed his belief that the Filipinos had simply
wanted to rid themselves of Spanish rule and that "they did not
look much beyond that."[11]

It would probably be more accurate to say that it was Dewey
who, in May and June of 1898, "did not look much beyond that,"
as he weighed the problems of destroying the Spanish power in
Manila. To the admiral, all political considerations were distinctly
secondary to the main task of destroying the Spanish fleet and
capturing the city. In this context, he thought of the Filipinos
primarily as allies against a common enemy. Despite later denials
and assertions to the contrary, there can be little doubt that Dewey
actively sought the aid of the insurgents in his campaign against
Manila. We know that as early as November, 1897, a member of
the junta had approached Rounseville Wildman, in Hong Kong,
with an offer of an offensive and defensive alliance should the
United States become involved in war with Spain. Wildman reported the proposal to Washington but the State Department was uninterested.[12] Then, in March of 1898 Dewey's squadron arrived in
Hong Kong. One of the officers of the gunboat *Petrel*, Lieutenant

9. Rounseville Wildman to Dewey, July 18, 1898, Philippine Insurgent Records, Records of the Bureau of Insular Affairs, in Record Group 126, National Archives.
10. New York *Evening Post*, March 28, 1901.
11. *Hearings Before the Committee on the Philippines*, 57th Cong., 1st Sess., Senate Doc.
No. 331, Pt. 3 (Washington, 1902), 2932.
12. Rounseville Wildman to Secretary of State, November 17, 1898, in RG 45, Area 10
file.

R. V. Hall, learned of the existence of the Filipino junta through "Mr. Levy," a Hong Kong merchant who had lived in the Philippines. Lieutenant Hall was instructed to meet with the insurgents and find out whether they had any information about the fortification of Manila.[13]

In the first meeting, arranged by Levy on March 2, the Filipinos pressed Hall for information as to what the attitude of the United States would be toward their political aspirations. Hall replied that he "had no authority to make any political arrangements," but that "if they wanted to go and help fight the Spanish, I would bring them a representative of the Commodore."[14] Following this meeting, Commander Edward P. Wood, the *Petrel*'s captain, visited the *Olympia* to report on Hall's conversation. He returned with instructions for Hall to "go back and find out if they wanted to go back to the Philippines, how many men they could muster and what arms they would need."

When Hall met the Filipinos three weeks later, the question of political arrangements was once again raised but Hall remained noncommittal. Under these circumstances, the insurgents appeared "rather reluctant to commit themselves" but said that they could raise five thousand men. After Hall's return, Commander Wood again visited the flagship and returned to report that Commodore Dewey was willing to transport the Filipinos and give them all the arms they wanted.

Ten days later, on April 4, Hall sent word to the Filipinos to send a representative to meet with Commander Wood. The meeting took place two days later at Aguinaldo's headquarters. The Filipino leader, who suspected that Mr. Levy might be a Spanish spy, was cautious. Again he raised the subject of American policy toward the Philippines. According to Aguinaldo, Wood assured him that "the United States neither needs nor desires colonies."[15] Still wary of Levy, who was acting as interpreter, Aguinaldo finally declared that he "did not care to take any part in this war." Wood was not

13. R. V. Hall to H. H. Caldwell, February 8, 1900, copy in Dewey Papers.
14. *Ibid.*
15. *Ibid.*

discouraged, however, and instructed Hall to "tell them when they are ready to talk they can send over to the *Olympia* and see me."[16] Any further talks were rendered impractical, however, by Aguinaldo's sudden departure for Singapore to escape a lawsuit.

While in Singapore, Aguinaldo was approached by the American consul general, Spencer Pratt, who persuaded him to return with Dewey to the Philippines. On April 24, Pratt telegraphed Dewey: "Aguinaldo, Insurgent leader here. Will come Hong Kong, arrange Commodore for general cooperation Insurgents, if desired." Dewey replied immediately: "Tell Aguinaldo come as soon as possible."[17]

Aguinaldo arrived in Hong Kong too late to sail with Dewey's squadron but a member of the Hong Kong committee, Jose Alejandrino, did accompany the American squadron to Manila. Upon Auginaldo's return the leading Filipino exiles in Hong Kong held a hurried meeting. The American victory was now well known and the Americans had reportedly offered arms to the insurgents. Still Aguinaldo was reluctant to return to the Philippines "without first making a written arrangement with the Admiral" and without knowing "the intention of the Americans." At the outbreak of the war he had cautioned his compatriots that the Americans might try to establish a colony in the Philippines.[18] In the end, however, Aguinaldo yielded to the urging of the other members of the junta and agreed to go to Manila. On May 19, the insurgent leader arrived at Cavite aboard the revenue cutter *McCulloch*.

During the next several weeks, Dewey continued to treat the insurgents as associates in a common cause, sharing intelligence, and turning over to them captured Spanish arms and ammunition. During May and June Dewey probably thought of the insurgents as nothing more than useful allies against the Spanish. Their political ideas were of little interest to him and, in any case, there was

16. *Ibid.*
17. Pratt to Dewey, April 24, 1898, Dewey to Pratt, April 24, 1898, in RG 45, Area 10 file.
18. Document 91, Philippine Insurgent Records, and Aquinaldo to insurgent leaders, April 29, 1898, both in RG 126.

little reason to believe that the United States would have any permanent involvement in the islands. Despite his close association with Theodore Roosevelt, Dewey was not an imperialist.[19] "Our government is not fitted for colonies," he declared to Frederick Palmer. "There will be resistance in Congress. . . . We have ample room for development at home. The colonies of European nations are vital to their economic life; ours could not be."[20] In any case, there was no reason for Dewey to expect that the United States would wish to permanently retain the Philippines. Congress had just passed the Teller amendment disavowing any intention to annex Cuba, and it was only logical to assume that if the American people did not desire an island ninety miles from their coast, they would not want a group of islands ten thousand miles away.

The Navy Department plans for war with Spain, while calling for cooperation between the insurgents and the navy, said nothing about retaining either Cuba or the Philippines. The capture of Manila was thought to be useful chiefly as a means of depriving Spain of the revenues of the colony and bringing her to the peace table on American terms. Dewey explained to his son that it was necessary to attack the Philippines because they "belong to Spain" and she "derives large revenues" from them.[21] The admiral's request for only five thousand troops from the United States clearly indicates that he had at that moment nothing more grandiose in mind than the capture of the city and had given no thought to conquering and holding the entire archipelago.

This probably explains Dewey's indifference to the political activities of the Filipinos during May and June. He attached very little importance to the decrees and manifestoes of the Filipino provisional government and forwarded them without comment,

19. On the eve of the war, when he was confident that his squadron would win an overwhelming victory, he still maintained to his son: "I don't see what we have to gain by war with Spain," (to George Goodwin, April 19, 1898, in George Goodwin Dewey Papers).
20. Frederick Palmer, *With My Own Eyes* (New York, 1934), 110. For a somewhat different interpretation of these events, see Nicholson, "Dewey and the Transformation of American Foreign Policy."
21. "Plan of Campaign Against Spain and Japan," June 30, 1897, in RG 38; Dewey to George Goodwin Dewey, April 16, 1898, in George Goodwin Dewey Papers.

often by slow mail. Even the Declaration of Independence by the Philippine Assembly in June, 1898, seems to have made no particular impression on him, and he later testified that he had not even bothered to read it!

When the Filipinos invited Dewey to attend their independence celebration, he politely declined but made no report of it to Washington. When Secretary of the Navy Long telegraphed him on June 14: "Report fully any conferences, relations, or cooperations, military or otherwise, which you have had with Aguinaldo and keep [the department] informed in that respect," Dewey replied: "The United States has not been bound in any way to assist Insurgents by any act or promise and he [*sic*] is not to my knowledge committed to assist us. . . . In my opinion these people are far superior in their intelligence and more capable of self-government than the natives of Cuba and I am familiar with both races."[22]

It was not until Brigadier General Thomas M. Anderson arrived with the first American troops at the end of June that Dewey learned that "there was any disposition on the part of the American people to hold the Philippines." Even after receiving this information, the admiral was not unduly disturbed. He was still privately opposed to keeping anything more than a coaling station in the Philippines; but these, he explained to friends, were his private thoughts as a citizen "which had no place in the public forum." In any case, his anxieties were mainly about what the United States would do.[23] Williams and Andre had assured him that the Filipinos were willing, even anxious, to be annexed to the United States. "Should the United States decide to retain the islands," wrote the admiral to his brother Edward, "I believe the insurgents will disband and accept the situation."[24]

The admiral's only official statement on the question of the Philippines during this period came in response to an inquiry by

22. Long to Dewey, June 14, 1898, in *Annual Report of the Navy Department, 1898, Supplement to the Report of the Chief of the Bureau of Navigation* (Washington, 1899), 103; Dewey to Long, June 27, 1898, *ibid.*

23. Thomas Anderson, "Our Role in the Philippines," *North American Review*, CLXX (February, 1900); Palmer, *With My Own Eyes*, 110; H. Wayne Morgan (ed.), *Making Peace with Spain: The Diary of Whitelaw Reid, September–December, 1898* (Austin, 1965), 41.

24. Dewey to Edward Dewey, September 29, 1898, in Dewey Family Correspondence.

the assistant secretary of the navy regarding the "desirability of the several islands" in case the United States should want to retain one or more after the conclusion of the peace treaty. Dewey replied noncommittally that "Luzon is the most desirable . . . contains most important commercial port . . . friendly natives, civilization somewhat advanced . . . possibly rich in minerals."[25]

This was all that Dewey was ever to say officially on the question of the Philippines. All through the autumn of 1898 as the question of annexation became more urgent, he retained his extraordinary "care not to express definite opinions on great subjects" which correspondents and government officials at Manila had come to know so well.[26] Even the American peace commissioners at Paris could get no inkling of the admiral's views on the future of the islands to guide them in their deliberations. "All of us had expected from the admiral some expression of his opinion with reference to the desirability of retaining the whole archipelago and of what he would prefer," observed Whitelaw Reid, one of the commissioners. "His letter appeared to be merely an amplification of the dispatch which he sent in reply to the first government inquiry as to which island would be preferable in case the government should desire to retain any."[27]

With the arrival of larger and larger numbers of American troops during July and August, relations between the Americans and the Filipinos grew more strained. The first detachment—2,500 men under General Anderson—arrived in Manila Bay on June 30 and established their headquarters at Cavite. Two weeks later, the cruiser *Boston* led the second American convoy carrying the troops of Brigadier General F. V. Greene into Manila Bay. They brought the total American strength in the islands to about 6,000 men.

Manila was by now closely besieged. Inside the city, thirteen thousand hungry Spanish troops and civilian volunteers occupied the old fortifications and a semicircular line of blockhouses and

25. Charles H. Allen to Dewey, August 13, 1898, and Dewey to Allen, August 18, 1898, both in Dewey Papers.

26. Frederick Palmer, "The Nation's Welcome to Admiral Dewey," *Collier's Weekly,* XXIV (October, 1899), 3.

27. Morgan (ed), *Making Peace With Spain,* 55.

trenches around the outskirts of the city. The seaward anchor of the Spanish line was a strong stone fort, Fort San Antonio de Abad, which had the only modern ordnance left to the defenders. All around the landward side, the Filipino insurgents occupied trenches and earthworks. Beginning as a small band who had accompanied Aguinaldo on his return to the Philippines, the Filipino army had grown in a few weeks to somewhere between ten and twenty thousand. The insurgents controlled the waterworks and all landward approaches to Manila. Within the city the Spaniards lived on horseflesh and the Chinese and Filipinos on dogs and cats.

A few miles behind the insurgent lines, in peanut fields fronting on the beach, the Americans established Camp Dewey. Here the American army, now grown to some ten thousand men with the arrival of the third contingent under General Wesley Merritt, set up its headquarters. With all the American expeditionary force now in the Philippines, it soon became clear to the Filipinos that the Americans expected to take possession of the capital without their advice or participation. Dewey advised the department on July 26 that the insurgents had grown "aggressive and even threatening toward the Army."[28]

Despite these developments, Dewey's advisers continued to assure him that most Filipinos wanted the United States to take the islands and that the insurgents were in a minority. Edouard Andre explained that the insurgent leaders had formerly been "mere servants or poor clerks without social position" and that it would be easy to come to an understanding with them "if they were assured that they would be maintained in positions similar to those they now occupy."[29]

General Merritt refused to hold any type of communication with Aguinaldo or even to recognize the existence of his government. On the other hand, the American army was still dependent on the Filipinos for wagons, ponies, and lighters to establish themselves ashore. Moreover, the insurgent positions blocked the American route of attack against Manila. Since the capture of Manila was to

28. Dewey to Long, July 26, 1898, in *Annual Report of the Navy Department, 1898, Supplement*, 118.
29. Andre to Dewey, August 29, 1898, in Dewey Papers.

be a purely American show, some way had to be found to persuade the Filipinos to "move over" and make room for the Americans without, at the same time, acknowledging the existence of the Philippine army. Merritt's method was to instruct General Greene, "on his own responsibility," to persuade the insurgents to evacuate their trenches to the immediate front of the Americans.[30] Greene succeeded in persuading General Mariano Noriel, commander of the sector, to evacuate the trenches by promising him "some pieces of modern artillery" for use against the common enemy. Aguinaldo agreed to the transfer, provided the American request was put in writing by General Merritt. Greene, who knew that Merritt had no intention of recognizing Aguinaldo by communicating with him, promised that the request would be forthcoming *after* the Americans occupied the trenches. When the written request failed to materialize, the Filipinos realized they had been duped. From this time on their attitude toward the American was one of unallayed suspicion.

The Spanish, in the meantime, were chiefly interested in assuring that the city would fall to the Americans and not the Filipinos. Dewey later claimed that as early as May, Spanish Governor-General Basilio Augustin had intimated to the British consul, Robert Rawson-Walker that he was prepared to surrender the city to the Americans.[31] But Dewey, who at that time had no troops to garrison the city, declined the offer. By late July, however, a considerable body of American troops had arrived and Dewey took up the negotiations in earnest through Consul Andre, who was close to the Spanish authorities.[32]

The Spanish governor-general was not averse to the idea of a bloodless capitulation, provided the insurgents could be kept out. In fact, throughout this period, the Spaniards displayed far more anxiety about the insurgents and their attempts to capture the city than they did about the Americans. General Fermin Jaudenes told

30. Greene, "The Capture of Manila."
31. Sargent, "Dewey and the Manila Campaign," 79.
32. This account is based primarily on Oskar King Davis, "Dewey's Capture of Manila," *McClure's*, XIII, 2 (June, 1899). Davis apparently had access to Andre's diary and he quotes from it liberally.

Andre that he "was willing to surrender to white people but never to Niggers."[33]

By mid-July, the Spaniards in the city had heard the news of Cervera's defeat at Santiago, and a few days later they learned that Admiral Camara's reinforcements had turned back for Spain. On July 23 the governor-general intimated to Andre that he might be willing to surrender to the Americans provided that the Americans agreed to keep the "Indians"out of the city and take the insurgent leaders into custody. Dewey refused to consider trying to capture the insurgent leaders, but he assured Andre that he would keep the "Indians"out of the city and that even Aguinaldo would not be permitted to enter if the Spaniards desired that he be kept out.[34] A week later, however, Augustin was dismissed by the Spanish government for sending a telegram to Madrid frankly describing the conditions in Manila and expressing doubt that the city could hold out much longer. The Spanish government replaced Augustin with General Fermin Jaudenes and ordered him to hold the city for Spain at all costs. Jaudenes, however, continued to negotiate with the Americans through Andre.

On August 4, the powerful monitor *Monterey* arrived in Manila Bay; and on August 6, Dewey and General Merritt prepared a letter to the governor-general, notifying him that they would attack the city at any time after forty-eight hours from the receipt of their dispatch. Dewey and Merritt addressed a second letter to Jaudenes on August 9 which pointed to "the inevitable suffering in store for the wounded, sick, women and children" and calling upon the governor for "considerations of humanity" to surrender the city. Jaudenes offered to consult with his government; Dewey and Merritt turned him down.[35] The attack on the city was scheduled for the next morning.

Before dawn on the morning of August 10, the ships of Dewey's squadron were cleared for action. All merchant vessels were ordered away from the city and the foreign men-of-war took up positions to have a better view of the battle. The moment for which the American sailors had waited for more than three months had

---

33. Davis, "Dewey's Capture of Manila," 180.
34. *Ibid.*, 173–74.
35. Chadwick, *Relations Between the United States and Spain*, II, 403.

finally arrived. All eyes were on the *Olympia* which was slowly getting underway. Suddenly, a signal fluttered from the flagship's masthead: "The attack is postponed." The army was not ready and General Merritt had requested more time. The bluejackets had some choice observations on the general's birth and lineage as they shut down their engines and dragged heavy shells back into place in the handling rooms.

Meanwhile, Andre had been working tirelessly to persuade the Spanish governor-general to capitulate. On the eleventh, he warned the governor-general that if a prolonged resistance was made, the Americans would be compelled to let the insurgents come into the city. He induced the governor-general to call a meeting of the Defense Council. The council agreed that the situation was hopeless but believed that they had to make some defense to satisfy the Spanish government. They promised Andre, however, that the big guns of the city's Lunetta battery would not fire unless the Americans fired first. It was also implied that the Spanish troops would not put up much resistance to the American army's advance on the city. They agreed that if Jaudenes desired to surrender, he would hoist a white flag above Fort San Antonio de Abad. The Americans agreed to fly the signal DWHB, the international letters for "surrender," as a signal for the Spanish to display the white flag.[36] On August 12, General Merritt issued General Order Number 4 to his commanders informing them of the details of the coming attack. "If a white flag is displayed . . . the troops will advance in good order and quietly. . . . It is intended that these results shall be accomplished without the loss of life."

On the morning of August 13, while—unknown to Dewey and Merritt—the peace protocol was being signed in Washington, the American ships again cleared for action. At 9:00 A.M., the *Olympia* signaled the ships to take their stations. The *Olympia*, with the *Raleigh* and *Petrel*, took station off Fort San Antonio de Abad while the larger ships of the squadron remained off the city front, well out of range of the shore batteries. At 9:30, the *Olympia* and her consorts opened fire on Fort San Antonio de Abad.

In the *Raleigh*, Captain J. B. Coghlan, who was privy to Dewey's

36. Davis, "Dewey's Capture of Manila," 179–82.

bargain with the Spanish, personally gave the range to his gunners as 7,000 yards, much too long to hit the fort. Lieutenant Casey Morgan, in charge of the forward guns, frantically protested that it wasn't half so far. "Never mind what it looks like!" snapped Coghlan. "I am giving the ranges." In the after five-inch gun house, however, a veteran gunpointer glanced quickly at the fort and declared "seven thousand, Hell!" Dropping his sight bar to 2,700 yards, he soon scored a hit. After this, the whole port battery knew the range and shells began registering on the fort. In disgust, Coghlan sounded "cease-fire" and took the ship out of action.[37]

At 11:00 A.M., J. M. Brumby, the flag lieutenant, ran up the signal DWHB. Twenty minutes later, a white flag could be seen flying from the walls of the city, and Andre's launch came alongside the *Olympia* to pick up the American representatives to arrange terms of surrender.

Ashore, things did not proceed as smoothly. The American advance got underway in a heavy rainstorm. A regiment of Colorado volunteers stormed the fort and found it deserted. A little to the north, the troops struck the El Camino road and advanced toward the walls of the city "not at all as if they were advancing upon the enemy but as if on march with their coffee coolers along and their rifles at right shoulder shift."[38]

Although the action was intended to be "bloodless," no one had bothered to explain this to the insurgents who, in any case, would not have been enthusiastic about a plan which was designed primarily to keep them out of the city. On the right of the American columns, the insurgents flowed and mingled with the Americans on the narrow road. Near the village of Singalong, the Americans came under heavy fire from the Spaniards who were endeavoring to stop the advance of the insurgents. Even while Brumby and the Spaniards were discussing the terms in the governor-general's office, two Americans were killed and several more wounded.

Dewey was furious: "The army need not have lost any [men] if they had not been too brash"; he wrote to his son. "The whole thing was agreed upon between the Spanish governor-general and

37. Davis, *Released for Publication*, 19.
38. Chadwick, *Relations Between the United States and Spain*, II, 413.

myself. . . . The Spanish carried out their part to the letter. So did my ships; but, as I said before, the army was too brash and rushed in too soon."[39] Nevertheless, the operation had been a great success. With almost no loss, Manila was in American hands and the insurgents had been kept effectively out of the city. The capture of the city had taken place two days after the United States had signed an armistice with Spain, but no one knew this in Manila until the sixteenth.

For Dewey, the end of hostilities with Spain did not mark the end of his difficulties. With the fate of the islands still uncertain, the tension and suspicion between the Americans and insurgents steadily increased. The primary responsiblity for dealing with the insurgents now rested with the army commanders. They refused to give the Filipino leaders any assurance about the political future of the islands. The Filipinos, in turn, began to plan quietly for an uprising against the Americans, should this prove necessary. In the meantime, they quietly accumulated arms and consolidated their control over Luzon and the outer islands. In mid-October, Dewey reported that the insurgents controlled most of the archipelago, which was in a state of anarchy.

Like most American commanders in the islands, Dewey had, by this time, concluded that the insurgents were incapable of establishing a stable government. "Now that the Spanish Power has been overthrown," observed General F. V. Greene, "he [Aguinaldo] cannot maintain independence without the help of some strong nation. Admiral Dewey fully concurs in these views."[40]

In November, however, Dewey received contrary evidence from two of his own officers, Paymaster W. B. Wilcox and Naval Cadet L. R. Sargent, who undertook an extended reconnaissance of northern Luzon during October and November of 1898. The two officers traveled hundreds of miles, visited seven provinces, and talked with several hundred people. Sargent reported that "it is a tribute to the efficiency of Aguinaldo's grovernment and to the law-abiding character of his subjects that Mr. Wilcox and I pur-

39. Dewey to George Goodwin Dewey, September 20, 1898, in George Goodwin Dewey Papers.
40. F. V. Greene to Secretary of State, September 5, 1898, in RG 45, Area 10 file.

sued our journey to Manila with only the most pleasing recollections of the quiet and orderly life we found the natives to be leading
under the new regime." The Filipinos "desire the protection of the
United States at sea but fear any interference by land. . . . On one
point they seem united, that whatever our government may have
done for them, it has not gained the right to annex them."[41] Nearly
every person the two officers encountered desired independence
with or without American protection.

Dewey sent the report on to the Navy Department with the
following endorsement: "In my opinion it contains the most complete and reliable information obtainable in regard to the present
state of the Island of Luzon." It seems likely that the Wilcox-
Sargent report significantly altered Dewey's view of the aims and
nature of the insurgent movement. Even Consul Williams was beginning to have second thoughts about the desire of the natives to
belong to the United States. "I shudder at the thought of local
war," he wrote to Dewey at the end of November. "Neither of us
will live to see it end if by shot and shell we attempt to conquer
these natives."[42]

Probably with the Wilcox and Williams findings in mind, Dewey
responded to a request from Washington for "suggestions as to the
government of the islands," by urging his government to promise
the Filipinos "a large and gradually increasing degree of autonomy
under American rule."[43] Again on January 7, 1899, he cabled the
Navy Department that the natives were "excited and frightened,
being misled by false reports spread by the Spaniards. Strongly
urge that the President send here as soon as possible a small civilian
commission to adjust differences."[44]

The same day, in a letter to Senator Proctor, Dewey expressed
the fear that the United States might become involved in war with
the natives. This would be a tragedy, he observed, for the Filipinos
were "little more than children."[45] To his son, Dewey confided that

41. W. B. Wilcox, "Report on a Reconnaissance of Northern Luzon," in Dewey Papers.
42. Williams to Dewey, November 29, 1898, *ibid.*
43. Dewey to Long, December 12, 1898, *ibid.*
44. Dewey to Long, January 7, 1899, in RG 45, Area 10 file.
45. Dewey to Proctor, January 7, 1899, in Dewey Papers.

"affairs are in a very critical state and we may be fighting the insurgents at any moment. We don't want a war with them if we can help it and perhaps it would be better to give up the islands rather than have one."[46] But it was already too late. On the night of February 4, an American and Filipino patrol exchanged shots near the village of Santol outside Manila. The next day, fighting erupted all around Manila. The civilian commission, dispatched at Dewey's suggestion, arrived to find a full-scale war in progress.

During the remaining four months of Dewey's stay in the Philippines, the navy played a relatively minor part in the insurrection, which was to continue in some parts of the islands for the next seven years. Dewey had been named a member of the Philippine Commission which President McKinley had appointed, at his suggestion, to investigate conditions in the Philippines. The commission included Professor Jacob Gould Sherman of Columbia University, who served as chairman; Charles Denby, formerly American minister in China; Dean C. Worcester, a young scientist who had visited the islands on zoological expeditions; and General Ewell S. Otis. The civilian commissioners arrived in March, two months after the outbreak of the insurrection, and began "quietly investigating."[47] In April, the commission began holding regular daily sessions in the Audencia and informal meetings at its headquarters at Number 92 Calle de Real.

Of the sixty-odd witnesses who appeared before the commission in public hearings, less than a dozen were Filipinos, and all of these were lawyers, bankers, physicians, and landowners. Many of them had not been outside Manila in years. The witnesses told the commissioners that only 5 percent of the population supported the insurgents, that the insurgents had "siezed control of the provinces much as robbers hold up a train,"[48] and that the Filipinos were "in general incapable of good government." It all sounded distressingly similar to the kind of "facts" Williams and Andre had reported

46. Dewey to George Goodwin Dewey, January 23, 1899, in George Goodwin Dewey Papers.
47. Jacob Gould Schurman to John Hay, May 20, 1899, Philippine Commission Records, in Record Group 59, National Archives.
48. Schurman to Hay, April 4, 1899, *ibid.*

to Dewey in the summer of 1898. If the admiral doubted the commission's findings, however, he kept it to himself. He made no dissent when the commission reported in January, 1900, that "while the peoples of the Philippine Islands ardently desire a full measure of rights and liberties, they do not generally desire independence."[49]

Dewey seldom attended the meetings of the commission. After the fall of Manila he continued to live aboard the *Olympia* and to conduct the business of the squadron from there. "Sphinx-like, immovable, the *Olympia* always surveyed us. She had become an institution like the cathedral and the Bridge of Spain." The admiral rose every morning at five and took a short walk on deck in the cool morning air before returning to his cabin for breakfast and the morning's business. After lunch he took a short nap and then called for his barge to take him to Manila for his daily drive. Soldiers on leave or convalescing in the capital often crowded the wharf to have a look at the famous Admiral Dewey as he stepped out of his barge and into his carriage.[50]

The admiral's favorite stopping place on his drives through the city was the home of H. D. C. Jones, manager of the Manila branch of the Hong Kong and Shanghai Bank. Mrs. Jones's sister, Beatrice, was renowned throughout the Far East for her beauty, and there is evidence to suggest that the friendship between her and Dewey was more than a casual one.[51] In any case, the Joneses undoubtedly helped to ease the monotony of the admiral's last months in the Philippines.

After a year in the tropics Dewey's health was poor and he was anxious to return home. In May, 1899, he finally secured permission to sail for New York in the *Olympia*.

49. *Report of the Philippine Commission* (4 vols.; Washington, 1899), I, 82; Dewey later told the Washington *Post* that he never read the *Report* (*Literary Digest*, XX, 15 [April 14, 1900].

50. Frederick Palmer, *George Dewey, USN* (New York, 1899), 15, 23; Barrett, *Admiral George Dewey*, 180–81.

51. Barrett, *Admiral George Dewey*, 181; Beatrice Jones to Dewey, May 20, 1899, in Dewey Papers.

CHAPTER V

Dewey for President

In the late afternoon of May 20, 1899, the *Olympia* steamed slowly past Corregidor and out into the open sea. It had been one year and twenty days since Dewey first arrived in the Philippines, and in all that time he had never left the islands. When the *Olympia* had gone to Hong Kong for a rest and refit, he had shifted his flag to the *Baltimore* and stayed on. Now, tired of the endless complications of the insurrection, worn out by the tropical climate, his hair turning gray, Dewey contemplated his return home with unconcealed relief. "I am not sorry to leave," he told a reporter. "I could not stand the care and responsibility much longer."[1]

At Hong Kong, the *Olympia* was dry-docked, scraped, and painted—a brilliant white and buff replacing her drab wartime gray. Dewey declined all but the most unavoidable social events and remained aboard until the ship went into dry dock. On June 11, the *Olympia* departed Hong Kong in a pouring rain amid salutes from the foreign men-of-war in the harbor. Secretary Long had given Dewey a blank check. He might choose his own route home, his own ports-of-call, the length of his visits, everything. It was to be a triumphal return home which would afford foreign powers a chance to view the admiral and newspapers a chance to make endless copy. To his brother the admiral explained that he had chosen the Suez-Mediterranean-Atlantic route "to give my Olympians an opportunity to see something of the world as a reward for good conduct after seventeen months on this station" and (by not

---

1. Halstead, *Life and Achievements of Admiral Dewey*, 446.

having to cross the United States from the Pacific Coast) "to escape as much of the circus racket as possible."[2]

The *Olympia* proceeded slowly from Hong Kong to Singapore, where Dewey was greeted by the outgoing United States consul, Spencer Pratt. Pratt was under intense criticism at home because of his supposed mishandling of Aguinaldo and the Philippine insurgents, but Dewey received him kindly and insisted that he attend the exclusive private dinner that the governor-general of Singapore was giving in the admiral's honor.[3]

From Singapore the *Olympia* steamed across the Indian Ocean and through the Red Sea to Suez. In the United States, the excitement over Dewey's impending return was intense. The admiral had lost none of his hero's aura during his year in the Philippines. Indeed, his very distance seemed to enhance his glamor. Swarms of newspapermen followed the flagship from port to port, reporting every detail of the admiral's daily rounds—whom he met, what he wore, even what he ate. One enterprising woman reporter somehow managed to steal onto the *Olympia*'s quarterdeck and, looking through a skylight into Dewey's cabin, commenced to take notes on how the great man washed and dressed himself. When the admiral happened to glance up through his skylight, the young woman "heard some language which might be classed as Old Testament wrath."[4]

At home, the country prepared to welcome its hero. The New York newspapers had collected seventy thousand dimes from worshipful school children; the dimes were to be melted down into a gigantic loving cup to be presented to the admiral. The city of St. Louis presented him with a silver punch bowl. From dozens of cities came invitations to visit and help dedicate their own Dewey statue or Dewey cannon or Dewey memorial. "I would do anything to escape it all." Dewey wrote to his son, "but I suppose that would be impossible."[5]

Only one incident marred the admiral's stately progress. At Tri-

2. Dewey to Edward Dewey, May 19, 1899, in Dewey Family Correspondence.
3. Palmer, *George Dewey*, 85.
4. Palmer, *With My Own Eyes*, 122.
5. Healy and Kutner, *The Admiral*, 250.

este, where the *Olympia* had put in to escape the heat of the Mediterranean summer, Dewey struck up an acquaintance with a Dr. Boyland, a fellow guest at the Hotel de la Ville, who said he was traveling for pleasure. In a conversation with Dewey, Boyland casually alluded to the recent recall of Admiral von Diederichs as commander of the German Pacific Squadron. That was all that was necessary to set Dewey off on a tirade against the Germans and their foreign policy. "Our next war," the admiral predicted, "will be with Germany." Boyland, who was an amateur correspondent for the New York *Herald*, excitedly telegraphed Dewey's remarks to his paper. The story arrived in New York so late that it was printed without any of the paper's regular editors seeing it. The next morning the whole world knew that the great Admiral Dewey had predicted an American war with Germany.[6] Dewey's remarks, which were all the more unfortunate for having been made while he was enjoying the hospitality of Germany's ally, Austria, caused a flurry in the United States and Germany. Dewey was under great pressure to deny the entire statement. Carl Schurz telegraphed indignantly that all German-Americans, who were among his "most ardent admirers," hoped that the story was not true.[7] The New York *Times* observed that Dewey's Washington friends were "annoyed beyond measure at the story and refused to believe it."[8]

Dewey was aghast. "The fellow didn't say he was a reporter," he told Frederick Palmer. "I should never have said anything of the kind if I knew he was a member of the press."[9] Still, the admiral refused to publicly disavow the statement. "It's true. I can't deny what I know I said."[10] He finally compromised by issuing the following statement: "I long ago gave up denying or affirming newspaper reports." This allowed Dewey's friends to represent the entire story as a fabrication and Germanophobes to quote it to their hearts' content.

The excitement of the story was soon forgotten as New York

6. New York *Herald*, July 28, 1899; Palmer, *With My Own Eyes*, 123; James Gordon Bennett to Dewey, July 31, 1899, in Dewey Papers.
7. Carl Schurz to Dewey, July 31, 1899, in Dewey Papers.
8. New York *Times*, July 30, 1899.
9. Dewey to Palmer, July 29, 1898, in Dewey Papers.
10. Palmer, *With My Own Eyes*, 124.

completed the final preparations for the hero's gala welcome. The Dewey Celebration Committee, headed by General Nelson A. Miles, worked frantically to complete the last-minute details, and the committee members solemnly debated whether the admiral ought to attend a public breakfast before the welcoming parade. The New York *Times* reported that bleacher seats along the parade route were selling at ten to twenty dollars apiece and building owners along the route were putting up their windows at from one to five hundred dollars. The *Times* reported the windows were "selling readily at these prices." At the last moment, the Grand Army of the Republic announced it was quitting the parade because it had been assigned a place to the rear of the National Guard.[11] With more than thirty thousand men scheduled to march, they would hardly be missed.

The admiral himself viewed the preparations with some trepidation. "I expect to anchor off Tompkinsville, New York on the 28th," he wrote his son from Gibraltar. "I expect to go to Washington to receive the sword on Tuesday the 30th, after that to Montpelier for a reception; after that to get out of everything I can."[12]

On September 26, having been delayed by a partially disabled propeller, the *Olympia* finally arrived off Sandy Hook, where the Atlantic fleet was waiting to welcome it. The next day, the fleet sailed up the Hudson River and anchored off Tompkinsville, New York. Dewey arose at 7:00 A.M. and breakfasted with his two aides. At 10:30 the tug *Nina* brought the first boatload of official visitors. These included the New York Welcoming Committee, Admiral William T. Sampson, Admiral Henry Erben, and Senator Proctor. Dozens of other uninvited guests clamored aboard the *Olympia* from yachts and small boats. "Hundreds of camera bugs crawled out on the after turret to try and get a look at the Admiral."

At 1:30, Governor Theodore Roosevelt arrived on General F. V. Greene's yacht *Wild Duck*. On board the *Wild Duck* were all of Dewey's old commanders from Manila: Captain Asa Walker of the *Concord*, N. M. Dyer of the *Baltimore*, Joseph B. Coghlan of

11. New York *Times*, September 19, 21, 1899.
12. Dewey to George Goodwin Dewey, September 10, 1899, in George Goodwin Dewey Papers.

the *Raleigh*, and others. The uninvited visitors, who by this time numbered in the hundreds, now milled about the lower decks hoping to catch a glimpse of the famous visitors. Suddenly a roar went up as the admiral emerged from the wardroom, followed by his guests, and prepared to descend a ladder. "The crowd pushed and jammed forward, men yelling and the women emitting little hysterical screeches of excitement."[13] The admiral and his party quickly retreated back into the wardroom. That evening, the Brooklyn Bridge was brilliantly illuminated by a thirty-six foot sign which read, "Welcome Dewey."

On Friday, September 29, the *Olympia* led the Atlantic fleet in a grand naval parade up the Hudson River. In one column steamed the battleships *Indiana*, *Massachusetts*, and *Texas*, with the armored cruiser *New York* and the other ships of the Atlantic fleet, all gleaming in their white and buff paint. The second column was formed by five torpedo boats and a long line of small craft led by J. P. Morgan's yacht *Corsair*. At one point, the parade of ships stretched from 110th Street to 60th Street. After leading the column as far as Grant's tomb, the *Olympia* turned and dropped anchor to allow the other ships a close look at Dewey's flagship. Sirens and whistles shrieked incessantly, and one correspondent estimated that the ships expended more ammunition in salutes that day than had been fired at the Spanish in Manila Bay.

The next day, the admiral led the long-awaited parade of more than 35,000 men down Fifth Avenue to the magnificent "Dewey Arch" at 23rd Street. Intended to symbolize naval victory, the seventy-foot structure was a wood and plaster model for a permanent arch to be erected later. A million dollar subscription drive was already underway to raise money for the permanent edifice which was to resemble the Arch of Titus in Rome. Beneath the arch, Dewey stood for over six hours reviewing the parade. This was followed by a monstrous reception at the Waldorf Astoria which continued into the following morning. That night the city was treated to eleven different fireworks displays, the most spectacular of which featured a 1,000 square-foot portrait of the admiral

13. New York *Times*, September 29, 1899.

formed by colored rockets.[14] Two days later, the hero was off to Washington and more of the same.

All along the route to the capital, crowds gathered to watch the admiral's special train speed by. At some crossroads settlements, the entire population gathered at the depot to salute their hero. The Washington reception was, if possible, even more grandiose than that of New York. As the admiral paraded through the streets, "women actually fainted in their excitement."[15] More than fifty thousand people watched as the secretary of the navy, in the presence of the president and the entire cabinet, presented Dewey with the jeweled Tiffany sword. In the evening, Dewey dined with the president while the General Post Office Building, as if to rival the Brooklyn Bridge, blazed forth in giant letters: "YOU MAY FIRE WHEN YOU ARE READY GRIDLEY." A few days later Dewey was off to Vermont by special train from Washington. In Montpelier the railroad had been obliged to construct more than a dozen new sidings at the capital's small railroad station to accommodate the trains carrying people to witness the state's salute to her most famous son. More than 35,000 were expected to crowd into the town for the ceremonies.

The admiral arrived late on the evening of October 11. Early on the morning of October 12, "Dewey Day," he slipped out alone to take a quiet walk through the town where he had been born. "I just wanted to see how old Montpelier looked," he told reporters on his return. "It was beautiful, simply beautiful."[16]

Dewey was at the height of his fame. Few, if any, Americans since the Civil War had enjoyed such adoration. Yet within a few months the admiral would change from a figure of universal awe and respect to an object of derision. Having no public-relations firm to advise him, and being, after all, human, the hero made a number of serious mistakes in what would now be termed "the projection of his image." The first of these was his marriage.

14. *Ibid.*
15. *Ibid.*, October 2, 1899.
16. "Admiral Dewey at Home," *Vermonter*, V (November, 1899); Gertrude Symons to Mary P. F. Partlou, October 13, 1899, in Dewey Day Collection, Vermont Historical Society, Montpelier, Vermont.

By 1899, Dewey had been a widower for more than twenty five years. During his years in Washington, he had sedately courted a few of the more eligible ladies of the city but with indifferent success. Among these ladies, one of the most sought after was Mrs. Mildred McLean Hazen, a wealthy widow and the daughter of Washington McLean, founder of the Washington *Post*. Mildred's husband, General William B. Hazen, had been a well-known Indian fighter and later chief signal officer of the army. After his death in 1887, the thirty-seven-year-old Mildred, who had no children, became one of the most eligible widows in the capital. She had been a close friend of Dewey for more than ten years, but there seemed little chance in the 1890s that an obscure navy captain could compete successfully with Mrs. Hazen's more prominent suitors.[17] As the hero of Manila Bay, however, Dewey was a far more formidable contender than he had been two short years before.

The admiral became a frequent visitor at the McLean home in Washington after his return to the capital, and on October 29 he proposed. According to Mildred, they were seated on the sofa when the admiral seized her hand and asked her to "be my dear wife and let me love you all I wish!"[18] Dewey's version is somewhat less dramatic. In his diary, for October 29, he recorded: "Unsettled, later clear. Lunched at the country club with Jesse Brown. Dined at Mrs. McLean's. Engaged." The engagement was announced to the press on the following day and less than two weeks later, the couple was married in great secrecy at St. Paul's Roman Catholic Church in Washington. They were attended only by Mrs. Washington McLean and Dewey's aide, Lieutenant Caldwell.

Mildred McLean Hazen was forty-nine years old when Dewey returned from the Philippines. Like many rich women of her day, she devoted inordinate amounts of time and energy to the pursuit of what was then called "social success." Like many such women, she was also a snob and not at all comfortable in the company of those she considered "underbred and common."[19] As the young wife of the American military attaché in Vienna, she had become

17. Healy and Kutner, *The Admiral*, 141–42.
18. *Ibid.*, 258.
19. Diary of Mildred McLean Dewey, November 12, 1901, in Dewey Papers.

a convert to Catholicism so as to be able to attend church with the Austrian upper classes. After her marriage to Dewey, she again became a Protestant.

One of the wealthiest women of her day, Mrs. Hazen was able to indulge fully her taste for fine clothes and jewelry. In one month her bill for handkerchiefs alone totaled $64.00.[20] A correspondent for the New York *Herald* described her at a White House reception: "She was the most dazzlingly ornamented woman among the hundreds who made their bow to the President . . . her jewels covering her corsage and her hair in bewildering splendor."[21] "On these occasions," she is reported to have declared, "too many jewels cannot be worn."[22] This was the woman who had just become Mrs. George Dewey. There was no woman less likely to have appealed to the broad mass of the hero-worshiping public or less inclined to try.

The wedding did not remain a secret for long. By the time the couple reached Philadelphia on the way to their New York honeymoon, the news was out. As the Deweys' train pulled into Philadelphia, a huge crowd gathered around the parlor car and cheered the newlyweds.[23] By the time they reached New York, an even larger crowd was besieging the Waldorf Astoria where the couple was to stay. The admiral and his lady finally managed to enter the hotel through a private entrance. The next day, when Dewey and his new wife emerged from the Waldorf for a walk down Fifth Avenue, they were almost immediately recognized by passersby, many of whom began to follow them. Soon there was a large crowd following them, and in an effort to shake off their pursuers, the admiral and his wife darted into Tiffany's under the guise of doing some shopping. The proprietor had his private carriage brought to the rear entrance and the Deweys drove back to the Waldorf. Outwardly, the admiral remained unperturbed, but inwardly he was furious. He remarked to the hotel manager that he refused to be treated as a curiosity. To friends, he remarked that his populari-

20. *Ibid.*, November 11, 1901.
21. New York *Herald*, May 6, 1900.
22. *Current Literature*, XXVII, 3 (June, 1900), 255.
23. New York *Times*, November 11, 1899.

ty was becoming something of a burden. He was soon to be relieved of it.

Among the many gifts showered upon the admiral on his return from the Philippines was a handsome house on Rhode Island Avenue, N.W., which had been purchased for the hero through popular subscription. Upon their return from New York, the Deweys moved into their new residence. Solicitous as always of his son's welfare, Dewey was anxious to make sure that, upon his death, the house would pass to George Goodwin. The admiral's attorney advised him that under the laws of the District of Columbia, it would first be necessary to convey the house to Mrs. Dewey who, in turn, could convey it to George.

Shortly after this legal process began, the press discovered that the house was to be conveyed to Mrs. Dewey. A "sudden storm of wrath" flared up against the Deweys and more intensely against Mildred who, it was rumored, planned to turn the house over to the Catholic church.[24] All the latent suspicion and jealousy of Mrs. Dewey, along with general anti-Catholic prejudice combined to bring a tide of insult and innuendo down on her head. So popular did the practice of smearing Mildred become that the Washington newspapers employed a full-time reporter who specialized in "Dewey dirt."[25] The admiral himself did not escape recrimination. "Is it quite gracious, quite courteous, that the hero should let the people's gift go so lightly away?" wrote an irate reader to the New York *Times*. The admiral's belated explanation that he had merely intended to deed the house to his son satisfied almost no one. Even the relatively restrained New York *Times* was skeptical: "The subsequent transfer [of the house] to his son appears to be so direct a consequence of public dissatisfaction that it will do little to mollify public feeling."[26]

Although the flurry eventually died down, Dewey's popularity never quite recovered from these two affronts to the public: his marriage and the deeding of his house. As Frederick Palmer shrewdly observed, Dewey's great mistake had been to marry in the

---

24. New York *Times*, November 25, 1899.
25. Diary of Mildred Dewey, November 12, 1900.
26. New York *Times*, November 21, 22, 1899.

first place. "The public itself was Dewey's sweetheart and it could brook no rivals."

Dewey himself was unable to understand the sudden change in public feeling; he was puzzled and disturbed by the sudden outpouring of vituperation. "I beg you my dear Admiral," wrote John Hay, "do not, I pray you, take the press so seriously."[27] But the admiral was still incredibly popular and this phenomenal popularity was directly responsible for perhaps the most bizarre episode of his career, the "Dewey-for-President" boom in the spring of 1900.

Today, Dewey's short-lived candidacy is a forgotten episode in the political history of the McKinley era.[28] Yet, to contemporaries, the idea of Dewey as presidential timber raised widespread hopes and fears, even among experienced politicians, and received extensive discussion in the press. Dewey's role was, in fact, the great unknown of the 1900 presidential election. Almost from the first, there had been talk of the hero of Manila Bay as a presidential candidate. Colonel Henry Watterson, publisher of the Louisville *Courier Journal*, and Joseph Pulitzer, influential publisher of the New York *World*, both undertook cautious Dewey-for-President movements. In March, 1899, the Reverend Henry Frank, pastor of the Metropolitan Independent Church of New York, delivered a sermon entitled "Dewey for President," in which he urged the hero's nomination "not as the candidate of any single party but as the unanimous selection of all parties combined."[29] Dewey, for the moment, would have none of it. In the autumn of 1899, he told a reporter that he had "no desire for any political office" and that he "would not accept nomination for the presidency."[30] In December, he wrote his brother Charles: "I have strong letters urging me

27. John Hay to Dewey, November 22, 1899, in Dewey Papers.
28. The most recent work, H. Wayne Morgan, *William McKinley and His America* (Syracuse, 1963), devotes only two pages to the Dewey boom. Margaret Leech, in her very detailed *In the Days of McKinley* (New York, 1959), devotes less than a page to the admiral's candidacy. J. Rogers Hollingsworth's admirable *The Whirligig of Politics* (Chicago, 1963) omits it altogether, as does William C. Spielman, *William McKinley* (New York, 1954). Paolo E. Coletta's *William Jennings Bryan: Political Evangelist* (Lincoln, Nebr., 1964), gives Dewey about a page and a half. For a discussion of recent scholarship on the politics of the era see Lewis Gould, "New Perspectives on the Republican Party," *American Historical Review*, LXXVII (October, 1972).
29. Henry Frank, "Dewey for President," copy in Dewey Papers.
30. Adelbert Dewey, *Life and Letters of Admiral Dewey*, 426.

Gentleman George Dewey, as Chief of the Bureau of Equipment, 1893.
(Official U.S. Navy Photo)

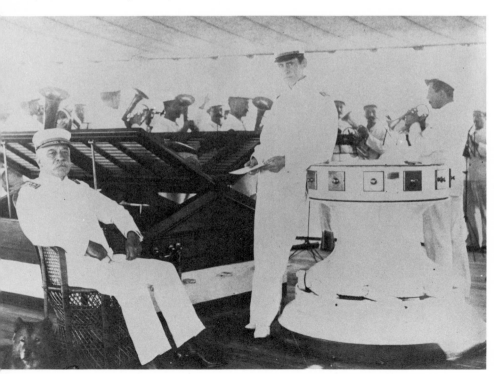

Dewey relaxing aboard the *Olympia* during the siege of Manila Bay, 1898.
(Official U.S. Navy Photo)

The *Olympia* in action at Manila Bay. (Official U.S. Navy Photo)

The *Olympia* in her peacetime white and buff paint. (Photo courtesy the Smithsonian Institution)

German warship *Kaiser*, von Diederich's most powerful ship at Manila Bay.
(Official U.S. Navy Photo)

Gunnersmate S. J. Skaw beside one of the *Olympia*'s five-inch guns. Skaw
is said to have fired the first shot at the Battle of Manila Bay. (Official U.S.
Navy Photo)

Wreckage of Spanish fortifications at Corregidor, 1898. (Photo courtesy National Archives)

Dewey and Frances Benjamin Johnston on the *Olympia*, reviewing the admiral's mail at Manila. (Photo courtesy Library of Congress)

President McKinley and Admiral Dewey at Dewey Day Parade. (Official U.S. Navy Photo)

Olympia's crew parades down Fifth Avenue at New York's Dewey Day celebration, September 26, 1899. (Official U.S. Navy Photo)

The first step towards lightening

"The White Man's Burden"

is through teaching the virtues of cleanliness.

Pears' Soap

is a potent factor in brightening the dark corners of the earth as civilization advances, while amongst the cultured of all nations it holds the highest place—it is the ideal toilet soap.

All sorts of people use it, all sorts of stores sell it.

One of many advertisements exploiting the Dewey craze after Manila.
(Photo courtesy Vermont Historical Society)

New York's Dewey Arch. (Photo in possession of the author)

Schley Court of Inquiry, Washington, D.C., 1901. (Official U.S. Navy Photo)

Dewey relaxing at Palm Beach, 1902. (Official U.S. Navy Photo)

to run for President. I had rather be an admiral ten times over."[31]
But the public remained unconvinced. It seemed to many that
Dewey was simply making the customary modest gestures of denial
expected of a candidate. Dr. R. A. Moseley, the new American
consul at Singapore, after a long chat with the admiral, remarked
to a friend: "My God, Dewey is a presidential candidate."[32]

It was certainly not a bad time for new faces in politics. The
conservative Democrats like Grover Cleveland and William C.
Whitney, who had never been able to stomach William Jennings
Bryan and his heresies, would naturally welcome a new contender.
Tammany, which had swallowed Bryan only with difficulty, was
also receptive. If imperialism was to be the big issue of the 1900
campaign, as it bid fair to be, then Dewey would be the ideal
Democratic candidate. He had never taken a public stand on the
issue of the Philippines, but he had repeatedly intimated to journalists that he favored their independence.[33] If he openly declared
himself an opponent of annexation, Dewey might well hope to
capture the Democratic nomination. On the other hand, no one
was certain that the hero *was* a Democrat! Indeed, his son, his
brother, and Senator Proctor had all claimed him as a Republican.
After all, he was a Vermonter and all his family had been Republicans.

If the admiral was indeed a secret Republican instead of a secret
Democrat, his presidential prospects were less bright, though by no
means unfavorable. McKinley and his supporters were in deep
trouble in Ohio, where the handpicked gubernatorial candidate of
the Mark Hanna machine was running into unexpectedly stiff opposition from the Democratic candidate, John R. McLean. Mc-
Lean was running on an avowed anti-imperialist platform. If he
should win the governorship, it would almost certainly be taken as
a repudiation, not just of the Ohio Republicans, but of McKinley's
foreign policy as well. It was no small wonder that Hanna ner-

31. Dewey to Charles Dewey, December 10, 1899, in Dewey Papers.
32. Leech, *In the Days of McKinley*, 654.
33. In August, he told the London *Daily News* that "the only way to settle the Insurrection and to assure prosperity in the Islands is to concede self-government to the inhabitants."
London *Daily News*, August 20, 1899; see also New York *Evening Post*, September 28, 1899.

vously remonstrated to reporters: "The practice of continually placing the name of Admiral Dewey on the list of prospective presidential candidates is indecent! It places this man of integrity . . . in the ranks of those shifting aspirants for presidential honors who have not the stamina to resist the flattery of political schemers."[34]

If the admiral did aspire to the presidency, the first weeks after his return were the ideal time for him to declare himself. With his immense popularity, with the Democrats undecided, and the Republicans in disarray, he would have an excellent chance. But as the weeks passed, Dewey made no move. He steadfastly refused to talk politics and brushed aside the cautious feelers of the professional politicians. In a private interview with President McKinley, he indicated that he did not, in fact, believe the Filipinos were presently capable of self-government.[35] And in November, 1899, he signed the preliminary report of the Philippine Commission, thus forfeiting his best campaign issue.[36] Three days later, the Republicans won handily in Ohio.

The moment of opportunity had passed. Yet this was not at all apparent to the apolitical admiral. Strangely enough, considering her long years of association with public men, it was not apparent to Mrs. Dewey either. Mildred was beginning to realize that being First Lady would provide even more opportunities for "social success" than being the wife of the Admiral of the Navy. Then there would be no more of these demeaning fights over precedence with the wives of cabinet officers and generals. Her social leadership would be unchallenged.[37]

Under the spur of Mrs. Dewey, the admiral became less positive in his denials. Newspaper speculation increased, but by April, 1900, no one had yet succeeded in inducing the admiral to make a positive statement. On the evening of April 3, a young reporter

34. Pittsburgh *Post*, October 2, 1899.
35. "Memorandum of Conversation with Admiral Dewey," reproduced in Charles S. Olcott, *The Life of William McKinley* (2 vols.; Boston, 1916), II, 96.
36. There is reason to believe, as the *Nation* alleged, that he never actually read it; *Nation*, April 12, 1900.
37. All of those who knew Dewey personally agree that it was Mildred's influence which led to his belated candidacy; cf. Sullivan, *Our Times*, I, 336.

for the Washington bureau of the New York *World*, Horace J. Mocke, was on his way home after a long day at work. Since his route took him past the admiral's residence, Mocke decided to call and see if he could get a statement from the admiral about the presidency. Scores of reporters had made similar attempts and Mocke was not very hopeful as he rang the Deweys' bell at 6:30 P.M. To his astonishment, he was ushered into the admiral's study where Dewey announced simply: "Yes, I have decided to become a candidate."

That same evening, at about 9:30 P.M., Samuel C. Blythe, head of the *World*'s Washington bureau, was startled to see Mocke burst into his office waving a piece of paper which he declared was an exclusive statement announcing Dewey's candidacy. Blythe immediately locked up the entire bureau staff and put the story on the wire to New York. Early the following morning, newspaper readers across the country were treated to the following remarkable interview:

"Yes," said the Admiral, "I realize that the time has arrived when I must define my position. When I arrived in this country last September, I said then that nothing would induce me to be a candidate for the Presidency. Since then, however, I have had the leisure and inclination to study the matter, and have reached a different conclusion, inasmuch as so many assurances have come to me from my countrymen that I would be acceptable as a candidate for this great office.

"If the American people want me for this high office, I shall be only too willing to serve them.

"It is the highest honor in the gift of this nation; what citizen would refuse it?

"Since studying this subject, I am convinced that the office of the President is not such a very difficult one to fill, his duties being mainly to execute the laws of Congress. Should I be chosen for this exalted position I would execute the laws of Congress as faithfully as I have always executed the orders of my superiors."

"On what platform will you stand?" asked the *World* correspondent.

"I think I have said enough at this time, and possibly too much," answered the admiral.[38]

Dewey's announcement was greeted by the politicians with min-

---

38. Healy and Kutner, *The Admiral*, 214.

gled incredulity and amusement. The appalling combination of
egotism, complacency, and naïveté revealed in the interview was
the subject of much comment in the press. His "view of the office
was considered absurd by many," and the *Times* reported that "a
repudiation of the statement was expected by everybody in public
office." The Washington *Star Republican* observed that "sincere
friends of the Admiral will regret the announcement."[39]

None regretted it more than Nathan Straus, a wealthy New York
politician and philanthropist who had been among Dewey's earliest
and most persistent backers. Heir to the great firm of L. Straus and
Son, the owners of Macy's Department Store, and brother of the
diplomat Oscar S. Straus, Nathan was primarily interested in problems of public health. His great achievement was the long and
arduous campaign which he waged, over more than two decades,
for compulsory pasteurization of milk; but he was also active in
politics and a strong Gold Democrat. He carried on an extensive
correspondence with Dewey, repeatedly urging him to run. It was
a severe shock to Straus when his hero finally decided to do so in
such an unorthodox way.

In despair, Straus sought the advice of Arthur Brisbane, editor
of the New York *Journal* and an experienced political observer.
Brisbane warned Straus that Dewey ought to "say as little as possible and nothing at all spontaneously. Every statement to the press
ought to be edited by competent politicians."[40] Brisbane was opti-
mistic about Dewey's prospects, provided that the admiral at once
declared himself to be a Democrat. There were important elements
of the Democratic party, Brisbane suggested, who disliked Bryan
and would welcome Dewey's candidacy. These included Gold
Democrats like Whitney and Senator Arthur P. Gorman of Maryland, Bryan-haters like David B. Hill of New York, Tammany, and
"many southern Democrats." In fact, prospects were not as unfavorable as they appeared. Although a few newspapers treated the
announcement with scorn, most were noncommittal. A few, like
the Philadelphia *Times* and the Boston *Herald*, regretted that Dew-

39. *Literary Digest*, XX, 5, (April 14, 1900), 444–45; New York *Times*, April 5, 1900;
Washington *Star-Republican*, April 5, 1900.
40. Arthur Brisbane to Nathan Straus, April 5, 1900, copy in Dewey Papers.

ey had not announced his candidacy sooner.[41] A few important ones like the New York *Times*, the Atlanta *Constitution*, the New York *World*, and Milwaukee *Journal* endorsed him. The Columbus *Press Post*, one of the leading Democratic papers of Ohio, observed that "if Dewey is nominated at Kansas City, he will certainly be the next president. The same cannot be said of Mr. Bryan."[42]

Even after tossing his hat into the ring, Dewey's desire for the presidency was something less than overwhelming. "I have yielded to the request of many friends," he informed his son. "In politics one can never know what may happen, although it looks as though Bryan may be the man. In that case I will be no worse off than I am now." Bryan himself refused to take the admiral's candidacy seriously. When reporters questioned him about Dewey's prospects the Great Commoner replied that he was "gratified to find one question he need not discuss."[43]

On April 4, the admiral, following Straus's instructions, dutifully admitted to reporters in Philadelphia: "Yes, I am a Democrat."[44] Dewey's brother-in-law, John R. McLean, the unsuccessful contender for the Ohio governorship, announced himself the admiral's campaign manager and proceeded to book a suite of rooms in Kansas City for a Dewey headquarters at the convention. "As the days pass everything is brighter and more hopeful," wrote Nathan Straus on the ninth, "and your candidacy gains force and dignity."[45] On the thirteenth, S. S. McClure endorsed him and the New York *Times* correspondent in Washington filed a column with the headline "Dewey Grows Stronger." There were rumors of secret meetings and back-room alliances. The mayor of New York was reported to have met secretly with Dewey in Philadelphia. Senator Gorman was reported to be masterminding his campaign strategy. The southern Democrats were reported about to bolt for Dewey.[46] "My friends tell me my 'boom' is on the increase and that I will

41. *Literary Digest*, XX, 5 (April 14, 1900), 444–45.
42. Columbus *Press Post*, April 5, 1900.
43. Dewey to George Goodwin Dewey, April 8, 1900, in George Goodwin Dewey Papers.
44. New York *Times*, April 6, 1900.
45. Straus to Dewey, April 9, 1900, in Dewey Papers.
46. New York *Times*, April 17, April 18, 1900.

surely be elected *if* we get the nomination at Kansas City," observed the admiral in a letter to George Goodwin; "I hear many of the state delegates will go to the convention uninstructed."[47] Democratic conservatives like William C. Whitney, convinced by this time that Bryan was "in" for 1900, were looking ahead to 1904 and were not inclined to risk dividing the party in a fight for Dewey.[48]

Yet as the days passed, no important Democratic politicians declared themselves for Dewey; no delegates committed themselves to him. The admiral committed a second blunder on May 6, when he confessed to reporters that he had never voted. The Bryan men, with most of the votes in their pocket, were content to sit tight until the brief flurry of publicity over the admiral's candidacy died down. Only a groundswell of popular opinion could have persuaded the professionals to switch their support to Dewey so late in the game, but the admiral's popularity was not what it had been the previous fall. Had the convention been held then, no candidate could have stood against him; but now, after the novelty had worn away, after his marriage, after the affair of the house, and after the hilarious "interview," there was no possibility of a popular revolt on his behalf. By mid-May his name had disappeared from the front pages and John R. McLean had announced his resignation. On May 18, the admiral threw in the towel, confessing to reporters: "I don't understand how I got the idea in the first place."[49]

The admiral's name was not long absent from the newspapers. In the summer of 1901 he was again thrust abruptly back into the limelight when he was named president of the Schley Court of Inquiry. Rear Admiral Winfield Scott Schley, along with Dewey, William T. Sampson, and Richmond P. Hobson, was one of the four popular heroes of the Spanish-American War. He had been second-in-command at the Battle of Santiago and his flagship, the *Brooklyn,* had led the pursuit of the escaping Spanish squadron and sustained the only casualties. Unfortunately, Schley had be-

47. Dewey to George Goodwin Dewey, April 19, 1900, in George Goodwin Dewey Papers.
48. Coletta, *Bryan,* 246.
49. New York *Times,* May 18, 1900.

come the victim of a bitter controversy fomented by the newspapermen and fed by the thoughtless remarks of younger officers.
The controversy was ostensibly over whether Schley or Rear Admiral William T. Sampson, commander of the American squadron at
Santiago, deserved the credit for the defeat of the Spanish fleet.
Partisans of both men often went so far as to attack the entire
conduct of Sampson or Schley in order to buttress the case for their
hero.

Nearly every action of the two men during the campaign was the
subject of intense controversy. Both were accused by partisans of
the other of poor judgment, incompetence, or downright cow-
ardice. Schley's admirers pointed out that Admiral Sampson had
actually been several miles away from Santiago at the time of the
battle, on his way to a conference with the army ashore. Sampson
had not returned until the fight was virtually over. Defenders of
Sampson retorted by criticizing Schley's conduct in the search for
Admiral Cervera in June, 1898. During the search Schley had
commanded a part of the American battle fleet known as the
Flying Squadron. Sent to the south coast of Cuba to search for the
Spanish fleet, Schley had spent three days blockading the wrong
port and then had almost allowed the Spaniards to escape from
Santiago because he believed that port to be empty.

The Sampson-Schley controversy was an extreme example of the
obsession with personal reputation, or honor, which characterized
the nineteenth-century officer corps. But it was more than that. The
controversy split the service in two, with every ship and station,
even every navy family, divided into "Sampsonites" and "Schley-
ites." The quarrel extended to the press, the Congress, and even the
administration, where Secretary Long was accused of being a
Sampsonite.

For a time the two admirals themselves attempted to ignore the
controversy and hoped it would eventually die out. In June, 1901,
however, almost three years after Santiago, new fuel was added to
the flames with the publication of Volume III of Edgar Stanton
MacLay's *History of the United States Navy*, the first two volumes
of which had long been in use as textbooks at the naval academy.
MacLay intemperately criticized Schley's conduct in the campaign

preceding the Battle of Santiago and flatly asserted that, during the battle itself, the admiral had behaved in a cowardly fashion. Admiral Schley now found it impossible to ignore the charges of his critics. In a letter to Secretary Long, he requested that the Navy Department "take such action as may bring this matter under the clearer and calmer review of my brothers in arms." Three days later, the department announced the formation of a Court of Inquiry to examine "the conduct of Rear Admiral Schley during the recent War with Spain."[50] Admiral Dewey was named president of the court, which was scheduled to begin its sessions in the fall of 1901.

To Dewey, with his intense aversion to public controversy, especially intraservice controversy, the presidency of the court was a most distressing assignment. A close acquaintance of both Sampson and Schley since his Annapolis days, Dewey found the controversy distasteful in the extreme. He had refused to take sides in this controversy and placed the blame for the quarrel squarely on the younger officers who posed as "friends" of Sampson.[51] As the ranking officer of the navy, however, he was the logical choice to head the court and could not well refuse.

The court began its investigation at noon on September 12, 1901. It received extensive coverage in the press, where it competed for headlines with the assassination of President McKinley. The proceedings were open to the public and large crowds attended the sessions which were held in the huge second floor workshop of the old gun factory at Washington Navy Yard. In all, the sessions lasted forty days and the proceedings filled two fat volumes, totaling more than nineteen hundred pages of small print.

Schley was represented by an able trio of lawyers led by Judge Jeremiah Wilson of Baltimore, who suffered a fatal heart attack early in the proceedings. His other lawyers were Isidor Rayner, a former senator and attorney general of Maryland, and Navy Captain James Parker. Early in the proceedings Schley's lawyers successfully challenged the presence of Rear Admiral Henry Howison,

50. *Record of Proceedings of a Court of Inquiry into the Case of Rear Admiral Winfield Scott Schley, USN* (2 vols.; Washington, 1902), I, 3, 4.

51. Dewey to George Goodwin Dewey, May 12, 1902, in George Goodwin Dewey Papers.

a reputed Sampsonite, as a member of the court of inquiry. Howison was replaced by Rear Admiral Francis M. Ramsay, so that the court of inquiry as finally constituted was composed of Dewey, Ramsay, and Rear Admiral Arthur E. K. Benham. The main points of contention concerned Schley's conduct during the search for Admiral Cervera's squadron and during the Battle of Santiago.

The court waded slowly through the evidence with many of the defense and government witnesses contradicting each other. Dewey, as president of the court, rigorously attempted to exclude any testimony or evidence bearing on the actions of Admiral Sampson on the grounds that only Schley's conduct was under review. This necessarily made the inquiry, for all its length and detail, a very incomplete one, and prevented the court from passing upon the most important public issue: the question of who ought to have the credit for the victory at Santiago.

Although the fact was never publicly mentioned, Rear Admiral Sampson was, by this time, too ill to testify. In a confidential letter to Secretary Long, Sampson's physician reported that the admiral was suffering from "a mental depression, the most constant symptom of which is a certain form of aphasia characterized by his mixing up words."[52] With Sampson unavailable, it was difficult, if not impossible, to thoroughly investigate the Santiago campaign.

On November 7, having examined more than three score witnesses, Rayner, chief counsel for Schley, rose to make his final plea on behalf of Schley. The courtroom was filled to overflowing and as Rayner delivered his speech describing Schley's unselfish service to his country and his patient sufferings at the hands of slanderers, many of the women wept. It was an address to the jury in the grand old nineteenth-century style and, at the conclusion, even the members of the court rushed up to the counselor to shake his hand.[53]

It did seem to reporters and other observers that the inquiry had gone far toward vindicating Schley. Consequently, the court's findings, issued on December 13, after more than six weeks of deliberation, came as a considerable surprise. The majority of the court

52. Henry G. Beyer to John D. Long, August 9, 1901, in Gardner W. Allen (ed.), *The Papers of John D. Long* (Boston, 1939), 56.
53. New York *Times*, November 8, 1901.

ruled that Admiral Schley's conduct in connection with the events
of the Santiago campaign prior to June 1, 1898, had been characterized by "vacillation, dilatoriness and lack of enterprise"; that the
maneuvers of the *Brooklyn* during the battle of July 3 "caused her
to lose distance and position with the Spanish vessels, especially
with the *Vizcaya* and *Colon*"; but that the commodore's personal
conduct was "self-possessed," and that he "encouraged in his own
person his subordinate officers and men to fight courageously."[54]
Dewey issued a lone dissenting opinion in which he declared: "The
passage from Key West to Cienfuegos was made by the Flying
Squadron with all possible dispatch . . . having in view the importance of arriving off Cienfuegos with as much coal as possible in
the ships' bunkers. The blockade of Cienfuegos was effective. . . .
The passage from Cienfuegos to . . . Santiago was made with as
much dispatch as was possible while keeping the squadron as a
unit. The blockade off Santiago was effective." The admiral went
on to pass on the very subject which he had rigorously excluded
from the investigation: the question of who was responsible for the
American victory. "Commodore Schley," Dewey asserted, "was
the senior officer of our squadron off Santiago when the Spanish
squadron attempted to escape. . . . He was in absolute command
and is entitled to the credit due to such a commanding officer for
the glorious victory which resulted in the total destruction of the
Spanish ships."[55]

Dewey's unexpected dissent delighted Schley's attorneys, who
promptly filed an appeal to the president. Secretary Long and
many of the officials of the Navy Department were furious with
Dewey. In an angry statement to the press, Long pointed out that
Dewey's dissent was not even logically consistent, since it "left him
in the position of agreeing with his associates on all the more
important matters which were considered by him and them and of
then expressing an opinion, while his associates expressed none, on
a matter . . . on which the full court had refused to hear any
evidence on either side."[56] Other critics were even less charitable.

54. *Record of Proceedings . . . Schley*, II, 1829–30.
55. *Ibid.*
56. Long, *The New American Navy*, I, 286–87. By his silence on several of the questions

"I never knew a court of inquiry or a council which was of any service whatever," wrote Charles Francis Adams. "The result of this last one merely further establishes a principle already proven. What was already bad enough is made, if possible, a little worse, than it was. Dewey may be great as an admiral but in the ordinary affairs of life he is not a success."[57] The controversy extended even to the august Metropolitan Club and when some members criticized Dewey's dissent, he resigned the presidency of the club as a protest. Mildred Dewey stoutly defended her husband against the charges of his critics. When the criticism was at its height, she asked the admiral for "a copy of his plain sailor's report" for a Christmas present.[58]

It is doubtful whether Dewey was aware of the technical defects of his dissent. Logical consistency in a controversy was not his strong point, as he had amply demonstrated in the Philippine controversy. His dissent was not so much a reasoned judgment as an impulsive, warmhearted gesture of support for an old friend who had been subjected to a cruel ordeal.

It was the new president, Theodore Roosevelt, who was to have the final word on the Sampson-Schley controversy. Replying to Schley's appeal, Roosevelt wrote that, in general, he concurred with the findings of the court. The question as to which of the two men was in command was "of merely nominal character" and "there is now no excuse from either side for any further agitation of this unhappy controversy. To keep it alive would merely do damage to the Navy and to the country."[59] To the end, Dewey was unrepentant. "I see the President condemns Schley," he wrote to George Goodwin, "but that does not make people agree with him."[60]

---

dealt with by the majority, Dewey had put himself in the position of technically agreeing with them.

57. Charles Francis Adams, Jr., to John D. Long, November 10, 1901, in Allen (ed.), *Papers of John D. Long*, 412.

58. Diary of Mildred Dewey.

59. *Record of Proceedings . . . Schley*, II, 1836.

60. Dewey to George Goodwin Dewey, February 7, 1902, in George Goodwin Dewey Papers.

CHAPTER VI

Admiral of the Navy

Dewey's position as admiral of the navy carried immense prestige but little real authority. In the years after the Civil War, there had been two other admirals of the navy, David Glasgow Farragut and David Dixon Porter. Though the objects of much veneration, neither had exercised any considerable influence upon the navy which they nominally headed. In his last years, Porter had been reduced to fuming impotence, a mere figurehead, seldom even consulted by the secretary of the navy.[1] What saved Dewey from a similarly ornamental role was not his superior political acumen (he was far less the politician than Porter) but the fortunate coincidence that his promotion to admiral of the navy came at almost the same time as the creation of what was to be the most influential body in the shaping of American naval policy: the General Board of the Navy.

As senior officer of the navy, Dewey was naturally selected to preside over the General Board as its first (and only) president. The accomplishments of the General Board over the next sixteen years were mainly the work of a small group of able younger officers who served as members of the board rather than serving Dewey himself. But without his prestige and authority, their brilliant projects would have come to little. "The General Board's real status depends largely upon you and your influence," wrote Captain Nathan Sargent to the admiral. "Your interest in its work and the

1. Porter to Stephen B. Luce, February 21, 1883, in Luce Papers, Library of Congress. For Porter's career in the Navy Department see Sprout, *Rise of American Naval Power*, 177–80; West, *The Second Admiral*, 315–28 and 336–38; and Hagan, *American Gunboat Diplomacy*, 19–24.

value attached to your advice both in and out of Congress gives it a prestige which it otherwise would lack."[2] Many years after Dewey's death Admiral Richard Wainwright recalled that "it was more the knowledge that Admiral Dewey was president of the board rather than any public knowledge of its composition and workings that gave weight to its decisions."[3] It was Dewey, moreover who was directly responsible for assembling talented young officers and putting them to work on questions of interest to the navy. Dewey himself was neither a remarkable thinker nor a brilliant innovator. His talents lay rather in channeling the energy and abilities of his more gifted young colleagues into projects of importance to the navy.

In managing the disparate and often antagonistic group of brilliant prima donnas who saw service with the General Board, Dewey proved himself to be an "organization man" par excellence. Few American military men before General Eisenhower proved so adept at eliciting the cooperation of their colleagues. Bradley A. Fiske, who served as a young staff assistant on the board, later recalled that the admiral "handled the board with exceeding skill, keeping himself in the background, never taking part in discussions but keeping a tight rein which all of us felt."[4] This is not to suggest that none of the ideas and policies of the General Board can be credited to Dewey; but his most important role was as the propagator of ideas rather than as the originator of them.

The General Board, which was created by executive order of Secretary Long on March 13, 1900, was the first American organization created to plan for war in peacetime. It was established in belated recognition of the fact that modern wars could no longer be fought in the leisurely, spasmodic manner of the age of sail. A reluctant, grudging concession to the age of machine warfare, the establishment of the General Board was the culmination of nearly twenty years of speculation and argument about the proper organization of the navy. The old system of administration, dating from 1842, whereby a civilian secretary and eight autonomous bureaus

2. Sargent to Dewey, October 20, 1905, in Nathan Sargent Papers, Library of Congress.
3. Richard Wainwright, "The General Board," USNIP, XLVI (August, 1922).
4. Bradley A. Fiske, *From Midshipman to Rear Admiral* (New York, 1919), 478.

ran the service, had proven itself clearly unsuitable for war, however admirable it might be in times of peace. The basic difficulty was that the eight bureaus—navigation, medicine, supplies and accounts, construction, yards and docks, and the others—all performed functions which were essentially technical in nature. This left to the secretary of the navy the tasks of directing the operations of the fleet, preparing war plans, and coordinating the work of the bureaus. As a civilian, with limited tenure and little military experience, he was seldom equal to the task.

During the Civil War, Secretary Gideon Welles had found it necessary to create the office of assistant secretary of the navy, filled by a former naval officer, to coordinate the work of the bureaus and advise the secretary on naval operations.[5] In the war with Spain, Secretary Long, like Welles, had been obliged to rely on an ad hoc organization, the Naval War Board, for advice on operations and strategy.

The navy's organizational shortcomings had been glaringly apparent ever since the early 1880s when the establishment of the Office of Naval Intelligence (ONI) and the Naval War College had provided forward-looking officers with a sounding board and a laboratory for their ideas about naval administration. Both of these organizations had, almost by default, begun to exercise some of the functions of a general staff, particularly in the area of war planning. The order which sent Dewey to Manila was, at least in part, the product of the primitive plans for war against Spain which these two organizations had developed in the late 1890s.

Both the War College and the ONI, however, were keenly aware of their own shortcomings in the area of general staff work, and both felt the need to replace the informal war-planning system of the 1880s and 1890s with a real general staff. In 1889, Captain A. P. Cooke had proposed that "a commission made up of officers from the Office of Naval Intelligence" be given powers "corresponding to the general staff of an army" to plan and direct the

5. For a discussion of the development of naval administration in the United States, see Charles O. Paullin, *Paullin's History of Naval Administration*, 1775–1911 (Annapolis, 1968), the best work on the subject. See also Sprout, *Rise of American Naval Power*, 151–202 and *passim*; Elting Morison, *Admiral Sims and the Modern American Navy* (Boston, 1942), 61–77.

operations of the fleet in war.[6] And at the Naval War College, Captain Henry C. Taylor, who served as president of the college from 1893 to 1896, had undertaken a systematic study of naval organization.

A brilliant and imaginative officer, Taylor has been somewhat overshadowed by his more famous colleagues Stephen B. Luce and Alfred T. Mahan. Even among specialists, Taylor's role in the development of the modern American navy is little understood or appreciated. It was Taylor, more than any other man, who was directly responsible for the creation of the General Board. At the War College, Taylor and his staff studied and compared the various forms of military organization then current in Europe. Like most military men in the late nineteenth century, Taylor and his colleagues had been impressed by the military achievements of the Germans in their wars with Austria and France. Not surprisingly, they concluded that what was needed was a general staff on the German model, though it would need to be "modified to suit the different political conditions in the United States."[7]

Taylor hoped that the nucleus of a general staff might be formed by combining the ONI and the Naval War College into an advisory board, but he was unable to interest the current secretary of the navy, Hilary A. Herbert, in the scheme. Although the secretary was, in fact, "using the College as a general staff and me [Taylor] as chief of staff,"[8] he was uninterested in any plans for permanent reorganization of the navy and could not "get his mind on it for ten seconds."[9] When the McKinley administration took office in 1897, Taylor and Admiral Luce pressed their plan upon Assistant Secretary Roosevelt who wrote to Taylor that he "entirely agreed,"[10] but Roosevelt was unable to persuade his chief, John D. Long, to take any action on the proposal.

6. A. P. Cooke, "Naval Reorganization," USNIP, XII (October, 1886).
7. Henry C. Taylor, "The Fleet," USNIP, XXIX (December, 1903), 803; for a more detailed account of Taylor's work at the War College, see Ronald Spector, "Professors of War: The Naval War College and the Modern American Navy, *1884–1917* (Ph.D. dissertation, Yale University, 1967), chapters V, VI, and X.
8. Taylor to Luce, January 13, 1896, in Luce Papers.
9. Taylor to Luce, June 22, 1896, *ibid.*
10. Roosevelt to Taylor, May 24, 1897, in Morison (ed.), *Letters of Roosevelt*, I, 617.

It was not that Long failed to understand the utility of a general staff. Rather, he and many other men in the administration and in Congress entertained grave doubts about the effect which such an organization might have on the continuance of civilian control of the military. Long feared that once a permanent chief-of-staff became entrenched in the Navy Department, he would usurp the powers of the civilian secretary who would then "lapse into a figurehead."[11]

The experience of the Spanish-American War, however, and the new worldwide responsibilities of the United States Navy clearly made some sort of reorganization unavoidable.[12] In February, 1900, Long asked Captain Taylor to report on "what concrete things should be done at present in the development of a general staff."[13] Taylor responded with an elaborate blueprint which included a chief-of-staff with broad powers to direct the work of the bureaus and a hierarchy of three boards with overall responsibility for "all questions relating to the fleet's efficiency."[14] Long promptly cut Taylor's proposal down to size. In March, 1900, he established the General Board of the Navy "to advise the Secretary of the Navy on war plans, bases, and naval policy and to coordinate the work of the War College and the Office of Naval Intelligence." The board had no legal existence but served at the pleasure of the secretary; it was not responsible for its recommendations and had no authority to implement them. Although the General Board did not meet his expectations, Taylor still viewed it as a promising first step.

Dewey had remained aloof from the debate over organization in the navy as was his habit in matters of controversy, but he shared Taylor's hopes for the General Board, believing it to be "the natural center and head of a general staff." He predicted that, whether

11. Long, *The New American Navy*, II, 186.
12. Daniel J. Costello in his study, "Planning for War: A History of the General Board of the Navy, 1900–1914" (Ph.D. dissertation, Fletcher School of Law and Diplomacy, 1968), 19–20, suggests that Long was also eager to find something to do with Admiral Dewey whose exalted rank made him too senior for almost any job in the navy.
13. Henry C. Taylor, "Memorandum on the Naval Assistant Secretary or General Staff," February 24, 1900, copy in Luce Papers.
14. *Ibid.*

it was established by statute or not, the General Board, with the passage of time, would "come to speak with great authority" on matters of naval policy."[15]

Although Long had been reluctant to establish the General Board, he did not hesitate to assign it a large sphere of authority once it had been established. In a letter to Admiral Dewey in March, 1900, Long outlined the duties of the board. These included war planning, advising the secretary on the disposition of the fleet and the location of naval bases, and cooperation with the army through "frequent consultation."[16]

Initially, the board consisted of eleven officers, six of whom (the admiral of the navy, the chief of the Bureau of Navigation, the chief of the Office of Naval Intelligence and his principal assistant, and the president of the Naval War College with his principal assistant) were to serve ex officio; the others were to be appointed by the secretary of the navy from among the line officers of the rank of lieutenant commander and above. After 1902, additional officers were assigned to the board as staff assistants. The Office of Naval Intelligence and the Naval War College also assigned an officer to work full-time on General Board matters.[17] Each member of the board received one vote, and the recommendations of the majority were forwarded to the secretary in the name of the entire board. Dewey adhered rigidly to this rule even when he found himself voting with the minority on an important issue.

Dewey chose the officers for service on the General Board with great care. In a letter for Secretary Long's signature the admiral outlined the qualities he sought in candidates for General Board duty. "Commanding officers who make recommendations . . . will have in view the professional aptitude of the officer, his intelligence and good judgment, and his qualities as a practical sea-going officer."[18] The young officers selected as "staff assistants" represented the professional cream of the navy. Many a future admiral was to

---

15. Dewey to Taylor, October 25, 1900, in Dewey Papers.
16. Long to Dewey, March 30, 1900, in Records of the General Board, Office of Naval History (Washington, D.C.), File 401.
17. Costello, "Planning for War," 29–31.
18. Long to Commander-in-Chief, South Atlantic Station, December 15, 1900, in Records of the General Board, File 401.

cut his teeth on strategic problems and concepts at the General Board during Dewey's long tenure.[19]

For the first four years after its establishment, the General Board was preoccupied with the problem of protecting the new American empire in the Caribbean and the Pacific. Secretary Long had instructed the board to give priority to "plans for the defense of our dependencies, including the strategic value of adjacent territory of importance and its military relation to our possessions, and to complete plans of campaign applicable to various war conditions in the Philippines and their neighborhood."[20]

Long did not specify, nor did the General Board ask, against whom our dependencies would have to be defended. Over the next fifteen years, except at rare intervals, the General Board was left entirely free to determine who the probable enemies of the United States might be. The guidance of the State Department was seldom sought and never offered; and as far as is known, no officer of the executive branch, aside from the service secretaries and the president, was ever consulted or permitted to comment on the political assumptions behind the board's war plans.[21] The essentially political question of determining America's friends and foes in international politics was thus left entirely in the hands of the naval officers of the General Board and its adjuncts, the War College and the Office of Naval Intelligence. Not all of these officers were as politically naive as Admiral Dewey; but almost all of them shared a peculiarly rigid and deterministic approach to questions of international politics that Dewey, with his own lack of political sophistication, tolerated if he did not encourage. So far as the admiral had views on international questions, they were mainly the views of these younger and more articulate officers of the board and the Naval War College.

At the turn of the century, the naval officer's view of internation-

19. *Ibid.*, 31–32.

20. Long to Dewey, March 30, 1900, *ibid.*

21. The navy was often reluctant to confide its plans to even the army. In 1911, when the president of the Army War College requested a copy of the Navy's Orange Plan, the Navy Department refused on the grounds that the plan was "highly confidential in character." President, Naval War College to Aide for Operations, May 6, 1911, in RG 80, File 9469, National Archives.

al politics was profoundly different from that of his fellow citizens. Few Americans at that time had any reason or saw any need to maintain a sustained interest in foreign affairs.[22] War, in particular, was regarded by most Americans as a great aberration which occurred only in the history books or, at worst, only in Europe and Asia. The naval officer, on the other hand, had perforce to pay constant attention to international affairs and what he saw did not make him sanguine. Contrary to most of his fellow citizens, he believed war to be an inevitable product of human weakness and depravity. Admiral Stephen B. Luce regarded war as simply "one of the many evils to which the flesh is heir."[23] "If we admit that there are so many bad people in the world that force must be exerted to guarantee a man his rights," observed Bradley Fiske, "then we must admit that . . . the exertion of force is necessary to protect a country in its rights."[24] Given the basic depravity of man, there was no reason to expect that wars would, in the future, be any less frequent than in the past.

Even granting the evil nature of man, it was hard to convince congressmen and other civilians that the United States was in any immediate danger of becoming involved in war, however inevitable it might be for mankind as a whole. It was difficult to imagine how the United States, separated from the great powers by the broad oceans, secure in her own hemisphere, with no powerful neighbors and no outstanding foreign quarrels, could become embroiled in war. To this objection, the military men had a ready reply. Wars, they explained, were not really undertaken for reasons of self-defense but for economic motives. As Mahan explained to readers of the *North American Review*, "the armaments of the European states are not so much for protection as to secure to themselves the utmost possible share of the unexploited regions of the world . . . the outlying markets of raw materials which shall minister to na-

---

22. Ernest R. May estimates that the "foreign policy public" of the late nineteenth century numbered between 10 and 20 percent of the "voting public" which itself was only a fraction of the population; see his *American Imperialism: A Speculative Essay* (New York, 1968), 24.

23. Stephen B. Luce, "The Benefits of War," *North American Review*, CLIII (December, 1891).

24. Bradley A. Fiske, "The Naval Profession," USNIP, XXVIII (1902), 71.

tional emolument."[25] Dewey had voiced much the same opinion in 1898 when he explained to his son that the "great fleets of war vessels" in the Far East were "all working for the same end: trade."[26] In the military view, economic competition was the real cause of war, and the expanding commercial interests of the United States were bound to bring this country into conflict with other nations. "The thing most apt to disturb the equilibrium of good feeling between two countries," declared Bradley Fiske, is "competition for money or its equivalent."[27]

A second belief which was discussed less often by naval officers, but which appears to have been fairly widespread among them, was that in questions of war and peace, public opinion or "sentiment" was of overriding importance. Naval officers stressed the extent to which public opinion and emotion, rather than rational political or military calculation, had influenced the conduct of past American wars. "In all wars in which the United States has been engaged," observed the Naval War College planning committee, "public opinion has been all-powerful; not only having actually brought about our wars, frequently against the wishes of the administration in power, but having also dictated the lines of campaign."[28]

To Dewey and the officers of the General Board, then, it seemed inevitable that the growing commercial interests of the United States or an upsurge of public feeling on some international issue would sooner or later result in war with a foreign power. Given these beliefs, it was also not difficult to determine who the future enemy would be. The foremost trading nation of the world was, of course, Great Britain; but Britain and the United States enjoyed unusually cordial relations in these years, and after 1899, the navy never seriously comtemplated the idea of war with England.[29]

25. Alfred T. Mahan, *Armaments and Arbitration* (New York, 1912), 22.
26. Dewey to George Goodwin Dewey, February 4, 1898, in George Goodwin Dewey Papers.
27. Fiske, "The Naval Profession."
28. "Solution to the Problem, 1901," in Records of the Naval War College, 19. In 1902, the War College officers asserted that "war is largely controlled by sentiment"; and in 1897, they expressed the fear that public opinion and panic could well dictate a faulty strategy. ("Problem, 1902," and "Problem, 1897," both in Records of the Naval War College.)
29. In 1899, the annual War College problem had involved a war between the United States on one side and Britain and Germany on the other.

France was also eliminated as a probable enemy "because of her unusually friendly" attitude. This left Germany as the state with the strongest motivation and capacity to interfere in the affairs of the New World. In keeping with their ideas of world politics, the officers explained that economic considerations would compel the Germans to challenge the Monroe Doctrine. With a rapidly increasing population, they would soon "outgrow their borders. Expansion is therefore a necessity that becomes more pressing with every year that passes."[30] The Germans were ardently desirous of acquiring colonies in South America where there were already large German-speaking communities. They were prevented only by the Monroe Doctrine from carrying out their wishes. It was probable that in the near future Germany would seek to remove this barrier to her colonial ambitions, if necessary, by force.[31]

Despite these careful arguments which appeared in every General Board assessment of international affairs, the officers' choice of Germany as a probable antagonist may well have been based more on suspicion and dislike of Germans than on any fine calculations of economic interest. As early as the Samoan crisis of 1889, some American naval officers had already become concerned about Germany's supposed expansionist designs. The establishment of German colonies in Africa in the 1880s and the German seizure of Kiaochow in the Far East seemed to them confirmation of their belief that the Germans were frantically searching for Lebensraum everywhere in the world. As early as 1897, the officers of the Naval War College had sketched out the main lines of what was to become the official navy view of Germany: the Germans desired colonies in the Western Hemisphere; they would attempt to intervene there under the guise of protecting the interests of their citizens or investments in the region; once they had established a coaling station in the Caribbean, they would seek to expand still further.[32]

The event which served to crystallize this suspicion of Germany

---

30. Costello, "Planning for War," 136.
31. "War Portfolio No. 1," p. 1, in Records of the General Board of the Navy.
32. Costello, "Planning for War," 129.

into outright dislike and fear was the Spanish-American War. Germany's open sympathy for Spain and her eagerness to acquire the remnants of the Spanish Empire in the Pacific earned her the lasting ill will of many American military men. This was particularly true of Dewey. The supposed slights he had received at the hands of the Germans at Hong Kong and their exasperating, not to say menacing, conduct during the siege of Manila, had made him an inveterate Germanophobe. For the rest of his life the admiral had few good words for "the Dutch," either in public or private.

Many of the officers who were to serve on the General Board from 1900 to 1917 were veterans of Manila Bay or had close friends who were, and their stories of German insults and intrigues lost nothing in the telling. Captain Charles S. Sigsbee, the chief intelligence officer during the early years of Dewey's tenure, was convinced that Germany had designs on Brazil, Cuba, Santo Domingo, the Danish West Indies, Venezuela, and Haiti. The Germans, he suggested, would not scruple to invade and annex Denmark and Holland in order to acquire their Caribbean real estate![33] Captain French E. Chadwick, president of the Naval War College, observed that Germany had designs on Brazil, and Lieutenant John M. Ellicott, a member of the War College staff, suggested that the Germans desired nothing less than "a complete chain of naval bases across the Atlantic and Pacific trending through the American Isthmus." In 1903, the Naval War College warned that the Germans had designs on the Philippines "because they lie on the route from the Carolines to Singapore and, with some of the Celebes Islands, rather feebly held by the Dutch, they would form a valuable and productive chain."[34] In the same year, Dewey himself reported a conversation with a German naval officer who freely predicted that "the next war between great powers would be between the United States and Germany." The Germans, Dewey

33. Charles S. Sigsbee, "Germany vs. the United States: Memorandum by the Office of Naval Intelligence," May 21, 1900, in Records of the General Board; Sigsbee even went so far as to suggest that the Navy Department investigate the number of sailors in the navy with German names.
34. French E. Chadwick, "Coal" (Lecture delivered to the Naval War College, March 19, 1901), in Records of the Naval War College.

reported, "believe they could win a naval war with the United States."[35]

During the first few years of the board's existence, these views were not far removed from those of many other government officials and congressmen who, as William L. Langer has observed, displayed "a pathological suspicion" of Germany and the kaiser.[36] Secretary of State Hay was convinced that "the Vaterland is all on fire with greed and terror of us . . . the jealousy and animosity felt towards us in Germany can hardly be exaggerated. They want the Philippines, the Carolines and Samoa; they want to get into our markets—and keep us out of theirs."[37] Brooks Adams, Henry White, and Henry Cabot Lodge were all strongly anti-German while Elihu Root, Hay's successor as secretary of state, predicted that "the American people will, within a few years, have either to abandon the Monroe Doctrine or fight for it, and we are not going to abandon it."[38] At a lower level, Assistant Secretary of State Francis B. Loomis warned the officers of the Naval War College that "the question of acquiring some sort of definite foothold in South America has not been wholly excluded from the thought of certain governments in connection with their plans for commercial and political expansion."[39]

Although Roosevelt, in his soberer moments, tended to belittle the more bizarre fears of his Germanophobe associates, he was still capable, on occasion, of giving voice to similar thoughts—as when he wrote to Lodge that "the Germans regard our failure to go forward in building up the Navy this year as a sign that our spasm of preparation . . . has come to an end; that we shall sink back, so that, in a few years, they will be in a position to take some steps in the West Indies or South America which will make us either put up or shut up on the Monroe Doctrine."[40] As late as 1906, he wrote

35. Undated 1903 memorandum, in Dewey Papers.
36. William L. Langer, *The Diplomacy of Imperialism*, (2nd. ed.; New York, 1951), 519.
37. Howard K. Beale, *Theodore Roosevelt and the Rise of America to World Power* (Baltimore, 1956), 393.
38. Dexter Perkins, *The Monroe Doctrine, 1867–1907* (Baltimore, 1937), 307.
39. Costello, "Planning for War," 135–36.
40. Roosevelt to Henry Cabot Lodge, May 27, 1901, in Lodge (ed.), *Selections from the*

to Oscar Straus that Germany "respects the United States only insofar as it believes that our Navy is efficient."[41]

The "men around the president" also shared, in some degree, the naval officer's belief that war might come at any time as a result of economic rivalries. Indeed, many naval officers who wrote on the subject claimed to have received their inspiration from the works of Roosevelt's friend, Brooks Adams, whose books, *America's Economic Supremacy* and *The Law of Civilization and Decay*, were the best-known arguments for the idea of international relations as a struggle for economic power. Henry Cabot Lodge warned the president that "we are putting terrible pressure on Europe; and this situation may produce war at any time. The economic forces will not be the ostensible reason but they will be the real cause."[42]

With the Venezuelan claims controversy of 1902–1903, American suspicion and fear of Germany reached a peak. German conduct was widely condemned in Congress, and newspapers in both countries talked openly of war.[43] When the controversy was settled amicably, however, most of the public seemed to lose interest in the German menace. Even Roosevelt conceded in 1905 that "the relations of the two countries have been, I am happy to say, growing more and more friendly."[44] After 1903, the kaiser and the German foreign office sedulously cultivated American goodwill with the result that historians of German-American relations have been able to find little of the overt hostility of the 1899–1903 period in the press or other public documents after 1905.[45]

Correspondence of Theodore Roosevelt and Henry Cabot Lodge, 1884–1918 (2 vols.; New York, 1925), I, 484–85.

41. Roosevelt to Oscar Strauss, February 27, 1906, in Roosevelt Papers, Library of Congress.

42. Lodge to Roosevelt, March 30, 1901, *ibid.*

43. For a detailed account of the controversy, see Perkins, *The Monroe Doctrine*, 319–94, and Beale, *Theodore Roosevelt*, 395–432.

44. Roosevelt to Cecil Spring-Rice, November 1, 1905, quoted in Beale, *Theodore Roosevelt*, 431.

45. See especially Alfred Vagts, "Hopes and Fears of an American-German War, 1870–1915," *Political Science Quarterly*, LI (March, 1940); Clara E. Schieber, "The Transformation of American Sentiment toward Germany," *Journal of International Relations*, XII (July, 1921); and Melvin Small, "The American Image of Germany, 1906–1914" (Ph.D. dissertation, University of Michigan, 1965).

By the end of the Taft administration, the apocalyptic visions of the Rooseveltian statesmen had been forgotten by nearly everyone but the military, who preserved the gospel of Brooks Adams and the vision of the German menace in all its original purity. The growing Anglo-German naval rivalry which bid fair to keep both fleets tied to their home waters did not add to the navy's sense of security. The Naval War College summer conference solemnly concluded that although "German writers have given the impression that Germany is preparing for war with England, [this] need not blind us to the fact that, when Germany's accelerated program is completed, she will still be unable to meet England successfully but will surpass us in naval strength. Germany will then be ready to take issue with us over the Monroe Doctrine."[46] In 1913 the General Board still insisted that "the steady increase of Germany's population . . . the steady expansion of German home industry" and "the desire of the Imperial Government for colonial expansion . . . all lead to the conclusion that when conditions at home are no longer considered bearable and Germany is strong enough, Germany will insist upon the occupation of the Western Hemisphere territory under the German flag."[47] The German threat, whatever it may have been in 1900, was practically nonexistent ten years later. The navy's failure to recognize this had serious consequences. It tied the navy to an unrealistic and outmoded strategy and made its war plans increasingly irrelevant.

In June, 1900, the admiral and his wife boarded the steamer for Newport, Rhode Island, to attend the summer sessions of the General Board. Although Newport was a summer headquarters for international society, the trip was in no way a social junket. Mildred, whose health was poor, refused all invitations and did not entertain, while Dewey stuck grimly to business. When he was asked to lead the Fourth of July parade, he curtly replied that "the monkey show days are past."[48] Every morning a gray torpedo boat appeared opposite the Dewey's house and anchored a half mile

---

46. "Solution to the Problem, 1904," in Records of the Naval War College.
47. War Plan Black, in Records of the General Board.
48. Mildred Dewey to George Goodwin Dewey, June 27, 1900, in George Goodwin Dewey Papers.

offshore. The admiral was rowed out to the ship in his barge and arrived at the Naval War College a few minutes later.

At the Naval War College, officers labored over endless studies and reports. Groups of instructors and students gathered about tables and boards where the "war game," a complicated method of simulating navy operations developed by the War College, was played out endlessly.[49] The object of all this effort was the selection of the best policy and strategy to be followed in an American war with Germany.

The studies continued through the fall and winter, long after Dewey and the General Board had returned to Washington. By the spring of 1901 the General Board, the college, and the Office of Naval Intelligence had developed a set of scenarios which were highly disconcerting. The War College had concluded that if the Germans dispatched all their available naval forces to the Caribbean at the outset of the war their fleet would be superior to any force that the United States could assemble during the first weeks of the conflict. The Germans would probably use this temporary superiority to seize a base for their forces in the Caribbean area. The naval planners had also concluded that the United States would be practically helpless to interfere if the Germans attacked some point in South America south of the Amazon River.[50] If a battle did take place the War College and ONI both agreed that the American fleet would almost certainly lose.[51] These grim considerations probably weighed more than a little on the admiral's mind during his first year as president of the board.[52]

49. For an account of the development of war gaming at the Naval War College, see Spector, "Professors of War," 130–41.

50. General Board Minutes, April 24, 1901, and June 25, 1901, in Records of the General Board.

51. "Report of the Tactical Committee of the Naval War College" (Secret), 1901, in Records of the Naval War College.

52. Taylor to Roosevelt (enclosing report of attaché with endorsement of Sigsbee), March 22, 1902, in Roosevelt Papers. For a fuller discussion of some of the possible implications of these conclusions, see Ronald Spector, "Roosevelt, the Navy, and the Venezuelan Controversy, 1902–1903," *American Neptune*, XXXII (October, 1972).

◇◇

CHAPTER VII

Damning "the Dutch"

Despite his recent declaration of Democratic sympathies, Dewey was pleased by McKinley's reelection in the fall of 1900. To his son he expressed the hope that "now that Bryan is out of the way my investments out west may be in fatter shape."[1] Mildred also expressed relief at Bryan's defeat. "I am mortally certain," she declared, "that he would have felt angry at George for being willing to be a candidate."[2] At the inauguration day ceremonies Dewey occupied a prominent place in the reviewing stand next to the president and vice-president. Mildred noted with satisfaction that "he had his *due* place, ranking [Army General Nelson A.] Miles."[3] A few months later however the Deweys were shocked and saddened to learn of the shooting of President McKinley by an anarchist in Buffalo, New York. On September 15, the president died of his wounds and his vice-president, Theodore Roosevelt, succeeded to the executive office.

Dewey had always enjoyed a warm personal relationship with Roosevelt, whose assumption of the presidency immensely increased Dewey's influence in the Navy Department.[4] Since Dewey communicated with the president mainly through private conversations, this influence is difficult to define or measure. It is possible that Roosevelt was not nearly as impressed with the admiral's ideas in private as he professed to be in public; but there is still ample reason to believe that Dewey's word carried considerable weight in the new administration.

1. Dewey to George Goodwin Dewey, November 15, 1900, in George Goodwin Dewey Papers.
2. Mildred Dewey to George Goodwin Dewey, November 17, 1900, *ibid.*
3. Mildred Dewey to George Goodwin Dewey, March 5, 1901, *ibid.*
4. "I have instructed the Secretary of the Navy to get into close communion with the Admiral," Roosevelt told Mrs. Dewey, "so that the service may have the benefit of his wisdom, sagacity and counsel." Diary of Mildred Dewey, no date.

Within a few months, Roosevelt had deftly maneuvered Long into retiring as secretary of the navy and replaced him with the able William H. Moody.[5] Moody was a man more to the liking of Roosevelt, who intended to push for a strong navy, and Dewey soon established a harmonious relationship with the new secretary. Dewey was even more pleased with the appointment of Rear Admiral Henry C. Taylor as chief of the Bureau of Navigation in 1902. Dewey heartily disliked the outgoing chief of the bureau, Rear Admiral Arendt S. Crowninshield. Crowninshield had opposed Dewey's appointment to the Asiatic Squadron in 1897, and had, in Dewey's opinion, slighted the achievements of his squadron in his annual report dealing with naval operations in the Spanish-American War.[6]

Roosevelt's presidency also brought social success to Mildred. Despite increasing bouts of ill health which rendered her partially deaf, she basked in the glow of White House society. "I saw the Prince [Louis of Battenberg], who sat just opposite me, watch my jewels many times," she exulted after a White House dinner. "I was correct, even to emeralds and diamonds and rings."[7]

Since Dewey held a life appointment, Mildred felt herself to be the social superior of the wives of cabinet officers and elected officials. "It is always the same with these women," she confided to her diary. "It is always 'Io Triumphe' while they are enjoying official position but very humble when it is over. All one needs to do is wait." She had an especially low opinion of Roosevelt's cabinet wives. "Mrs. Root is a vulgar, brusque person. Mrs. Shaw is a crass vulgarian and underbred. Mrs. Cortelyou is the sort of woman one meets in sewing machine shops, behind the counter. Mrs. Bonaparte is a nonentity. Mrs. Metcalfe is nil but kindly. If there are others, I forget them."[8]

The newspapers had long since ceased to carry any unflattering references to the Deweys, a fact which Mildred attributed to a species of divine intervention. "It has not paid those who tried to

5. For a good discussion of Moody's appointment and his administration, see Paul T. Heffron, "Secretary Moody and Naval Administrative Reform, 1902–1904," *American Neptune*, XXIX, (October, 1969), 1.
6. Dewey to Crowninshield, January 26, 1900, in Dewey Papers.
7. Diary of Mildred Dewey, November 13, 1905, p. 127.
8. *Ibid.*, November 18, 1904, p. 73, and March 2, 1906, p. 152.

ruin George," she observed. "Long is despised, Crowninshield condemned [that is—retired], McKinley murdered, Hanna dead, Cor-
bin dying—all archplotters! It behooves us to live clean and be true
since the heavens themselves keep ward of George."[9]

For Dewey, the days were much the same. He would arrive at
his office at 9:00 A.M. and depart at 12:30. After a nap, he would
take his pair of matched sorrels for a drive and return home at 5:45
for dinner. He normally retired early and "slept all evening."[10] At
home, Mildred had tastefully decorated the admiral's sitting room
in Delft blue and white. On one wall was his five-star flag and on
the other a large photograph of Cavite and the sunken Spanish
ships. Dozens of carriages every week stopped near the house on
"K" Street "to see where the hero lives." But Dewey's comfortable
life was destined to be disturbed once again, this time by an international crisis over Venezuela.

The worst fears of the navy's Germanophobes seemed ready to
materialize in December, 1901, when the German ambassador,
Theodore von Holleben, informed the State Department that his
government might have to use force to collect debts long owed to
its citizens by the Venezuelan government. The government of
Venezuela was then in the hands of General Cipriano Castro, a
particularly irresponsible and unscrupulous demagogue, even by
Latin American standards. His government had long since ceased
to honor its international obligations, either financial or legal, and
by mid-1901 the European powers had begun to consider chastis-
ing the dictator with force.

Von Holleben's note expressly disavowed the intention of acquiring or permanently occupying any Venezuelan territory, but he
indicated that his government was seriously considering a blockade
of Venezuelan ports. If this measure failed to make Castro more
reasonable, the Germans "would have to consider the temporary
occupation of different Venezuelan harbor places and the levying
of duties in these places."[11]

The German note produced no great stir in the State Department. Secretary of State Hay repeated the long-standing American

9. *Ibid.*, November 18, 1905, p. 130.
10. *Ibid.*, February 4, 1902, p. 22.
11. Perkins, *Monroe Doctrine*, 325.

objection to the acquisition of territory in the New World by a non-American power, but raised no objection against the collection of debts by force. If the State Department reaction was mild, however, the navy's verged on paranoia. The War College had already predicted that Venezuela or one of its nearby islands would be the site the Germans would most likely choose to establish a naval base.

The General Board hastily dispatched Commander John E. Pillsbury to Venezuela to investigate the situation. In January, 1902, Pillsbury reported that "six German officers had arrived incognito at Port of Spain," in order to gather intelligence on the area. From conversations with them, Pillsbury concluded that "Germany means to put all possible pressure on Venezuela."[12] This was enough for Taylor and Dewey, who confidently expected war in the near future. They reassured themselves that at least the forthcoming goodwill visit of Prince Heinrich of Prussia, brother of the German emperor, to the United States would delay the war "for a time." "We need the delay," wrote Taylor, "to get our enlisted men in trim."[13] On January 1, 1902, Taylor informed the president that the General Board was "perfecting plans for a sudden descent on the Spanish Main should this be necessary."[14]

Under these circumstances, Dewey naturally gave special attention to the combined fleet maneuvers which the General Board and the War College were planning for the winter of 1902–1903 in the Caribbean. Whether the maneuvers were planned with the Germans in mind or as a genuine naval exercise cannot be unequivocally determined. It is possible that President Roosevelt, who well understood the diplomatic uses of naval parades, may have originated the idea himself. In July, 1902, Secretary Moody informed the navy bureau chiefs that the president was particularly interested in the success of the forthcoming maneuvers.[15] On the other hand, the General Board was genuinely anxious to test some of its ideas and the findings of the Naval War College. Dewey took a

---

12. Pillsbury to Taylor, January 16, 1902, in Dewey Papers.
13. Taylor to Dewey, January 31, 1902, *ibid.*
14. Taylor to George B. Cortelyon, January, 1902, in Roosevelt Papers.
15. Seward W. Livermore, "Theodore Roosevelt, the American Navy and the Venezuelan Crisis of 1902–1903," *American Historical Review*, LII (April, 1946), 458.

personal interest in planning the main search problem for the winter exercises, and the maneuvers themselves were based squarely on the War College Games of 1901.[16]

At Roosevelt's suggestion, Dewey agreed to take personal command of the combined squadrons. It the maneuvers were designed to impress the Germans, the appointment of Dewey was a clever step. The president was well aware of the psychological effect Dewey's presence would have on the Wilhelmstrasse. He hoped to use both the admiral's enormous prestige and his reputation for standing up to "the Dutch" to good effect. "I have been very anxious that this . . . effort . . . should be under your direction," he wrote to Dewey in June. "Your standing, not only in this nation, but abroad, is such that the effect of your presence will be very beneficial outside of the Service."[17]

The appointment was announced early and in a way designed to have maximum effect. "DEWEY GOING TO SEA," proclaimed the New York *Tribune*. Other press reports described the fleet as "the greatest assemblage of warships the United States has seen,"[18] and explained that the combined North Atlantic, European, and South Atlantic squadrons would participate.

In September, as the Venezuelan situation worsened, Dewey was summoned by telephone to the White House from a meeting of the General Board. Roosevelt, dressed in pajamas, received the admiral in his bedroom. According to Mrs. Dewey, "the President said he was glad that George had agreed to assume command in the Caribbean. 'It will put pride in the people and arrest the attention of the Kaiser,' the President told George in strictest confidence— what had better not be written now."[19] The admiral received his orders to proceed to the fleet advance base at Culebra on November 18. One week later, the British and German governments informed the State Department that they had resolved to use force against Venezuela.

Dewey joined the fleet on December 8, the day of the final

16. Dewey to Secretary of the Navy, July 22, 1902, in Records of the General Board; New York *Times*, December 3, 1902.
17. Roosevelt to Dewey, June 14, 1902, in Dewey Papers.
18. New York *Herald*, September 18, 1902; New York *Times*, November 6, 1902.
19. Diary of Mildred Dewey, September 24, 1902, p. 50.

British and German ultimatum to Venezuela. Two days later, the allies seized or sank the gunboats of the Venezuelan navy and landed troops at the town of La Guaya. On the thirteenth, they bombarded a fort at Puerto Cabello.

The actions of the European powers, who on the sixteenth were joined by Italy, aroused much excitement in the United States. Newspapers carried detailed accounts of the British and German actions and some expressed concern for the Monroe Doctrine. The official American attitude remained unchanged: the United States did not object to the forcible collection of debts, only to the acquisition of territory. When the Venezuelan government suggested arbitration, however, the United States took up the suggestion with alacrity as a possible way out of an awkward and potentially dangerous situation.

Under pressure from the United States, the European powers eventually agreed to arbitration "in principle." Several more weeks of argument ensued over the nature of the arbitration. During this time, the allies maintained their blockade of the country and the Germans twice bombarded points on Venezuelan soil. On February 19, the powers finally agreed to lift their blockade and the worst of the crisis had passed.

The precise nature of Roosevelt's diplomacy during these weeks has been widely debated. In 1916, the president, in a famous letter to William R. Thayer, claimed that he had warned the German ambassador that he would order Dewey's fleet to the coast of Venezuela unless the Germans agreed to arbitration.[20] The consensus of recent scholarship seems to be that Roosevelt did issue some sort of warning to the Germans, although not perhaps in the dramatic manner which he later recalled.[21]

Whatever the nature of the president's dealings with Germany, there can be little doubt that Dewey's presence as commander of the fleet was an important psychological factor. Throughout the

20. Roosevelt to William R. Thayer, in Thayer, *Life and Letters of John Hay* (2 vols.; Boston, 1916), II, 411–12.
21. See Beale, *Theodore Roosevelt*, 339–69; Livermore, "Theodore Roosevelt," 453–71; and Paul S. Holbo, "Perilous Obscurity: Public Opinion and the Press in the Venezuelan Crisis, 1902–1903," *Historian*, XXXII, 3 (May, 1970), 428–48.

Venezuelan episode, American newspapers pointed with confidence to the proximity of the fleet and to Dewey's role as commander. The Chicago *Daily Tribune* observed: "It would not be surprising if he should take a notion to drop into Venezuelan waters with a force at his back far superior to the warships of Great Britain and Germany combined. . . . Admiral Dewey, it must be remembered, had trouble with the Germans at Manila."[22]

The significance of the president's choice of Dewey to command the American fleet was not lost on the German embassy. The admiral had recently enhanced his long-standing reputation as a Germanophobe by refusing to attend a dinner in honor of Prince Heinrich during the prince's visit to America. The German chargé in Washington, Wilhelm von Quadt, perhaps succumbing to the wilder rumors in the press, informed his government that the Christmas dispersion of the American ships to various West Indian ports was a precaution against Dewey's taking some rash action against the Germans on his own initiative.[23]

The actual maneuvers were far less dramatic than the publicity surrounding them. Dewey assumed command of the fleet on December 8, just as the combined European, North Atlantic, and South Atlantic squadrons were completing an elaborate search problem designed to test whether an invading fleet from Europe could reach Puerto Rican waters undetected. True to the War College predictions, the "raiding force," under Rear Admiral George M. Sumner, easily eluded the much larger force of Rear Admiral F. J. Higginson and slipped into Mayaguez, Puerto Rico.[24]

On December 10, the combined fleets, consisting of seven battleships, more than a score of cruisers and gunboats, and the torpedo flotilla of seven torpedo boats, engaged in maneuvers and exercises in the waters off Puerto Rico.[25] These maneuvers continued until the twentieth when the ships were dispersed for the Christmas holidays, the battleships going to Trinidad and the Virgin Islands,

22. Holbo, "Perilous Obscurity," 431.
23. Alfred Vagts, *Deutschland und die Vereinigten Staaten in der Welt-Politik* (New York, 1935), 1622.
24. *Report of the Secretary of the Navy, 1903* (Washington, 1904), 64.
25. *Ibid.*, 627.

and the smaller vessels to other West Indian ports.[26] The fleet reassembled on December 29 for more exercises and drills. These lasted until January 5, when Dewey hauled down his flag and returned to Washington.[27]

The performance of the fleet was hardly such as to strike terror into the hearts of foreign observers. In a memorandum, Dewey's aide, Commander Nathan Sargent, observed that "the formations, both in line and in column, were ragged, distance and guide being badly kept, speed not well regulated and turns unskillfully executed."[28] The 1902 exercises marked the end of the heterogeneous cruising squadrons, scattered over different parts of the globe, which had been the basic units of the American fleet since the Civil War. The experience of the maneuvers proved that these "show-the-flag" squadrons were not effective as fighting units because of the great variety of ships included in a single "squadron." Shortly after the close of the Caribbean exercises, all the American battleships not in the Pacific were reorganized into one great battleship squadron of the North Atlantic Fleet. The squadrons on distant stations were organized into homogeneous divisions of cruisers and gunboats.

Dewey himself thought the maneuvers an immense success. In his official journal for January 3, 1903, he exulted: "The work laid out so long ago and with such care . . . is now ended and successfully accomplished. When one considers the technical success of the mobilization of so large a naval force 1,500 miles from home, and the effect on foreign powers, particularly at the present moment of the demonstration against Venezuela, it can only be considered as . . . adding immensely to our naval and national prestige."[29] To George Goodwin he observed, "I have no doubt we would have had considerable trouble had it not been for this splendid fleet *on the spot*."[30]

26. *Ibid.*
27. Livermore, "Theodore Roosevelt."
28. Sargent, "Memorandum for the Chief of Staff," January 12, 1903, in Records of the General Board.
29. "Journal of the Commander-in-Chief," December, 1902–January, 1903, in Dewey Papers.
30. Dewey to George Goodwin Dewey, January 4, 1903, in George Goodwin Dewey

Back home in Washington, the admiral was even more enthusiastic. The maneuvers of the American fleet, he told a reporter, "were an object lesson to the Kaiser more than any other person. . . . Think of it, fifty-four warships including colliers and all. Germans could not possibly get a fleet over here that could fight such an aggregation."[31] Forgetting his own earlier warnings about the strength of the German fleet, the admiral remarked that the efficiency of the German navy had been "greatly exaggerated."[32]

The Newark *Evening News* carried the interview on Friday, March 27. On Saturday, Captain William S. Cowles, the president's brother-in-law, called on the Deweys with "an important message" from the White House. The president was distressed over the *Evening News* story and thought that Dewey had better deny the whole affair, but the admiral would not be pressured into denying his own words as he had in 1899. He stubbornly stood his ground and told Cowles that the account "was in the main correct." The captain then urged that Dewey go to see the president at once.

The admiral, accompanied by Cowles, arrived at the White House to find a number of people waiting to see the president; but when Roosevelt emerged from his office, he immediately motioned the admiral into the room. According to Mrs. Dewey's diary, "he asked George about the matter—if it were true, etc." The admiral said that he believed he was having a friendly talk and had not known his words were to be quoted. "He asked the President what he was going to do." He said, "anything you want me to." The admiral repeated his determination not to back down. "I did not expect to be quoted," he told Roosevelt, "but Mr. President, you know how it is." Roosevelt exclaimed, "Don't I though!" and the interview was at an end.[33] Later that day, the White House issued a carefully worded statement which, while admitting the authenticity of the interview, stressed the fact that it had not been intended for publication.

Papers.
31. John Gary Clifford, "Admiral Dewey and the Germans: A New Perspective," *Mid-America*, 49, 3 (July, 1967), 218; New York *Times*, March 28, 1903.
32. New York *Times*, March 28, 1903.
33. Diary of Mildred Dewey, March 28, 1903.

For his part, Dewey was rather proud of the incident. "I suppose most of the Western papers, catering to the large German population out there, did not like what I said," he wrote to his son. "But in the East I have had nothing but compliments. . . . *I am standing by it.* The President was delighted and said to me much more than I had said to the newspaperman."[34]

Although Dewey's "interview" aroused anger among the more jingoistic elements in Germany, the general reaction was more restrained than in 1899. The German Foreign Office, anxious not to disturb its satisfactory relationship with the United States, a relationship which had already been somewhat strained by the Venezuelan episode, took no official notice of the affair.[35] In the United States, the Dewey faux pas received comparatively little attention and failed to arouse the torrent of chauvinistic feeling which his 1899 pronouncements had elicited. The New York *Times* expressed the feeling of many when it observed that it was disagreeable for a bluff old sea dog to have to call on the president and assure him that, though he was correctly quoted and meant what he said, his words were not intended for human ears. "Your true sea-dog is a guileless creature but his luminous sayings cease to be effulgent, just as jokes cease to be funny, when they have to be explained."[36] By the middle of April, the papers were full of Roosevelt's "Western Tour" and the incident had been forgotten.

In July, 1903, Dewey was given a new task when Secretary of War Elihu Root and Secretary of the Navy William Moody agreed to establish a Joint Army-Navy Board composed of four army and four navy officers "for the purpose of discussing and reaching common conclusions regarding all matters calling for the cooperation of the two services."[37] Dewey, as senior officer of the armed forces, served as chairman.

Although often regarded by historians as an early version of the Joint Chiefs of Staff, the Joint Board, during Dewey's day, was

34. Dewey to George Goodwin Dewey, April 7, 1903, in George Goodwin Dewey Papers.
35. New York *Times*, March 31, 1903.
36. *Ibid.*
37. General Order No. 107, July 20, 1903, in Elihu Root, *Military and Colonial Policy of the United States* (Cambridge, 1916), 431.

more in the nature of a liaison committee. The board had no
executive authority and could only discuss questions referred to it
by one of the service secretaries. There was no staff and all the work
was done by ad hoc committees drawn from the permanent members. More elaborate studies had to be undertaken by the war
colleges. The Joint Board was nevertheless destined to play an
important part in strategic planning during the latter part of the
Roosevelt administration.

The amicable settlement of the Venezuelan episode and the general waning of public interest in the German menace failed to shake
Dewey and his comrades from their conviction that war with Germany was imminent. In secret sessions in Washington and Newport the General Board continued its studies of the probable course
of the future German-American conflict.[38]

In preparing for a war with Germany, Dewey and his colleagues
were plagued with an almost insoluble problem: what was the
proper peacetime disposition of the battle fleet? If war with Ger-

---

38. The reader who has followed the convolutions and calculations of Dewey and his
fellow strategists this far may wonder whether there was any substance to the fears and
suppositions of the navy about the Germans. Until a few years ago, historians of German-
American relations tended to dismiss the warnings of the General Board as nothing more
than jingoistic imaginings. But there were jingoes on both sides of the Atlantic. Today,
thanks to the work of such scholars as John A. S. Grenville, Holger H. Herwig, and David
Trask, we know that the German military and naval staffs did indeed prepare war plans
against the United States, and that these plans were, in fact, somewhat farther along in their
development than those of the United States against Germany. By a curious irony, the chief
of the German admiralty staff was Vice Admiral Otto von Diederichs, the man who had
confronted Dewey at Manila Bay a few years before. Von Diederichs inherited a theoretical
strategic plan for war against the United States, prepared in 1898 by Lieutenant Edward
von Mantey. The admiral lost no time in developing von Mantey's scheme into a full-fledged
"operations plan" for a combined naval and military attack against one of the East Coast
cities of the United States, probably New York. Count Alfred von Schlieffen, the chief of
army general staff, was having none of this, however. Schlieffen estimated that it would
require upwards of 100,000 men for a successful direct invasion of the United States and
suggested a preliminary landing in Cuba as an alternative. Finally, in the spring of 1903,
a "final" operations plan, "Operationsplan III" was agreed upon by the two services. The
plan called for a lightning seizure of Culebra and Puerto Rico as the first step in a war
between Germany and the United States. German naval forces in East Asia and the Pacific
were to carry out an immediate assault on the Philippines. The American Naval War
College, with a tiny staff and a rudimentary intelligence system, had thus successfully
predicted the correct German strategy—two years before the Germans themselves had
actually thought of it. Holger H. Herwig and David Trask, "Naval Operations Plans Between Germany and the United States of America, 1898–1913," *Militargeschichtliche Mitteilungen*, No. 2 (1970), 9–12; see also Grenville and Young, *Politics, Strategy, and American
Diplomacy*, 305–307.

many was likely, then the Atlantic was the proper station for American battleships; but the necessity to defend the Philippines and the generally unsettled political conditions in East Asia argued for the continued presence of American naval strength in the western Pacific. It was this problem which was to chiefly occupy the naval planners during the remainder of Roosevelt's first term.

The Naval War College argued that all the battleships had to be combined into a single fleet to be deployed at the point of maximum danger, the East Coast; but though the War College's arguments were unanswerable from a strategic point of view, there were pressing political reasons for the continued presence of American naval forces in the Far East. The Russians and Japanese were edging toward war over Manchuria, which the Russians had occupied during the Boxer Rebellion and now refused to evacuate. The United States, concerned for the future of the Open Door in Manchuria, supported Japan in her efforts to ease the Russians out of at least the southern half of the province. In December, 1903, the Japanese foreign minister informed Admiral Taylor that the Japanese government considered the continued presence of American battleships in East Asia "of the greatest weight and influence during the negotiations [between Russia and Japan]."[39]

From his own experience in the Far East, Dewey was convinced of the need for naval forces in the Pacific. He had already advised the secretary of the navy in 1901 that "the growing interest of the United States in the East will probably necessitate the keeping of a large naval force in the Pacific." Both Admiral Taylor and Dewey's aide, Commander Nathan Sargent, were in agreement with this view, and both believed that American forces in the Atlantic were sufficient to deter, for the moment at least, any German moves against the West Indies.[40] Even Alfred Thayer Mahan, who had done more than any man to instill in the navy an appreciation for the importance of concentration, declared that "to remove our fleet—battle fleet—from the Pacific would be a confession of weakness."[41] The navy's other elder statesman, Rear Admi-

39. Taylor to Dewey, December 2, 1903, in Dewey Papers.
40. Taylor to Theodore Roosevelt, February 9, 1903, in Roosevelt Papers; Sargent, "Memorandum on the Disposition of Our Naval Forces" (1902), in Dewey Papers.
41. Alfred T. Mahan to Taylor, December 7, 1903, cited in Costello, "Planning for War,"

ral Stephen B. Luce, also held this view. "It seems to me that the storm center is now in Asiatic waters," he wrote to Taylor on the same day as Mahan. "It seems to me our diplomacy in the East requires the moral support of material force. . . . As to the Atlantic, I have no fears at present. It is not easy to see how the balance of power on this side of the world can be disturbed; or if it is, can be confined to two opponents. I do not share the common apprehension of Germany."[42]

Alone among the strategists, Luce saw the significance of the elaborate system of alliances and counteralliances into which the European powers were gradually locking themselves. He alone justified the retention of the fleet in the Pacific, not on the grounds that American strength in the Atlantic was sufficient to deter the Germans, but on the grounds that the balance of power in Europe would prevent Germany—or any other European power—from interfering in the affairs of the New World.

The conflicting positions of his naval advisers prompted Secretary of the Navy Moody to ask Dewey for a definite statement on the distribution of the fleet.[43] For more than two weeks, the General Board debated the question, with Rear Admiral Charles S. Sperry presenting the case for the War College and Taylor heading the opposition. In truth, the navy was caught between two of its own dogmas: its commitment to the strategic "truths" of Mahan, which demanded concentration at the point of greatest danger, and its belief that economic rivalry was the all-important issue in international relations. One dogma suggested concentration in the Atlantic against Germany; the other suggested a continued presence in East Asia, the scene of the most naked economic rivalries. The result, as in many other debates presided over by Dewey, was a compromise. The board declared that "as a general principle," the proper policy on distribution of the fleet was to concentrate all battleships in the Atlantic but that "under present conditions, viz the imminence of war between Russia and Japan, the presence of a battle squadron in the East is necessary."[44]

296.
42. Stephen B. Luce to Taylor, December 7, 1903, in Luce Papers.
43. Moody to Dewey, November 20, 1903, in Records of the General Board, File 420.1.
44. Dewey to Moody, December 5, 1903, in RG 80.

No one·was really satisfied with this compromise, which kept a fraction of the American battle fleet in the Pacific and the remainder in the Atlantic. American interests in East Asia were too important to be left unsupported, whatever the danger to Latin America. Yet, to divide the fleet between the two oceans was strategically unsound. In the end, Dewey and his colleagues would not be satisfied until the United States Navy was large enough to assure its superiority over any probable enemy in *either* ocean. What the naval strategists really desired was a navy strong enough for two oceans; and, as early as 1903, the General Board had begun to consider what such a navy would entail. In January of that year, the board met in extraordinary session to formulate a long-range building policy for the United States.

There was some difference of opinion as to the proper size of the battle fleet. The more conservative officers recommended thirty or forty battleships as the proper number, but Captain Samuel Pillsbury and Commander Nathan Sargent demanded "a gradual increase in the number of battleships until we have one for each state in the union."[45] After some debate, the board voted unanimously to recommend a fleet of forty-eight first-class battleships as the ultimate goal. The ships were to be laid down at the rate of four a year. In addition, the board desired to have one scout (light) cruiser and one destroyer for every battleship, with one armored cruiser for every two battleships.[46]

The board's recommendations were embodied in a letter to the secretary of the navy in February, 1903. The letter also recommended a corresponding increase in the personnel of the navy, so as to properly man the new ships.[47] In 1904 and 1905, the General Board virtually repeated its recommendations, calling for an immediate start on at least three battleships and three scout cruisers per year.[48]

In later years, congressional and other critics of the navy were

45. General Board Minutes, January 31, 1903, I, 237, in Records of the General Board.
46. *Ibid.*
47. Dewey to Secretary of the Navy, February 9, 1903, in Records of the General Board.
48. Dewey to Secretary of the Navy, October 28, 1904, October 28, 1905, in Records of the General Board.

to charge that the General Board desired a fleet of forty-eight battleships simply to have a ship for each state. There was more than a little truth in this charge. Naval planners like Pillsbury and Sargent, who were convinced that the navy ought to be vastly expanded in the face of the German menace, apparently hit upon forty-eight as a nice large number. Once the "goal" had been set, the General Board must have seen little reason to revise it downward in the face of growing naval armaments abroad. To revise the goal upward would have been an exercise in futility since Congress had failed to appropriate the necessary funds for even forty-eight ships.

Nevertheless, the General Board's recommendations were not wholly unreasonable. For Dewey and his colleagues, the proper yardstick against which to measure American fighting strength was the German navy. As Dewey frankly stated in a letter to the secretary of the navy in October, 1904, "There is one nation in particular with whom we must be prepared to show that we have the ability to pursue this policy [the Monroe Doctrine]. In laying down and pursuing a building program, the question will always be greatly simplified if we bear in mind the clear proposition to prepare for a struggle with this power. Such a struggle is inevitable unless we studiously direct our efforts to prepare for it."[49]

The "enemy," of course, was Germany, which at this time had embarked upon an ambitious program of naval expansion embodied in the famous Fleet Law of 1900. The law provided for a long-range building program which would provide the German navy with a fleet of thirty-eight first-line battleships and more than fifty cruisers by 1920. The Naval War College and the General Board believed that, at least until the completion of the Panama Canal, the American battle fleet would have to be 50 percent stronger than the German. Germany possessed interior lines and might strike either in the Pacific or the Atlantic; hence the request for forty-eight battleships.

On a more fundamental level, Dewey and his colleagues must have believed that, because of its constantly expanding commercial

---

49. "Memorandum for the Secretary of the Navy," January 26, 1904, in Records of the General Board.

activities, the United States was bound to come into collision with *some* power sooner or later. Therefore, in the long run, nothing short of a navy able to operate in both oceans would be satisfactory. The officers of the War College rather tortuously expressed this idea in the "Solution to the Problem" for 1909. "The time will probably come," they observed, "when our Pacific commerce will have advanced to the point demanding the maintenance of a strong battle fleet there. But when this time comes, we must also have a paramount fleet in the Atlantic. The U.S. will then be at the zenith of her power and will control the world."[50]

To Dewey and his fellow strategists, the logic behind their demand for a fleet of forty-eight battleships seemed well nigh irrefutable. Unfortunately, it did not appear so to large segments of the American public. The little navy congressmen and senators who would have to vote the gigantic appropriations requested by the General Board remained unconvinced about the necessity for any such extraordinary expansion. Little concerned with the German menace or the dangers of an expanding foreign commerce, these men were aware that the United States Navy of 1904 with its twenty-odd battleships and ten large armored cruisers, either completed or under construction, was second only to that of Britain in size. They also knew that the shipbuilders, the arms makers, the "Steel Trust," and the naval officers themselves had more than a little personal interest in large naval appropriations.

For 1904, Congress authorized only one battleship and two armored cruisers. By 1905, even President Roosevelt was ready to call a halt to the spiral of increasing appropriations. During earlier years, the president had threatened, pleaded, and cajoled Congress into record appropriations. By 1905, however, he was prepared to concede that "it does not seem necessary that the Navy should, at

---

50. "Solution to the Problem, 1909," in Records of the Naval War College. A more unusual argument for a large battle fleet was presented by Lieutenant Commander Washington Irving Chambers. In a memorandum prepared for Dewey's signature, Chambers actually envisioned offensive operations by the United States against the Germans in the North Sea. "Blockade is what they fear more than anything else. In the North Sea we could bring the fleet to combat and throttle the resources of our enemy in the shortest space of time." Chambers to Dewey, January 26, 1904, in Records of the General Board.

least in the immediate future, be increased beyond the present number of units."[51]

In vain, the General Board recommended three battleships in 1905 and three more in 1906. Congress reluctantly approved two in 1905 and only one in 1906. But new developments in world affairs were soon to upset the calculations of both the board and its congressional critics.

51. On Roosevelt's ship-building policy, see Sprout, *Rise of American Naval Power*, 259–83.

CHAPTER VIII

"Let Us Have Neither Cliques Nor Grudges"

On July 26, 1904, Rear Admiral Henry Clay Taylor died suddenly while on a visit to Canada. Dewey had lost his ablest collaborator. No other member of the General Board ever enjoyed the trust and respect which the admiral of the navy felt for Taylor, and while Taylor was alive Dewey actively supported his colleague's great aim: the development of the General Board into a true naval general staff.

In June, 1901, at Taylor's suggestion, Dewey had sounded out Secretary Long on a scheme to create a general staff within the Bureau of Navigation which would carry out the policies of the General Board and coordinate the work of the bureaus. Long was not enthusiastic and expressed the fear that such an arrangement would interfere with "the continued good work of the Board" and the principle of "simplicity of departmental organization."[1] In 1904, with William H. Moody now secretary of the navy, Dewey addressed a memorandum to President Roosevelt on the advantages of a general staff for the navy. A general staff, wrote Dewey, "would go far toward assuring us a greater efficiency of personnel, a knowledge of our nautical resources, a surety of war plans, a readiness for offensive operations and generally, a thorough preparedness for hostilities."[2]

The admiral believed that the General Board, together with the

---

1. Dewey to Long, June 28, 1901, and Long to Dewey, July 10, 1901, both in Records of the General Board; Costello, "Planning for War," 50–51.
2. "Memorandum for the President from Admiral Dewey Concerning the Proposed General Staff for the Navy," June 3, 1904, in Records of the General Board.

Office of Naval Intelligence, the War College, and the Bureau of Navigation could form the basis of a de facto general staff, but a chief of staff was needed to direct the whole. A chief of staff could be created without legislation simply by relieving the chief of the Bureau of Navigation of the "countless routine duties of that position" so that he could "devote himself to the more important ones of general efficiency of the fleet and thorough readiness for international complications."[3]

Roosevelt pronounced Dewey's memorandum "conclusive,"[4] but in the matter of administrative reform both the president and his service chief preferred to make haste slowly. It was not until the spring of 1904 that Secretary Moody, with considerable trepidation, proposed to the House a bill which provided for the legislative recognition of the General Board as a permanent organ of the Navy Department and the appointment of a "chief-of-staff" to be selected from among the members of the General Board.[5] At Dewey's suggestion Moody later changed the title "chief-of-staff" to the more innocuous one of "military advisor."

Moody and Taylor urged Dewey to agree to accept the position of "military advisor" should it be created. They believed that such a move would go far toward assuring the success of the proposed legislation. The admiral demurred, claiming that his advanced age (sixty-six) would not permit him to accept such a demanding position.[6] Dewey's refusal was probably also prompted by his distaste for intraservice controversy and his unwillingness to hazard his prestige on anything as controversial as the general staff issue.

Dewey testified in favor of the bill during the hearings held by the House Naval Affairs Committee, but the measure failed to reach the floor of the House. Three months later Taylor was dead, and Moody had left the Navy Department to assume the post of attorney general.

---

3. *Ibid.*
4. Roosevelt to Dewey, June 4, 1902, in Roosevelt Papers.
5. *Hearings before the Committee on Naval Affairs, House of Representatives, on Appropriations for 1905 and on H.R. 15403* (Washington, 1904). Hereinafter cited as *Committee on Naval Affairs Hearings.*
6. Taylor to Moody, April 10, 1904, in Moody Papers, Library of Congress; Taylor to Dewey, n.d. 1904, in Dewey Papers; *Committee on Naval Affairs Hearings,* 914.

With Taylor's death the movement for administrative reform in the Navy was taken up by more radical and less cautious officers. The "insurgents"[7]—young officers like Bradley A. Fiske, Albert L. Key, William S. Sims, and Philip Andrews, and older men like Stephen B. Luce, William J. Barnette, and William Swift blamed the faulty organization of the Navy Department for everything from the poor state of navy gunnery to the faulty design of American battleships; and in a large measure they were right. These men regarded the General Board as a promising start, but nothing more, toward their ultimate goal of subordinating the interests of the bureaus to the needs of the seagoing navy. To properly prepare the navy for war and direct its operations, the reformers demanded a full-fledged general staff, on the German model, with complete legal responsibility for the direction of the navy. Over the next decade the gap between these insurgent officers and their opponents, the more conservative officers and those associated with the bureaus, was to grow even wider. As he had done throughout his career, Dewey endeavored, with decreasing success, to maintain a middle position, sometimes siding with the insurgents, sometimes with their opponents.

The first challenge came from the insurgent camp. Late in 1905 a cabal of General Board officers led by Barnette and Swift had devised still another scheme to establish a general staff for the navy. Their plan was to have a clause inserted in the naval appropriations bill assigning all the administrative and routine duties of the chief of the Bureau of Navigation to his principle assistant, leaving the chief of the bureau free to function as a chief of staff.

In January, 1906, the reformers, without prior consultation with Dewey, presented their scheme before a meeting of the General Board. The admiral was furious. Departing from his usual policy of noncommittal neutrality in board meetings, Dewey denounced his colleagues for attempting to "seize executive power." The plan was "a personal slap in the face," declared Dewey, his voice shaking with anger, "and with this he rose and left the room."[8] The

---

7. This term is borrowed from Elting Morison's *Admiral Sims and the Modern American Navy*.
8. Diary of Mildred Dewey, January 27, 1906; Costello, "Planning for War," 72–75.

following day, Dewey refused to go to his office or attend further meetings of the board; and it required the combined efforts of Rear Admiral George E. Converse, the chief of navigation, Captain Nathan Sargent, and Mrs. Dewey to prevent him from resigning from the board.[9] The insurgents, frightened by the possibility of having Dewey's prestige used against them, were temporarily quiet.

The plan which Dewey had reacted against so violently was, ironically, almost the same plan he had endorsed in 1902 in his general staff memorandum to the president. The admiral's radical change of attitude can partly be attributed to the fact that in 1902 he was endorsing an open and aboveboard scheme of his admired friend, by which in all probability Taylor would become chief of staff; in 1905, however, he was presented with a plan deliberately designed to sneak by Congress and the secretary. It was a plan designed also to supplant Dewey as the real, if not the symbolic, head of the navy. As Captain Barnette confided to Admiral Luce, "my plan presumes the status quo so far as Dewey is concerned (unfortunately). . . . Dewey, so long as he acts, will of course be the President of the General Board, but the Chief of Bu Nav [Bureau of the Navy] has the power and *is* therefore the executive head."[10] After 1906 Dewey's enthusiasm for a general staff cooled rapidly.

At the same time that the admiral was confronted with troubles from the "left wing" of the officer corps he was also having his problems with the "right"—the entrenched bureaus. From the beginning the General Board had sought to have a voice in determining not only the numbers and types of warships, as they had done in their 1903 report, but also the characteristic speed, size, and armament which such warships ought to have. This brought the General Board into direct collision with the Bureau of Construction and Repair and with the Board on Construction which it largely controlled. Dewey and the officers of the General Board believed that the officers of the Bureau of Construction needed the advice and guidance of the seagoing line officers who would actual-

9. Diary of Mildred Dewey, January 27, 1906.
10. Barnette to Luce, October 15, 1905, cited in Costello, "Planning for War."

ly operate and fight the ships.[11] The design specialists in the Bureau of Construction, however, were incensed that the General Board would presume to tell them their business.

The controversy came to a head at the beginning of 1906. Charles J. Bonaparte, current secretary of the navy, had angered the members of the General Board by submitting their suggestions on ship characteristics to the Board of Construction for comment and then adopting the construction board's views on the subject. To Dewey this was intolerable. He had had a low opinion of Bonaparte ever since the latter had succeeded Moody and Paul Morton as secretary of the navy in 1905, and the Board of Construction imbroglio merely served to confirm the admiral's opinion. "Mr. Bonaparte is not a hustler as his predecessor [was]," wrote Dewey to Nathan Sargent. "And so there is not much to show for what we are doing."[12]

The full wrath of the admiral of the navy now descended upon the hapless Bonaparte. "George is worried over Bonaparte's crazy-headed actions," recorded Mildred in her diary. "He says he is a crank and has been hurtful to the Navy." At a dinner party given by Henry Cabot Lodge, the usually genial Dewey angrily declared that "the Navy is going to hell!"[13] Three days after the Lodge dinner Dewey met with President Roosevelt. The admiral repeated his charges that Bonaparte was a "crank" and threatened to resign unless he was replaced, preferably by the assistant secretary, Truman H. Newberry.[14]

Roosevelt was evidently impressed with Dewey's complaint. Although he did not actually replace Bonaparte until the end of 1906 the secretary was conspicuous by his absence from the Navy Department during the balance of the year. As Dewey wrote to Nathan Sargent, "Mr. Bonaparte is at the Department very little of late and the assistant secretary, Mr. Newberry, is practically doing the work, which is gratifying to us as we are all much pleased with

11. For a fuller discussion of the feud see Costello, "Planning for War," 43–49, 75–88, and *passim*, and Morison, *Admiral Sims and the Modern American Navy*, 176–216 and *passim*.
12. Dewey to Nathan Sargent, December 26, 1905, in Dewey Papers.
13. Diary of Mildred Dewey, January 17, 1906.
14. *Ibid.*, January 20, 1906.

his work."[15] After Bonaparte's nomination as attorney general, Dewey charitably allowed that "the last report of Mr. Bonaparte . . . was a great improvement over the very original ideas he first expressed, but he is probably much better fitted to be an attorney general."[16]

Dewey had won his battle with Bonaparte but the underlying board-bureau quarrel which had brought on the confrontation was far from settled. Nor was the dissatisfaction of the insurgents allayed by what they considered to be the board's overly cautious methods. As 1906 drew to a close the admiral of the navy appealed for unity in the navy in his Christmas message to the service: "Let us have neither cliques nor grudges but all stand together for the good of the country."[17] The navy was indeed in need of unity, for it was about to face its gravest international challenge since the Venezuelan crisis.

The petty bureaucrats and political hacks of the San Francisco School Board were probably unaware that they were setting off an international crisis of major proportions when, in October, 1906, they ordered the establishment of a separate school for pupils "of the Mongolian race" and ordered the Japanese residents in their city, both aliens and citizens, to send their children to this school only. The board's action was simply one more in a long series of discriminatory measures enacted against Orientals in California and neighboring states where feelings against the Japanese, who reportedly competed with American workers for jobs, ran high. When challenged, the board pointed out correctly that its measures merely brought the San Francisco school system into line with existing state laws which provided for segregated schooling. Nevertheless, the school board's order touched off a diplomatic crisis.[18]

In Japan, news of the order produced a burst of rage and indignation which was reflected in bellicose editorials and letters in the nationalist press. The Japanese government filed a formal protest,

15. Dewey to Nathan Sargent, June 5, 1906, in Dewey Papers.
16. Dewey to Willard S. Brownson, January 15, 1907, *ibid.*
17. Costello, "Planning for War," 81.
18. The best treatment of the school board crisis is still Thomas A. Bailey, *Theodore Roosevelt and the Japanese-American Crises* (Stanford, 1934).

claiming that the order violated the most-favored-nation provisions of the Japanese-American Treaty of 1894. Secretary of State Elihu Root shot off a telegram to Ambassador Luke Wright in Japan informing the Japanese government that the president had ordered the justice department to investigate the legality of the school board's actions. At the same time, the White House announced that Secretary of Commerce and Labor Victor I. Metcalf, a Californian, would go to San Francisco to confer with the local authorities. In his briefcase, Metcalf carried a memorandum from Root which painted in lurid colors the effects of an American-Japanese conflict. The memorandum spoke of the loss of Hawaii and the Philippines, a Japanese occupation of the Pacific coast, and the ruin of America's Pacific trade.[19]

In all their lofty calculations of geopolitical advantage, the balancing of trade rivalries, the weighing of national policies, Dewey and his colleagues had never considered the possibility that simple race hatred might suddenly involve the country in war. Prior to 1904 the General Board had always considered the United States' most likely antagonist in the Pacific—as in the Atlantic—to be Germany, with Russia a close second and Russia's ally, France, a more distant third. England and Japan were considered likely allies.

The outbreak of the Russo-Japanese war actually increased the navy's sense of security. In 1904, the Naval War College's Special Committee on Naval Policy reported to the General Board that Russia would be crippled by the war; France was "well satisfied" with her holdings in Indochina, and England "acquiesced wholly in our Caribbean and Asiatic expansion." As for Japan, she was "likely to be crippled by the war unless she can get an indemnity."[20] Dewey's trusted aide, Captain Nathan Sargent, who was then serving a tour in the Far East, graphically described the financial and economic exhaustion of Japan in his letters to the admiral.[21]

19. Braisted, *The United States Navy in the Pacific*, 192; Bailey, *Theodore Roosevelt*, 84. Both Braisted and Bailey believe that the Root memorandum was drafted primarily to impress the Californians with the danger of war with Japan.

20. "Report of the Special Committee on Naval Policy, 1904," in Records of the Naval War College.

21. Cf. Sargent to Dewey, October 20, 1905, in Nathan Sargent Papers, Library of

After the conclusion of the war, the American naval attaché, Commander Frank Marble, continued to report on the friendly disposition of Japanese officials toward the United States.[22] The sudden confrontation with Japan, therefore, came as a considerable surprise to Dewey and his colleagues. When Roosevelt, through Assistant Secretary Newberry, asked about the navy's readiness for war with Japan, Dewey confidently replied that the General Board had a plan already prepared.[23] In fact, the navy's war plans for the Far East, as we have seen, had never contemplated a war with Japan at all.

In private, Dewey was much less sanguine. Mildred noted in her diary: "It looks ugly with Japan and George is very blue. Says we are not ready. It is not the fault of the Navy but of [Senator] Hale who killed the bill for the ships."[24] Lack of ships was not really the problem. The United States Navy enjoyed a comfortable superiority over Japan in battleships and armored cruisers. The heart of the difficulty was the lack of an adequate operating base anywhere in the Pacific, together with the General Board's firm belief that naval assets had to be kept in the Atlantic to counter any aggressive moves by Germany.

The army and navy, acting through the Joint Board, finally got around to the problem of war with Japan in January, 1907.[25] A few weeks later, the San Francisco School Board, having enjoyed a cross-country junket to Washington to "confer" with the president, agreed to rescind its obnoxious order. Shortly thereafter, the Japanese government privately promised to issue no more passports to Japanese coolie laborers desiring to go to the United States.

In May, tempers flared again when a San Francisco mob attacked and wrecked a Japanese restaurant and damaged other Japanese places of business. The Japanese press gave extensive coverage to what it referred to as the "Second San Francisco Inci-

---

Congress.

22. Braisted, *The United States Navy in the Pacific*, 185.

23. Roosevelt to Newberry, October 26, 1906, Dewey to Newberry, October 29, 1906, both in Roosevelt Papers.

24. Diary of Mildred Dewey, October 27, 1905, p. 114.

25. Braisted, *The United States Navy in the Pacific*, 199.

dent." Within two weeks of the riots, opposition leaders in Japan were speaking openly of war "with the United States."[26] On June 20, President Roosevelt asked Assistant Secretary of War Robert Shaw Oliver to report to him on "what plans had been made by the Joint Board, the War Department and the Navy in case of trouble with Japan."[27]

The Joint Board met on June 19 with Dewey in the chair. By this time, the navy's studies were fairly well advanced. In April, the General Board had concluded that despite friction with Japan, the entire battle fleet must remain in the Atlantic. To send part of the ships to the Pacific would be to violate Mahan's principle of concentration. It would be better to station the *entire* fleet in the Pacific, provided that bases for them on the West Coast and in the Philippines had been completed. In June, 1907, however, the "Two-Ocean Navy" and the Pacific bases were still far off.

For the present, the Joint Board agreed that the United States would have to assume the defensive in the Pacific until the battleships could be brought around from the Atlantic. When war with Japan seemed imminent, the larger ships of the Pacific fleet would have to withdraw from Asiatic waters and join the battleships from the Atlantic. The gunboats, monitors, and small torpedo boats which made up the balance of the Pacific fleet would concentrate at Olongapo in the Philippines. There, the gunboats' armament and crews would be landed to help in the defense of Subig Bay, to which all the land forces would also be ordered. They were expected to hold out as long as possible while the American battle fleet fought its way back across the Pacific. It was not a very promising plan, but it was the best that could be devised under the circumstances and it formed the basis for American military planning for years to come.

A more spectacular outcome of the military's deliberations, however, was the decision to send a fleet of sixteen of the newest American battleships on a practice cruise to the Pacific. The move had been discussed in naval circles for some time and the General

26. Bailey, *Theodore Roosevelt*, 194, 201.
27. Fred C. Ainsworth to Elihu Root, July 6, 1904, in Records of the Adjutant General of the Army, Record Group 94, National Archives.

Board had recommended such a cruise on June 18, the day before the meeting of the Joint Board. On June 27, when General W. W. Wotherspoon and Captain Richard Wainwright called on the president at his home in Oyster Bay to discuss the Joint Board plans, Roosevelt affirmed his intention to send the battle fleet to the Pacific in October. He also approved the Joint Board's other recommendations, although he assured the two officers that he "definitely had no apprehension of war with Japan."[28]

Dewey had also concluded that there was little danger of war with Japan. As he wrote to Admiral Brownson: "In my opinion the whole agitation [over the Japanese] is due to the labor organizations who rule the entire Pacific Coast . . . but whether just or unjust we must make up our mind that . . . the Japanese must be kept out . . . if any friction results the Navy will bear the brunt of it. But I do not think it likely matters will reach a critical stage for a long time to come; probably not until trade competition accentuates the situation."[29] Nevertheless, the admiral welcomed the voyage of the battle fleet as a graphic demonstration of American naval power and a spectacular means of pointing up the need for a two-ocean navy.[30]

While the fleet was on its much publicized voyage around the world, a debate, which was to have a far more lasting effect on American naval power in the Pacific, was quietly reaching a climax in the halls and offices of the State, War, and Navy Building on Pennsylvania Avenue. The question at issue concerned the proper site for the much needed American naval base in the Western Pacific.

This problem had occupied the General Board from its inception in March, 1900, when Secretary Long had set as its first task the study of "possible war situations in the Philippines and vicinity."[31] After more than a year of study, the General Board had determined that Olongapo on Subig Bay was the proper site for the future Far

---

28. Ainsworth to Root, July 6, 1909, *ibid.*
29. Dewey to Brownson, January 15, 1907, in Dewey Papers.
30. Dewey to Secretary of the Navy, September 1, 1907, in Records of the General Board.
31. Long to Captain C. H. Stockton, March 30, 1900, in RG 45, Area 10 file.

Eastern base. Like the Spanish Captain del Rio, the board believed that a powerful fleet in Subig Bay would render an attack on Manila too hazardous to be undertaken.[32] The Army Corps of Engineers expressed reservations about the defensibility of Olongapo from the land side but, for the moment, the question remained an academic one, for Congress refused to appropriate any money for the site during 1900. It remained equally tightfisted during 1901 and 1902.[33]

Dewey committed his personal reputation and influence to the success of the Subig Bay project. As a commander in the Philippines, he had been much impressed with the strategic advantages of Subig. He had had a special translation made of Captain del Rio's memorandum and kept a copy of it in his personal papers. When Congress failed to appropriate money for the base at Olongapo, Dewey made a rare personal appeal to Secretary of the Navy Moody to use his influence to obtain funds for a start on construction.

The admiral pointed to the "threatening aspect of affairs in the East" where war between Japan and Russia seemed every day more imminent. "We are entirely dependent [for bases] in the East on the courtesy of other nations," Dewey observed. This fact pointed up the "urgent necessity for docking facilities" on the Asiatic station. He enclosed a letter from General Nelson A. Miles, the commanding general of the army, endorsing the Subig Bay location and declared that "all experts have agreed on Subig Bay as the proper site."[34] In a second letter to Moody, one week later, the admiral was even more emphatic: "Had the Spanish been in Subig Bay, and that bay been properly defended, my victory at Manila would have been much more difficult." Subig Bay "should be made into an impregnable naval base of the first order."[35] Congress, however, was unimpressed. No funds were forthcoming in 1903. At the end of that year, Dewey referred to the defenseless condition of the

32. Dewey to Long, November 9, 1901, *ibid.*
33. For details of the board's efforts on behalf of Subig, see Braisted, *The United States Navy in the Pacific*, 118–24.
34. Dewey to Moody, June 8, 1903, in RG 80, File 11406.
35. Dewey to Moody, June 15, 1903, *ibid.*

Philippines as a "constant subject of anxiety to American military planners."[36] The admiral's letter bore the date December 7.

It took the Russo-Japanese War to jolt Congress out of its complacent mood. On February 8, 1904, Japanese destroyers and torpedo boats slipped past the Russian defenses at the great naval base at Port Arthur and put half of the Russian battle fleet out of action. The attacking force escaped with light losses. War had not even been formally declared and the defenders were caught napping.

Impressed by these events, which received extensive newspaper coverage in the United States, the House and Senate approved an appropriation of $862,395 for a start on the naval base at Olongapo and an additional $700,000 for the army for fortifications in the Philippines. The secretary of war promised that half of the army appropriation would be spent on the defense of Subig Bay.[37]

Just as it appeared that the Far Eastern Base was finally becoming a reality, a new obstacle loomed. Like many Spanish officers before them, a large number of American officers serving in the Philippines looked askance at Subig Bay as the site for the principal American base. Dewey described the situation from his point of view in a letter to the commander of the Asiatic Fleet.

> Upon arriving at Manila you will encounter the Olongapo-Cavite question to which Taylor and I, the General Board, War College and all your predecessors have given so much thought and in which all emphatically declared in favor of Olongapo. . . . You will find in Manila a strong Army sentiment and civil sentiment as well . . . enthusiastic in favor of retaining Cavite as it now is. And of all the advocates of this plan General [Leonard] Wood, usually so clear-headed in most matters, is the most ardent. He and his followers reason that Manila *is* the Philippines and can only be protected by fortifications at Corregidor and a fleet in Manila Bay. Such fallacious reasoning hardly needs contradiction.[38]

Whether because of reluctance to leave the comforts of the capital as their opponents claimed, or because of strategic considerations as they themselves claimed, the army officers vigorously

36. Dewey to the Secretary of the Navy, December 7, 1903, in Records of the General Board.
37. Braisted, *The United States Navy in the Pacific*, 176.
38. Dewey to Willard Brownson, October 26, 1906, in Dewey Papers.

urged the government to concentrate all of its defenses, including the fleet, in Manila Bay. The chief among these champions of Manila Bay, as Dewey noted, was Major General Leonard Wood, the commanding general of the Philippine Department.

Wood was probably the only military man in the government with sufficient prestige and influence to challenge Dewey on such an important issue. Superficially, the two men had a great deal in common. Wood, like Dewey, had made his reputation in the Spanish-American War, where he had served as colonel of the famous "Rough Riders" and later as governor-general of Cuba. Like Dewey, he had behind him many years of service in the doldrum period of the 1880s and 1890s. He had served as a surgeon with the Indian-fighting army on the frontier and distinguished himself in the last campaign against Geronimo. But, as with the admiral, it was not Wood's combat record but his valuable connections which were to give him his great opportunity. As official physician to the president and the secretary of war during the late 1890s, Wood had made the acquaintance of many men of substance, including Theodore Roosevelt.

Roosevelt and Wood were close personal friends. In the Subig Bay matter, the general, never a stickler for form, put his recommendations into a personal letter to the president. Wood believed that a defending fleet could be "bottled up" in Subig Bay while the enemy reduced Manila and Luzon.[39] Rather than waste men and resources at Olongapo, Wood urged the government to concentrate all appropriations on improving the defenses of Manila.

To buttress his case, Wood persuaded Rear Admiral William M. Folger, commander of the Philippine Squadron, who also opposed the Subig Bay project, to write to the Navy Department about the disadvantages of Subig as a naval base. Folger pointed out that the Spanish authorities had also been divided over the proper location for a naval base. Subig Bay might be a useful base for a fleet attacking Manila, he contended, but it was useless for the purpose of defending the city. "The enemy will leave a vessel or two to

<hr />

39. Wood to Roosevelt, June 1, 1904, in Roosevelt Papers.

watch the rat trap at Subig and then take Manila."[40] The correct
course was to block the entrance to Subig Bay with mines and old
ships and to fortify Manila. The defending squadron could then
take refuge behind the defenses of the city.

The president turned the two letters over to Dewey and the
General Board for comment. The old admiral threw himself into
the task with rare energy, drafting the reply personally with the help
of the General Board. Dewey began by reminding the president
that the General Board, the Joint Board, and every commander-in-
chief of the Asiatic Squadron had agreed "that the best site is Subig
Bay and Manila is one of the worst."[41] Then he proceeded to
demolish one by one the points raised by Wood and Folger. Manila
Bay could never be completely closed to an attacking fleet; the
channels at the entrance to the bay were too broad and deep to be
defended by mines and shore batteries. On the other hand, "with
the American fleet based upon, not bottled up in, Subig Bay," the
enemy must either divide his forces between Subig and Manila or
risk an attack on his flank. The fact that Manila was the great prize
of the campaign did not make it necessary for the mobile naval
forces to be kept there. This would make no more sense than "a
boxer trying to defend himself by holding his fist against his
breast."

The boxing analogy may have appealed to Roosevelt. In any
case, he pronounced Dewey's report an "admirable" statement of
the case.[42] Folger and Wood were told to mind their own business
and the cabinet endorsed the General Board's findings.[43] Despite
this resounding bureaucratic victory, however, the construction of
the Far Eastern base continued to lag. Nathan Sargent, who was
with the Asiatic Squadron at this time, wrote to Dewey in January,
1905, that "not much progress is being made at Olongapo." In
March, he predicted that "even if unlimited money were supplied,
it would still take ten years to carry out the [General Board's]

40. Folger to William H. Moody, June 1, 1904, in RG 80.
41. Dewey to Theodore Roosevelt, August 4, 1904, General Board Letterpress, in Records of the General Board.
42. Roosevelt to Dewey, August 5, 1904, in Dewey Papers.
43. Braisted, *The United States Navy in the Pacific*, 177.

plans" for a naval base. In a later letter he reported "great opposition to Olongapo by nearly everyone in the Philippines."[44]

Congress had lapsed back into its usual niggardliness. Only $300,000 more was appropriated for Subig Bay in 1905 and 1906. In March, 1906, Dewey called on the president to protest a bill in the House of Representatives which would have appropriated $600,000 for "insular defense but nothing for Subig."[45] In desperation, the General Board decided to cut back its estimates and plan for a much smaller base which could be completed in a shorter time.

This was the state of things when the Japanese-American crisis again called the whole scheme into question. Army officers who had always had reservations about Subig now raised the question of the site's vulnerability to a land attack. Before 1905, when Germany, Russia, or France had been considered the most probable enemies, only a naval attack on the Philippines was believed likely. With Japan now the most likely antagonist, a large-scale amphibious invasion of the Philippines had become a real possibility.

Among the features of the Russo-Japanese conflict that had most intrigued military and naval men alike had been the ability of the Japanese, late in the war, to cripple the Russian squadron in Port Arthur without actually capturing that port. They had accomplished this by means of exceptionally powerful mortars mounted on the hills surrounding the city. Accurately directed by forward observers, these giant weapons had poured a deadly rain of shells onto the Russian men-of-war, rendering the harbor untenable. Military men noted that Olongapo was remarkably similar to Port Arthur, with high, but not impassible, hills surrounding it.

General Leonard Wood was quick to grasp the implications of the new situation. In a series of hard-hitting letters to the War Department, Wood pointed to the remarkable similarities between Port Arthur and Subig. Both were surrounded by high peaks. Enemy artillery on these peaks could command the entire harbor and render it untenable to warships just as the Japanese had done at

---

44. Nathan Sargent to Dewey, January 27, 1905, March 24, 1905, May 29, 1905, in Sargent Papers.
45. Diary of Mildred Dewey, March 1, 1906.

Port Arthur. Wood estimated that it would require a line of defense thirty-five to thirty-six miles long and upwards of eighty thousand men to hold the peaks against the enemy. "The peaks themselves constitute no barrier. There is not a foot of land that is not practicable for men on foot."[46]

In words that were to sound strangely prophetic forty years later, Wood declared that "if a surprise attack comes from Japan, it will come in great force and with shattering rapidity. We will have almost no time to get ready." He also contended that such an attack would only be undertaken if the enemy had command of the sea. If he had it, the question of a naval base would be academic and "the question then becomes one of time." Wood believed that Manila was more suited to withstand a prolonged siege than Olongapo. Taking its cue from Wood, the Army War College undertook extensive studies of the defense of the Philippines during the summer of 1907 and reached similar conclusions.[47] A team of army artillery experts sent to the islands the following autumn confirmed that Subig was untenable against an attack from the land side.

The army's case was now as unanswerable as the navy's had been four years before. At the meeting of the Joint Board on January 31, 1908, the navy began a strategic retreat. In a face-saving memorandum, the Joint Board resolved that although Subig Bay was the most suitable site for a base from the naval point of view, the army had "determined" that it could not be defended. Therefore the main base would have to be at Manila. However, the navy might retain its temporary base at Olongapo pending the establishment of one at Manila.

This formula satisfied both the army, which was relieved of the responsibility for defending Subig Bay, and the navy, which was reluctant to move its ships to Manila. It did not, however, satisfy the president, who was furious with such backing and filling. In a blistering letter to the secretary of the navy, Roosevelt "called the

46. Wood to Adjutant General, May 6, 1907, cited in Louis Morton, "Military and Naval Preparations for the Defense of the Philippines During the War Scare of 1907," *Military Affairs*, XII (Summer, 1949).
47. "Memo for the Third Division," enclosure in Taft to Theodore Roosevelt, March 5, 1908, in Roosevelt Papers.

attention of the Joint Board to the grave harm done the Army and Navy by such vacillation and one-sided consideration as has been shown in the treatment of the Philippine problem." He went on to say:

> For years I had been informed by many Army officers and nearly all naval officers that Subig Bay was the one point in the Philippines which could be made impregnable. . . . I am now advised that the recommendations I have repeatedly acted on in the way of advising Congress are all wrong . . . and by way of explanation, I am further informed that it is not the province of the Navy to advise on Army matters. . . . Now I have a very high opinion of our Army and Navy officers . . . but they justify their most trenchant critics when they act in this manner. This year a great many Congressmen and Senators have said to me [that] they disbelieved in a General Staff for either Army or Navy because of the curious attitude of the Joint Board in this Philippine matter.[48]

The president announced that he had ordered a full inquiry into the whole matter of the Philippine base site.

Roosevelt's strongly worded letter was almost a personal slap at Admiral Dewey. It was Dewey who had been most closely associated with the Subig Bay project, and it was he who had repeatedly railroaded it through the Joint Board despite the muted objections of some of his colleagues. The admiral might urge in his defense, as indeed he did during the subsequent inquiry, that the change in the status of Japan from that of "sure friend" to probable enemy had fundamentally altered the military prospects in the Far East.[49] Nevertheless, the Philippine fiasco remained an egregious example of failure in interservice cooperation, the very cooperation which Dewey, as chairman of the Joint Board, was expected to foster.

Personally, Dewey remained convinced of the utility of Subig. He was described by an associate as "very resentful" over the army's abandonment of the site and "very picqued and sulky when the President took the Army view."[50] Officers of the General Board

---

48. Roosevelt to Metcalf, February 11, 1908, in Morison (ed.), *Letters of Roosevelt*, VI.
49. Dewey to Secretary of War, March 5, 1908, in Roosevelt Papers.
50. Willaim L. Rodgers to Stephen B. Luce, November 2, 1908, in Luce Papers.

talked of avoiding any future attempts to settle important interservice matters through the Joint Board. Captain William L. Rodgers appealed to Admiral Stephen B. Luce, the edler statesman of the navy, to try to do something to counter Dewey's "feeling of aloofness" and "soothe the wounded feelings of the Navy."[51] Dewey had not abandoned hope for Subig Bay, however. During the Taft administration he was to come forward with still another scheme for salvaging the base at Olongapo.

If Dewey had utterly failed to take the possibility of American-Japanese antagonism into consideration in his planning for the Far East, he did foresee, albeit somewhat imperfectly, the revolution in battleship design which coincided with the period of Japanese-American tension. The revolution, it may be said with some precision, began on February 10, 1906, when King Edward VII, standing in a chilly winter rain at Portsmouth dockyard, officially christened a new British battleship. This battleship, the *Dreadnought*, was being constructed in secrecy and with great speed, so much speed in fact that the big guns earmarked for ships which had been begun a year or two before were taken over to arm the *Dreadnought*. Less than a year after her launching, the new ship had completed her trials and was declared ready for service.

The *Dreadnought* was the cumulative result of nearly three years of intense study by the Admiralty of new developments in gunnery and steam engineering. Her displacement was 17,900 tons, larger than that of any battleship afloat. Her speed of twenty-one knots was two knots faster. But it was her novel armament which attracted most attention. In place of the usual mixed collection of light, medium, and heavy caliber guns which her contemporaries usually carried, the *Dreadnought* mounted only guns of the largest caliber. (The American *Connecticut* class, for example, the latest battleships in the round-the-world fleet, had a main armament of four twelve-inch, eight eight-inch, and twelve seven-inch guns.) The *Dreadnought*'s main armament consisted of ten twelve-inch guns, mounted in five double turrets, and her only other armament was

51. *Ibid.*

some light anti–torpedo-boat weapons. Armed in this way, she was approximately two and a half times as powerful as any contemporary battleship, and her superior speed would enable her to keep the battle at a range where the smaller intermediate batteries of her conventional opponents would be ineffective.[52] The new battleship thus rendered all previous vessels obsolete.

The creation of the *Dreadnought* had been made possible and perhaps inevitable by the rapid progress in naval gunnery which had taken place in the years since 1900. At the time of the Spanish-American War, the standard battle range was about two thousand yards, about the same as in the War of 1812. At this range the armament of ships like the American *Connecticut* made some sense since the smaller six- and eight-inch guns could fire more rapidly than the large twelve- and thirteen-inch guns of the main battery. Each gun on a warship was loaded, aimed, and fired individually, and hits depended upon the skill of the individual gun captains and pointers.

In general, naval gunfire was wildly inaccurate. At the Battle of Santiago the Americans had fired more than 9,000 rounds in order to obtain 120 hits. The Spanish, of course, had done worse.[53] Beginning around 1900, however, naval gunnery began to improve greatly in speed, range, and accuracy. New methods of training seaman gunners, an improved telescopic sight, and the introduction of the range-finder all made possible rapid progress in the field. By 1904 British battleships were firing at ranges of 8,000 yards, and ranges of over 10,000 yards were considered feasible.[54]

The man who took the lead in introducing the innovations in naval gunnery into the United States Navy was Lieutenant Commander William S. Sims, the same officer who, as an attaché in Paris during the Spanish-American War, had kept Dewey informed

52. The best discussion of the development of the dreadnought type is in Marder, *Anatomy of British Seapower.*
53. Morison, *Admiral Sims and the Modern American Navy,* 194.
54. Marder, *Anatomy of British Seapower,* 522–23.

on the progress of Admiral Camara's squadron.[55] As inspector of target practice from 1902 to 1909 Sims revolutionized the navy's gunnery. By 1906 American battleships were scoring 77 percent hits on a small thirty-by-sixty-foot target at a range of over five miles.[56]

Sims's methods were greeted with skepticism by some of the more conservative officers, but Dewey enthusiastically supported him from the first. Shortly after his return from the Caribbean maneuvers in 1903 the admiral told the New York *Herald* that the United States was in danger of falling behind in naval gunnery; Dewey praised the measures Sims was taking to improve American marksmanship. The *Outlook* described Dewey as constantly "lecturing the Navy on the quality of its gunnery."[57] In October, 1906, the admiral went so far as to write personally to the commander of the Asiatic fleet explaining Sims's innovations and urging that they be adopted.[58]

Dewey was quick to see the implications of the new gunnery for the future design of battleships. At the new, longer ranges the intermediate batteries of six-, seven-, or eight-inch guns were now superfluous, indeed worse than superfluous since they interfered with accurate spotting of shell splashes and complicated the problem of fire control. In the descriptions of the battles of the Russo-Japanese War which he read in letters from Nathan Sargent, Dewey saw confirmation of his view that the mixed-caliber battleship was doomed. In September, 1905, the admiral told the New York *Herald* that the Russo-Japanese War pointed to the need for "more big ships, more big guns and good shooting." Battleships like the U.S.S. *Oregon* of Spanish-American War fame were excellent for their time, the admiral explained, but "modern battle is fought at a range of three or four miles. At that distance your eight-inch guns

55. See Chapter III.
56. Morison, *Admiral Sims and the Modern American Navy*, 236–37.
57. New York *Herald*, February 19, 1903; *Outlook*, February 28, 1903.
58. Dewey to Brownson, October 26, 1906, in Dewey Papers.

are nothing but so much dead weight." The American navy now required "ships of 18,000 tons carrying twelve-inch guns, with a few three-pounders for defense against torpedo boats."[59]

The General Board had been interested in the idea of an all-big-gun ship since 1903. In the summer of that year, the Naval War College, as a result of its war game studies, had concluded that the so-called intermediate batteries of six-to-eight-inch guns should be done away with and that the weight saved should be used for more guns of the largest caliber.[60] The General Board had the War College's studies before it when it made its recommendations for a long-range building program in the fall of 1903; but the board, after much discussion, decided to play it safe. Their recommended design called for a conventional battleship of sixteen thousand tons, eighteen knots speed, and a mixed armament of four twelve-inch guns and eight eight-inch guns.

The board was impressed with the new type ship, however, and believed that "the idea merited careful study." In January, 1904, the board requested the Navy Department to direct the Bureau of Construction and Repair to prepare a design for a battleship carrying twelve heavy guns "of which none shall be less than ten-inch and at least four of twelve-inch caliber."[61] Thus more than a year before the British Admiralty, the General Board had already begun to plan a battleship on the all-big-gun principle.[62]

The Bureau of Construction was assigned the design project in January, 1904. By the end of September, the bureau had still not produced a design. In October, when Roosevelt, prompted by Commander Sims, inquired into the feasibility of an all-big-gun

59. New York *Herald*, September 22, 1905.

60. William L. Rodgers "Memorandum in Regard to the Tactical Advantages of Suppressing the Intermediate Battery of Battleships and Armored Cruisers," in Records of the Naval War College.

61. Dewey to Secretary of the Navy, January 26, 1904, in Records of the General Board.

62. Arthur Marder has pointed out that although the Americans started earlier, the British were first with the idea for a *uniform calibre* all-big-gun ship. See Marder, *Anatomy of British Seapower*, 541–42.

design, the Bureau of Construction observed complacently that "from time to time suggestions have been made as to the desirability of reducing the armament of battleships to heavy guns and a light battery." Nevertheless, "nothing has transpired during the past year which would justify extensive changes in the main battery of vessels building or recently designed."[63] Three months later the British completed the final design for the *Dreadnought*.

By the end of October, 1904, Dewey and his colleagues had become convinced of the superiority of the *Dreadnought*-type battleship. In an official paper for the secretary of the navy, they recommended that future battleships be given a main armament of ten-inch or twelve-inch guns and no intermediate battery at all. The board was obliged to frame its recommendation "in somewhat general terms" as the Bureau of Construction's design was still not available.[64] Under repeated badgering by the General Board and the secretary, the Bureau of Construction admitted that it had no design at all, claiming that "it has been impracticable to do more than get out a sketch design of the several [possible] arrangements of battery." The following month, the sketch designs were "lost in transit" while being delivered to the General Board.[65]

Despite the lack of a design, the General Board's confidence in the all-big-gun ship was now so strong that on September 30, 1905, it recommended that the displacement of the newest battleships, the *Michigan* and the *South Carolina* be increased to eighteen thousand tons so as to accommodate a main battery of ten twelve-inch guns.[66] "I am glad the board is such a unit with regard to the battery of big guns," wrote Captain Sargent to Dewey. "I was early converted to that doctrine and the lessons of this last war confirm it."[67]

Unfortunately, other makers of naval policy were not as convinced as Dewey about the inevitability of the big-gun battleships.

63. Morison, *Admiral Sims and the Modern American Navy*, 161–62.
64. Dewey to Secretary of the Navy, October 28, 1904, in Records of the General Board.
65. Dewey to Secretary of the Navy, June 10, July 11, 1905, *ibid.*
66. Dewey to Secretary of the Navy, September 30, 1905, *ibid.*
67. Sargent to Dewey, October 20, 1905, in Sargent Papers.

Little-navy congressmen and senators noted that the new ships
would be larger and more costly than battleships of the conventional type; and the bureaus, as might be expected, raised numerous
technical objections. President Roosevelt himself was reported to
have doubts about the all-big-gun ship.[68]

Dewey did his best to counter these doubts and objections by
statements to the press and talks with influential members of Congress. In March, 1906, he urged the House Naval Affairs Committee to approve construction of the U.S.S. *Delaware*, the first true
American dreadnought.[69] The New York *Herald* predicted that
"Dewey's advocacy of big battleships will have great influence in
Congress despite the President's vacillation." Two senior members
of the committee were reported to have changed their minds on the
matter because of the admiral's testimony.[70] But the small battleship forces also had their naval authority, the redoubtable Alfred
Thayer Mahan.

As the most eminent American naval publicist Mahan was a
powerful voice for the opposition. The celebrated historian summed up his doubts about the value of the all-big-gun battleship in
an article entitled, "Reflections, Historical and Other, Suggested by
the Battle of the Japan Sea," which appeared in June, 1906,[71] and
for a time it appeared that the opposition of the world-renowned
writer had tipped the balance in favor of the antidreadnought
force.

In December, 1906, however Mahan's arguments were demol-
ished in a persuasive and closely reasoned article by William S.
Sims.[72] Sims's arguments were enough to convince Roosevelt once

68. Roosevelt to Rear Admiral G. A. Converse, September 10, 1906, in Records of the
General Board.
69. Diary of Mildred Dewey, March 24, 1906.
70. New York *Herald*, October 5, December 8, 1905.
71. Alfred T. Mahan, "Reflections, Historical and Other, Suggested by the Battle of the
Japan Sea," USNIP, XXXII (June, 1906), 447–71.
72. William S. Sims, "The Inherent Tactical Qualities of All-Big Gun, Large Calibre
Battleships of High Speed, Large Displacement and Gun-Power," USNIP, XXXII (December, 1906), 1337–66.

and for all, and in February the president told George E. Foss, chairman of the House Naval Affairs Committee, that he believed completely in the dreadnought type of battleship. Significantly Roosevelt cited Admiral Dewey's advice as the deciding factor in his decision to ask for the new type of warship.[73] In a sense, the president was correct, for while Sims's technical arguments carried weight with Roosevelt and his naval advisers, only Dewey's name could match the prestige of Mahan with Congress and the general public. Had the admiral not thrown his weight to the side of the dreadnought forces, the outcome of the debate may well have been different. As it was, the appropriation for the *Delaware* authorized in 1906, was finally approved by Congress early in 1907. A new era in naval technology had begun.

Although he had fought long and hard for the dreadnought design and for Sims's gunnery reforms, Dewey still refused to join Sims and his fellow insurgents in their wholesale attack upon the organization and materiel of the navy. In the spring of 1908, when Sims and Commander Albert L. Key, former naval aide to the president, attacked the design of the *Delaware* and her sister ship the *North Dakota* as embodying many of the same defects as earlier American battleships, Dewey demured.[74] In his public statements, Dewey continued to praise the efficiency of the navy and to minimize the defects in its material even after a joint General Board-War College conference convened by order of the president at Newport confirmed Key's criticism of the ships.

Dewey's refusal to condemn publicly the battleships and the ineffective bureau system which produced them angered the insurgents. In a letter to Sims, Commander Key suggested that "Dewey and [Rear Admiral Robley D.] Evans ought to be roasted for their statements. It is simply an outrage that any officers of the line, who ought to be the most active in attempting to reorganize the depart-

---

73. Roosevelt to George E. Foss, December 19, 1906, in Roosevelt Papers.
74. For details of this controversy, see Morison, *Admiral Sims and the Modern American Navy*, 201–14.

ment and place the fleet on an efficient basis, consider merely their own personal interests, want to be on the popular side, and combine to perpetuate . . . the present organization. . . . They say one thing to the department and the directly contrary thing to the public. . . . They are attempting to deceive their fellow countrymen, who pay the bills, about defects well known to every foreign naval attaché in Washington."[75]

Key's letter admirably summed up the insurgent case against Dewey. But it was not merely concern for his personal interests which made the admiral minimize in public evils he himself had campaigned against in private. As he had demonstrated in the Schley controversy and would demonstrate again during the preparedness controversies of the Wilson era, Dewey detested displaying the navy's dirty linen in public. His interest in administrative reform was slight, but even in matters in which he believed strongly, the admiral was unwilling to put his prestige, or that of the navy, on the line. The dislike for controversy he had demonstrated throughout his career persisted, as did his solicitude for his personal prestige, or "honor." This made him shy away from the noisy all-or-nothing confrontations in which the insurgents delighted.

75. Key to William S. Sims, November 27, 1908, in William S. Sims Papers, Library of Congress.

CHAPTER IX

Studies in Orange
and Black

On February 22, 1909, Theodore Roosevelt boarded the presidential yacht *Mayflower* to welcome the round-the-world fleet on its return to Hampton Roads. A few days later, Roosevelt was a private citizen and his good friend and protegé, William Howard Taft, sat in the White House.

The navy and the world were much changed since Dewey and Roosevelt had assumed their duties eight years before. As Walter Millis has aptly observed, "things were getting serious."[1] The arms race in Europe was quickening. In the navies of the world, long gray dreadnoughts were replacing the older battleships with their gleaming white paint and giant ram bows. In the Far East, the Japanese and Russians were concluding a businesslike agreement to divide control of Manchuria between them and exclude the other powers. It was a world that was becoming more and more unlike the simple, mechanistic world which existed in the minds of Dewey and his advisers in the War College and the General Board.

The admiral of the navy was now nearly seventy-one years old and beginning to feel the effects of his years. "I write with difficulty nowadays," he wrote George Goodwin in December, 1909, "and avoid it as much as possible."[2] Outwardly, however, little had changed at the house on Rhode Island Avenue save for the addition of electric lights in the spring of 1908. Dewey still rose at 7 A.M. and walked the seven blocks from his house to his office near the

1. Walter Millis, *Arms and Men* (New York, 1956), 197.
2. Dewey to George Goodwin Dewey, December 4, 1909, in George Goodwin Dewey Papers.

White House. Commander John M. Ellicott, on his way to duty at the State, War, and Navy Building would often see the admiral on pleasant mornings seated on a park bench in Lafayette Square talking to children.[3] On clear afternoons, the admiral would exercise his horses or go for walks.

Almost to the end, Dewey remained unenthusiastic about the new automobiles which were beginning to be acquired by fashionable Washingtonians. "He calls them very stiff names and curses their noise and dirt," wrote Mildred to George Goodwin.[4]

Dewey's opinion of the automobile was not improved by an incident in Rock Creek Park. While riding in the park one autumn day, the admiral and his groom had watched in dismay as a horseless carriage "capsized," spilling its occupants into Rock Creek. Dewey and his groom managed to rescue the passengers who were all unhurt and pleased to have such an illustrious rescuer. The admiral, in fact, had been the cause of the accident since the driver of the car, in his eagerness to get a closer look at the hero of Manila Bay, had run his vehicle into a tree.[5] The admiral's distaste for automobiles was not, however, shared by Mrs. Dewey, who, in 1910, acquired a beautiful Packard limousine worth over sixty-five hundred dollars. "The only one of its type in Washington."

Dewey never enjoyed the close personal relationship with President Taft that he had enjoyed with Theodore Roosevelt. An experienced administrator, the new president preferred to leave military matters to his service secretaries and their military advisers. Fortunately, in the new secretary of the navy, George von Lengerke Meyer, the service gained one of its ablest civilian heads. Meyer quickly gained the respect and cooperation of Dewey and the General Board by meeting frequently with them and soliciting their advice on important matters. It was Meyer who finally achieved the control over the semiautonomous bureaus which navy reformers from Luce and Taylor to Sims and Bradley Fiske had always dreamed of.

In the last months of his presidency, Roosevelt, at the urging of

3. Ellicott, "Contacts with the Hero of Manila Bay," 72.
4. Mildred Dewey to George Goodwin Dewey, August 20, 1906, in George Goodwin Dewey Papers.
5. Mildred Dewey to Goerge Goodwin Dewey, September 2, 1906, *ibid.*

Sims and Key, had appointed two high-level commissions composed of retired officers and former secretaries to report on the organization of the Navy Department. The recommendations of the commissions were placed before the Congress which paid little attention to them, but when Meyer took up his duties, the reports provided him with a detailed blueprint for reform. The new secretary appointed still a third board, under the chairmanship of Rear Admiral William Swift, which largely endorsed the conclusions of its predecessors.

Without waiting for Congress to reconvene, Meyer moved to reorganize his department by executive order. The secretary established four divisions in the Navy Department, all headed by line officers who were referred to as aides. The most important of these was the aide for operations, a sort of embryo chief-of-staff, who was responsible for fleet operations and for coordinating the war-planning activities of the War College, the General Board, and the Office of Naval Intelligence. The other aides were charged with responsibility for personnel, inspections, and matériel.

Although reformers like Luce and Sims considered even the aides system inadequate, it was still radical enough to earn the resentment, jealousy, and suspicion of the bureau chiefs and their longtime allies in the House and Senate. There was talk among some of the members of the House Naval Affairs Committee that Meyer had exceeded his authority and that his reforms ought to be submitted to Congress for its approval.

At this point Dewey came to the aid of the secretary, characteristically taking a stand midway between the insurgents, who thought the aides system inadequate, and the congressmen who wished to limit it still further. In a letter addressed to Representative George A. Loud, but actually aimed at House Naval Affairs Committee Chairman George Foss, Dewey expressed the hope that "you will help see to it that Mr. Meyer's plan has an unrestricted trial." The admiral warned that "if the committee does change the plan, which the President has approved, it will become responsible to the country. I should think you would rather leave such responsibility to the Secretary."[6] The committee took the admiral's hint and Meyer's

6. Dewey to Representative George A. Loud, January 31, 1910, in Dewey Papers.

reforms stood unchallenged, but congressional friends of the bureaus successfully blocked every attempt to enact them into law.

While the insurgents had seen Meyer's assumption of office as an opportunity to press for a general staff, Dewey looked upon it as an opportunity to attempt to retain Subig Bay as the Far Eastern base of the navy. In two long memoranda for the secretary, Dewey called attention to the fact that when thirty battleships were in commission it would be safe to form a separate Pacific fleet to be based on the West Coast. The army had repeatedly declared that it could not defend Subig against a land attack. Very well, the establishment of a Pacific fleet "would probably prevent such an attack." The presence of an American battle fleet "anywhere in the Pacific would make a Japanese invasion of the Philippines too dangerous to consider."[7]

Unimpressed, Meyer issued an order directing that arrangements be made for the establishment of a naval base at Manila Bay. Dewey replied petulantly that, although the board would undertake to plan for a base at Manila, it would "in no wise [retreat] from its position previously recorded, that Olongapo is the desirable location for the base and station."[8]

President Taft, who as secretary of war had presided for three years over the army-navy debates on the Philippines, had no desire to bring on another confrontation. To Meyer, the president confessed that he was really "not stiff in the matter of having the thing at Manila."[9] He did want a definite recommendation from the Joint Board which would, he hoped, lay the argument to rest.

With Dewey in the chair, the outcome in the Joint Board was never in doubt, but the navy had to make important concessions to the army. They assured the generals that the cooperation of the army in the defense of Subig was not required, because the Pacific fleet would arrive in the islands early enough to forestall an invasion. In fact, the establishment of a Pacific fleet and the anticipated opening of the Panama Canal made a large base in the Philippines unnecessary. A small repair station at Olongapo would suffice,

7. Dewey to Secretary of the Navy, June 21, 1909, in Records of the General Board.
8. Braisted, *The United States Navy in the Pacific*, 63.
9. *Ibid.*, 69.

with the main base to be located at the new naval station at Pearl Harbor, Hawaii.[10]

It is doubtful whether Dewey himself believed these arguments. In 1909, the Pacific fleet was still nothing more than a gleam in the eye of a few General Board and War College planners, and the navy's confident assurance that it could defend the Philippines from Hawaii convinced no one. Nevertheless, they provided Taft, Meyer, and the army with a satisfactory way of concluding the interminable debate on Pacific bases. In his annual report of 1909, Meyer noted with gratification that "past differences" between the services over the Philippines "had been entirely overcome."[11]

The secretary reckoned without General Leonard Wood, the old foe of Subig Bay who, in the spring of 1910, became the chief of the War Department General Staff. The new chief-of-staff almost immediately opened a guerrilla campaign against the navy's plans for the Western Pacific. He repeatedly attacked the weakest point in the navy's position: their contention that no major base was necessary west of Hawaii. The army pointed out that if "as a result of an indecisive engagement our fleet finds itself in Philippine waters with a number of crippled ships . . . our entire fleet would be forced to withdraw to Pearl Harbor, a distance of 5,000 miles for a period of several months."[12]

Despite appeals to the service secretaries, to the president, and even to members of Congress, Wood was unsuccessful in reopening the debate on Subig. As Wood finally realized, not even the president was willing to challenge the formidable Admiral Dewey on a question of naval strategy.[13]

In his dogged determination to have a base in the Philippines at Subig Bay and nowhere else, Dewey had prevailed, but only by placing himself and the navy in the absurd position of arguing that no first-class base was needed in the Western Pacific. Wood and Dewey, by their mutual intransigence, had helped lay the foundation for the American disasters in the Pacific in World War II.

10. Dewey to Dickinson, November 8, 1909, in Dewey Papers.
11. *Annual Report of the Navy Department, 1909* (Washington, 1910), 30.
12. Braisted, *The United States Navy in the Pacific*, 69.
13. *Ibid.*, 70.

While problems and tensions in the Far East had occupied much of Dewey's attention after 1905, he never wavered in his conviction that Germany was the most likely foe of the United States in any future war. In the spring of 1905, Mildred recorded his belief that "the outlook is black for war with Germany. . . . She is trying to grab Denmark and Holland and that means islands in the Caribbean and that means war for us."[14]

Most American naval officers agreed with this view. Admiral Mahan warned the readers of *Colliers* that a conflict between the United States and Germany was "almost sure to arise."[15] American attachés in South America continued to report on German machinations there and the Naval War College continued to make Germany the most frequent subject of its studies.[16]

President Taft and his secretary of state, Philander C. Knox, did not share Roosevelt's apocalyptic views of world politics or his extremes of Anglophilia and Germanophobia. Nevertheless, Taft was "not fond of the Germans" and particularly disliked their opposition to his schemes for international arbitration. Taft's undersecretary of state, Francis M. Huntington Wilson, the number-two man in the State Department, was "an inveterate German-hater."[17] Just as Francis Loomis was obsessed with the German penetration of Latin America, Wilson was keenly interested in what he believed to be German attempts to dominate the Middle East.

In such a political atmosphere, the naval men had no difficulty sustaining the belief that the German navy was their most likely antagonist. The distinction between the views of the civilian officials who saw the Germans as international troublemakers or economic rivals and the views of the naval planners who saw the Germans as an immediate military danger to the United States, was

14. Diary of Mildred Dewey, June 16, 1905.
15. Alfred T. Mahan, "Germany's Naval Ambitions," *Colliers*, XLII, 5 (April 24, 1909).
16. See, for example, W. W. Wotherspoon to Chief of War College Division, October 28, 1912, and Stimson to Chief of War College Division, October 28, 1912, both in Records of the Army General Staff, Record Group 165, National Archives; "War Plan Black, General Considerations," in Office of Naval History.
17. Archie Butt to Clara Butt, December 21, 1908, cited in Melvin Small, "The American Image of Germany, 1906–1914" (Ph. D. dissertation, University of Michigan, 1965).

lost on Dewey and his associates. War plans against Germany continued apace.

Under Secretary Meyer, the General Board's earlier strategic studies were consolidated into two principal war plans, "Black" for war with Germany and "Orange" for war with Japan. Although hardly real war plans in the European sense, they were still far more complete and sophisticated than the rough and unfinished plans which the General Board had prepared during its first half-dozen years. A joint product of the Naval War College, the General Board, and the Office of Naval Intelligence, the Orange and Black plans really amounted to astute "Estimates of the Situation" which were to form the basis of the navy's plans and preparations until the end of the First World War.

The Orange plan was begun in the spring of 1910 and completed in 1911. It was really two plans, one based on the assumption that the American battle fleet would be in the Atlantic at the outbreak of war, the other based on the assumption that it would be in the Pacific. If the fleet were in the Atlantic, the results might well be disastrous. In the three months it would take the Americans to reach the Pacific, the Japanese could capture all the American possessions in the Pacific including Guam, Midway, Kiska, Samoa, the Philippines, and Hawaii. To avert such a disaster, the planners hoped that the American fleet, if in the Atlantic, might get a head-start and depart for the Pacific "during the period of strained relations." Much time and thought was given to choosing the American route of advance across the Pacific. The middle route via Hawaii and Guam to the Philippines was judged the most desirable because it involved shorter lines of communication and a wider choice of objectives.[18]

The decisive battle between the two fleets was expected to take place in the vicinity of the Philippines. The planners were some-what at a loss to say how the war was to be concluded if the Japanese refused to make peace after the destruction of their fleet. They believed that "attacks against Orange home territory would likely prove fruitless." American war efforts would therefore be

18. "War Plan Orange," in Office of Naval History, 61, 25.

confined to "the isolation of the Orange home territory, the invest-
ment and capture of outlying Orange possessions and . . . threats
at the repatriation of Korea."[19]

To Dewey and the other Germanophobes on the General Board,
the Orange plan was merely a prudent exercise. Their real attention
and interest was centered on the Black plan for war with Germany.
Unlike the Orange plan, the origins of which can be fixed with
some precision, the exact beginning of the Black plan cannot be
determined.[20] Apparently, Secretary Meyer's efforts at systematiz-
ing war plans furnished the impetus for the General Board, sometime around 1910, to pull together its earlier exercises and studies
on Germany into a complete war plan. As it finally emerged about
1913, the Black plan was the most complete of all American pre-
World War plans and the closest to European models. The heart
of the Black plan, as Warner Schilling has observed, was an elaborate series of mobilization timetables.[21] There were three sets of
timetables, one for each of the possible locations of the American
battle fleet upon the outbreak of war.

Years of study and war gaming at the Naval War College had
convinced American planners that no German attack on the home
territory of the United States could possibly be successful with the
entire American fleet in the Atlantic. The best the Germans could
do in such a situation would be to attempt to seize a base in the
West Indies. The most likely sites were believed to be Samana Bay
in the Dominican Republic or Margarita Island off the coast of
Venezuela, and the board hoped to use submarines and mines to
deny these anchorages to the enemy. In the meantime, the active
American fleet was to be mobilized in Chesapeake Bay. The reserve
fleet was expected to be ready one week later. The plan called for
the entire fleet to start for Culebra, Puerto Rico, on M plus fifteen,
or two weeks after the outbreak of war.

Under these conditions, the General Board was confident of

19. *Ibid.*, 42.
20. The Black plan preserved in the Office of Naval History is obviously the product
of long evolution. The pages have different type faces and sections have been arbitrarily
replaced, corrected, and updated.
21. Warner R. Schilling, "Admirals and Foreign Policy, 1913–1919" (Ph. D. dissertation,
Yale University, 1954), 24.

success. In fact, it believed that it would be "suicidal for Germany
. . . to attempt a descent upon American possessions in the Caribbean in the presence of the full American fleet at Culebra with a
moderate train protected by the advance base armament and with
ample supplies in fortified ports nearby." Since an attack on the
American coast was also out of the question, there was no other
conclusion possible but that Germany would not come at all. "It
may be doubted if, under the assumed conditions of readiness of
the United States, Germany would resort to hostilities."

The Black plan was therefore a plan for a war which would never
take place if the plan were followed. It was all unbelievably neat
and logical. It was also somewhat unrealistic. There was, first of all,
the matter of the "assumed conditions of readiness of the United
States." The Black plan called for the reserve fleet to be fully
mobilized within fifteen days after the outbreak of hostilities. The
planners themselves conceded, however, that sixty to ninety days
was a more realistic estimate.[22] Moreover, there were not enough
trained personnel to properly man the reserve ships which would
have to be rapidly commissioned after M-Day. But these were
minor administrative difficulties compared to the problems that
would be created for the Americans if their battle fleet were in the
Pacific or divided between the two oceans. In this case, the General
Board believed that the Germans would be able to seize most of
the Caribbean.

The planners warned the Navy Department that it must "avoid
any normal distribution of the Blue fleet that makes possible the
outbreak of war when the fleet is in the Pacific."[23] They did not
explain how this was to be accomplished while still preparing effectively for the possibility of war with Japan. Had the outside observer been permitted to examine the highly secret war plans which the
navy was perfecting after 1911, he might have been struck by the
fact that the Black plan for war with Germany predicted disaster
if hostilities were to begin with the fleet in the Pacific, while the
Orange plan for war with Japan predicted disaster if war should
find the fleet in the Atlantic. Both plans insisted that the battle fleet

22. "War Plan Black," 51.
23. *Ibid.*, 111.

could not be divided. This schizophrenic outlook was to character-
ize all of the General Board's deliberations upon the disposition of
the fleet until American's entry into the World War.

There were equally cogent reasons for maintaining the battleships in either ocean and the navy's strategists were almost equally
divided over the question. By the end of 1910, the situation was so
confused that the Naval War College was at work upon an elaborate scheme to maintain a Pacific fleet on the West Coast at the
same time that the aide for operations, Rear Admiral Richard
Wainwright, was organizing the battleships into an Atlantic battle
fleet of four divisions.[24]

Secretary Meyer impatiently ordered the War College officers to
keep their mouths shut. The fleet would remain in the Atlantic.[25]
Citizens of the West Coast—like Congressman S. H. Piles of California, who demanded to know when they would see some of the
naval protection for which they were constantly urged to vote—
were blandly assured by Dewey that "a battle fleet in the Pacific
. . . is contemplated when circumstances permit."[26]

At the heart of the navy's dilemma was the unalterable fact that
the strategists did not know, and because of their position could not
know, whether war with Japan or Germany was more likely. This
question was really in the realm of foreign policy. As early as 1908,
when President Roosevelt asked the advice of the Joint Army-
Navy Board on the question of retaining the battle fleet in the
Pacific, Dewey had pointed out that "the question of concentration
depends upon the country's international relations. . . . What
may be the facts determining the country's international relations
only the administration can decide and until this knowledge is
communicated to the Joint Board it cannot intelligently [make]
recommendations."[27]

One way around this difficulty was suggested by a group of
officers at the Naval War College. They proposed a "Council of

24. "Answer of the Reconciling Committee to Question 10, August 31, 1910," enclosure
in Sperry to Wainwright, November, 1910, in Records of the Naval War College.
25. Meyer to Dewey, November 18, 1910, in Records of the General Board.
26. Dewey to S. H. Piles, February 7, 1910, in Records of the General Board.
27. Dewey to Roosevelt, June 4, 1908, in Roosevelt Papers.

National Defense," to be composed of the secretaries of war, state, and the navy; the chairmen of the House and Senate military and naval affairs committees; the chairmen of the foreign relations committees; the chief-of-staff of the army; the aide for operations; and the presidents of the war colleges. The function of this council of national defense was to be nothing less than the coordination of the foreign and defense policies of the United States. The cabinet officers would advise the military men as to current foreign policies, the military men would point out their military implications, and the representatives of Congress would provide the means.[28]

In 1912, a bill embodying these proposals was actually introduced in the House of Representatives by Richmond P. Hobson, the perennial congressional spokesman of the navy. The bill had little chance of passing but the ideas it represented were significant and had they been adopted they might have marked a new approach to political-military collaborations in the United States.

Dewey's approach to the problem was in keeping with his performance in other controversies. As his 1908 letter to the president clearly showed, the admiral was aware that the navy needed some sort of positive political guidance, but he was unwilling to embrace a solution as radical as that proposed by the Naval War College. "It is a fact well understood," wrote Dewey to the president of the War College, "that all commanders should thoroughly understand the [foreign] policy of the country. But since they are the prime instruments of war, and the object of war is to defeat the enemy, and that object is best attained when defeat is complete, a commander-in-chief should rarely be influenced by ulterior motives."[29] For Dewey a council of national defense like a naval general staff seemed too much a departure from traditional American practice to warrant serious consideration.

Although naval questions continued to occupy a good deal of Dewey's time during the Taft years, the admiral also devoted con-

28. F. K. Hill, "Co-ordination Before and During War," Naval War College lecture, 1910; "Report of the First and Second Committees, Summer Conference, 1912," both in Records of the Naval War College.
29. Dewey to president, Naval War College, June 19, 1912, in Records of the General Board.

siderable attention to the preparation of his autobiography. Although the hero of Manila Bay had received numerous letters from publishers urging him to allow them to publish his memoirs, he had taken little interest in the idea until 1911. By that time, as he explained to George Goodwin, "so much incorrect stuff [had] been published that, after much thought, I decided to go ahead."[30]

Frederick Palmer, one of Dewey's favorite journalists from his Manila days, was chosen by Scribners to act as the admiral's ghost. Palmer prepared most of the preliminary drafts based on conversations with Dewey and on documents provided by him. When a chapter was completed the author would take the manuscript to Dewey's house where Palmer, Mildred, and the admiral would all gather in the study to read the work and make comments and corrections. The book appeared in the fall of 1913 and enjoyed a modest popularity. "I hear the Scribner's book has had a good sale, for which I am very glad," wrote the admiral to his son. "I have given the world the true story of Manila Bay."[31]

The *Autobiography* was hardly that. Palmer and Dewey had relied heavily on secondary sources for their account and had deliberately "softened the truth about Prussian brusquerie" at Manila in order to accommodate "Prussian super-sensitiveness."[32] The old admiral disliked "the Dutch" as much as ever, but he had learned the perils of making provocative statements about them to the public.

30. Dewey to George Goodwin Dewey, March 12, 1912, in George Goodwin Dewey Papers.

31. Dewey to George Goodwin Dewey, November 10, 1913, in George Goodwin Dewey Papers.

32. Palmer to Dewey, February 6, 1912, in Dewey Papers.

CHAPTER X

"I Am Only Suffering from Anno Domini"

In November, 1913, Mildred Dewey triumphantly recorded the news that the admiral of the navy "was the only military man" invited to the White House wedding of President Woodrow Wilson's daughter, Jesse. But this signal honor was more an indication of the Democratic president's lack of regard for the military than of his admiration for the hero of Manila Bay. Associates of President Wilson later recalled that he had a "sentimental attachment" to the navy.[1] If so, it was an attachment of a most peculiar kind, for the new president was probably less interested in the army and navy than any chief executive since the 1880s, and his appointment of William Jennings Bryan as secretary of state positively flabbergasted the professionals in both wings of the State, War, and Navy Building, many of whom, like Dewey, considered the Great Commoner "a dangerous revolutionary."[2]

It was, however, the new secretary of the navy, Josephus Daniels, who was ultimately to cause the most consternation and hand-wringing among naval officers. A crusading, progressive newspaper editor from Raleigh, North Carolina, Daniels "entered the Navy Department with a profound suspicion that whatever an admiral told him was wrong and that every corporation with a capitalization of more than $100,000 was inherently evil."[3] He promptly infuriated the seagoing officers with his order banning

1. Braisted, *The United States Navy in the Pacific*, 123.
2. Dewey to George Goodwin Dewey, September 4, 1908, in George Goodwin Dewey Papers.
3. Ernest K. Lindley, *Franklin D. Roosevelt* (Indianapolis, 1931), 56.

191

beer and wine from the wardrooms. Captain Bradley Fiske predicted darkly that this ill-starred measure would soon drive officers to "the use of cocaine and other dangerous drugs."[4] The captain was somewhat ahead of his time.

Strangely enough, Dewey and the secretary of the navy hit it off splendidly from the first. As editor of the Raleigh *News and Observer*, Daniels had vigorously defended Dewey when he was criticized for deeding his house to his wife, and the victor of Manila Bay remained his personal hero.[5] At his first meeting with the General Board, Daniels insisted that the admiral preside while he sat humbly at his right.[6] A warm friendship soon developed between the admiral of the navy and the man he was soon calling "the best Secretary we have ever had."[7] With characteristic flexibility, the admiral, who had rejoiced at the triumph of Theodore Roosevelt in 1904 and the defeat of Bryan in 1908, described himself to Daniels as "in principle a Democrat."[8] Even Mrs. Dewey, who had little good to say about most cabinet couples, had nothing but praise for Mr. and Mrs. Daniels. They remained friends and correspondents for many years after the admiral's death.

The Deweys were even more enthusiastic about young Franklin D. Roosevelt, a cousin of Theodore, who had been appointed assistant secretary of the navy. "The secretary this morning brought his new assistant to call upon me and to see your father's treasures," wrote Mildred to George Goodwin. "Mr. Roosevelt is a very handsome young man . . . most charming and enthusiastic. . . . I predict that if this young man lives he is going far."[9]

The admiral's admiration for the Wilson administration was, however, largely confined to Daniels and Roosevelt. The "New Freedom" domestic measures confused and worried him. "The

4. Fiske, *From Midshipman to Rear Admiral*, 119.
5. Josephus Daniels, *The Wilson Era: Years of Peace* (New York, 1944), 502–503.
6. *Ibid.*
7. Mildred Dewey to Senator Lee S. Overman, February 10, 1917, in George Goodwin Dewey Papers.
8. Daniels, *The Wilson Era*, 50.
9. Mildred Dewey to George Goodwin Dewey, n.d., 1913, in George Goodwin Dewey Papers.

new tariff has been introduced and the President will tell Congress what he thinks of it," he wrote to George Goodwin. "I fear it will hurt your investments."[10] By the end of 1913 Dewey was so worried by "the tariff, hard times, and the high cost of living" that he begged his son not to expend money on Christmas presents for himself and Mildred.[11]

Far more serious matters than the tariff or the high cost of living were on the admiral's mind in 1913, however, for April of that year saw the beginning of another crisis with Japan. As usual, the Californians were at the root of the trouble. Their latest product was a bill, then under consideration in the California legislature, that would prohibit "aliens ineligible to citizenship" from owning land in the state. Since the Japanese, along with the Chinese and the Koreans, were legally ineligible to become citizens, the bill was a thinly veiled slap at the Japanese. When the bill passed the lower house on April 15, 1913, it touched off demonstrations and angry speeches in Japan. In a few days, a full-fledged war scare was on in the United States. "It looks as if the Japanese are determined to find a reason for declaring war on us.," wrote Dewey to George Goodwin; "perhaps they want the Philippines and Hawaii."[12]

Secretary of State Bryan, hurriedly dispatched to the West Coast, was unable to dissuade the Californians from passing the Webb Bill on May 3, 1913. By this time, the General Board was urging the Navy Department to recall all its large ships from foreign stations, prepare the reserve fleet for mobilization, and concentrate the Asiatic fleet at Manila.[13] On the same day that the General Board's recommendations were received by the Navy Department, the Japanese government presented a very urgent and explicit formal protest against the "unfair and discriminatory Act of the California Legislature." The note "used terms as strong as peaceful diplomacy would allow."[14]

The Japanese note was presented to the cabinet on May 13,

10. Dewey to George Goodwin Dewey, April 7, 1913, *ibid.*
11. Dewey to George Goodwin Dewey, December 15, 1913, *ibid.*
12. Dewey to George Goodwin Dewey, April 19, 1913, *ibid.*
13. Dewey to Secretary of the Navy, April 29, 1913, Dewey to F. D. R., May 8, 1913, in Records of the General Board, File 425.
14. Arthur S. Link, *Wilson: The New Freedom* (Princeton, 1956), 296–97.

together with a warning from the General Board drafted by Admiral Bradley Fiske, the aide for operations. In it he predicted the loss of the Philippines, Hawaii, and possibly Alaska in the event of a surprise Japanese attack. The president observed that this was a possibility but that the Japanese would not be able to "keep them."[15] Both the president and Daniels turned down Fiske's request that, as a minimum precaution, the three American cruisers in Chinese waters be withdrawn to the Philippines. They feared such a move might be misinterpreted by the Japanese.

Undeterred, Fiske next turned to the Joint Army-Navy Board. With the help of General Leonard Wood, he succeeded in persuading Dewey and the other members of the board to send an unsolicited letter to the secretary of war, repeating the earlier warnings and recommendations of the General Board and, in addition, recommending that the Pacific fleet be sent to Hawaii.

The effect on Secretary of War Lindley M. Garrison was all that might have been wished, but Daniels was still unimpressed. He refused to join Garrison in endorsing the views of the Joint Board, pointing out, quite correctly, that no conceivable precautions could prevent the ultimate fall of the Philippines in the event of war.[16]

When the cabinet convened again on May 16, the stage was set for a showdown between the two service secretaries. Garrison presented the Joint Board's views, adding that Manila "could be defended for a year" if the ships then in Chinese waters were sent to the Philippines. In the ensuing discussion, Garrison intimated that the views of the civilian cabinet members on military matters "were not very valuable" and that the board members were "the people competent to pass on such matters." This was too much for Secretary Bryan. Growing redder every second, he "thundered out that the military could not be trusted to say what could or couldn't be done 'till we actually got into war . . . if the ships were moved about it might actually bring on war." The president quickly said that there would be no war and that he would accept personal responsibility for keeping the navy's ships where they were.[17]

15. Fiske to Daniels, May 13, 1913, in Fiske Papers, Library of Congress; David F. Houston, *Eight Years in Wilson's Cabinet* (2 vols.; New York, 1926), I, 66–67.

16. Link, *Wilson: The New Freedom*, 297.

17. Houston, *Eight Years in Wilson's Cabinet*, 66–67.

Wilson and Bryan were perfectly correct, of course. Despite their lack of military expertise, they grasped the essential fact, which seemed to elude Fiske, that the risk of war which would result from any provocative moves by the navy far outweighed any marginal advantages that might accrue from these preparations. But Fiske was to prove himself even more obtuse. On May 17, only one day after the cabinet had turned down his proposals, the aide for operations forwarded a second letter to the president against the advice of Secretary Daniels.

The second letter brought down the president's wrath, not only on Fiske, but on the general and joint boards as a whole. Wilson was incensed at what he considered an attempted usurpation by the military of his authority as commander-in-chief. He warned Daniels that any more such incidents would lead him to abolish the joint and general boards. The Joint Board was not to meet again unless convened by personal order of the president. Dewey had not shared Fiske's extreme apprehension, but he had allowed himself to be stampeded into officially backing the admiral's recommendations with the authority of the Joint Board. He therefore shared at least part of the responsibility for the disastrous consequences.

As for the Japanese-American crisis, it finally petered out in a long and futile exchange of notes between Bryan and the Japanese aimed at hitting upon some face-saving formula acceptable to Japan. Such a formula was never found. The Japanese-American crisis made a strong impression on Dewey. It left him with a profound feeling of uneasiness about Japan which he perceived for the first time as a real threat to the United States. "It looks as if the trouble with Japan is over for the present," he confided to George Goodwin in June, 1913, "but I shall not be easy in my mind until the [Panama] Canal is opened and our fleet is in the Pacific."[18]

On June 12, 1913, Admiral Dewey suffered a slight stroke. After a long rest cure, he was again able to resume his duties, but old friends declared that he was never again the man he had been. He no longer attended all the meetings of the General Board which were presided over in his absence by Rear Admiral Charles J.

18. Dewey to George Goodwin Dewey, June 19, 1913, in George Goodwin Dewey Papers.

Badger. In important cases, Badger would take the General Board papers to Dewey's house on Rhode Island Avenue for the admiral's advice and approval. Dewey continued to take an active interest in the work of the board, attending its meetings as often as his health would permit.

An avid newspaper reader, the admiral watched with intense interest the rapidly deteriorating political situation in Europe during the critical summer of 1914. "It seems to me as if this terrible war must, in the end, benefit our people in every way," he wrote to George Goodwin not long after the outbreak of hostilities. "Our people must learn to rely on themselves and not the outside world. We can produce anything we need right here at home and we must learn to do so." The admiral watched with surprise and growing contempt as the much-vaunted German navy remained inactive at its bases. "Germany seems to have her hands full. Her war fleet . . . is content to remain behind mine fields and fortifications. *That is not the way to wage an aggressive war.*" [Italics in original.][19]

Dewey's last years as president of the General Board were not to be peaceful ones. As had often happened before, he was caught up unwillingly, and to some extent unwittingly, in the midst of a great controversy over naval policy. What made the situation even more uncomfortable for the admiral was that the two principal protagonists were both men he liked and admired: his chief, Josephus Daniels, and his younger protégé, Admiral Fiske. As so often before, Dewey managed to give both men the impression that he wholeheartedly supported their views. The long controversy between Fiske and Daniels over the proper development and organization of the navy had begun even before the outbreak of the World War. It soon became entangled in what is usually known to historians as the "preparedness" controversy.

The agitation over "preparedness," meaning, specifically, the preparedness of the armed forces for war, was the product of both legitimate concern over the unprecedented international situa-

19. He wrote to George Goodwin Dewey that he was spending much of his August vacation time reading the newspapers; Dewey to George Goodwin Dewey, August 16, 1914, *ibid.*

tion and the desire on the part of Republicans and navalists to embarrass the Wilson administration. The opening gun of the preparedness battle was a resolution introduced into the House of Representatives by Augustus P. Gardner of Massachusetts, the son-in-law of Henry Cabot Lodge, on October 16, 1914, calling for an investigation of the state of the country's defenses. The instigator of Gardner's proposal was none other than Franklin Roosevelt, the assistant secretary of the navy who, along with Fiske, had supplied the congressman with background information on the navy's deficiencies. Gardner's theme was quickly taken up by Republican politicians and newspapers as well as the pro-navy faction of the House and Senate.

The administration was unimpressed. On November 6, 1914, Daniels advised the General Board that there were to be no references to the European situation in its public recommendations on the building program for 1914–1915. At its meeting in November, Admiral Fiske informed the board that the president had decided that no department was to ask for larger appropriations for the coming year. Both Daniels and Wilson believed that no emergency existed and the secretary did not want "any reference to emergency steps" in the board's paper on the building program which was to be published as an appendix to the annual report of the secretary of the navy.[20]

A heated discussion ensued. Admiral Fiske and his supporters were determined to make some reference, at least, to the navy's chronic shortage of personnel and to what they believed to be the very real possibility of the United States becoming involved in war. To the objection of Rear Admiral Victor Blue that it was the responsibility of the administration to decide whether war was probable, Fiske heatedly replied that the members of the General Board were all experienced men of the world whose average age was fifty-nine years. It was their business "to make our own opinion as to the probability of war and advise the secretary about it."[21]

At this point Dewey offered a compromise. He urged the board

20. "General Board Proceedings," November 6, 10, and 11, 1914, in Records of the General Board; Fiske Diary, November 11, 1914, in Fiske Papers.
21. Fiske Diary, November 11, 1914, *ibid.*

to remove a paragraph on "the immediate need of the Navy for trained personnel" and all references to the World War from its published report. Its views on these subjects could then be submitted to the secretary in a confidential letter. Fiske was disgusted with this "compromise" but once the admiral of the navy had spoken, there was little the aide for operations could say to dissuade the other members of the board from following his lead.[22]

Having succeeded, with Dewey's aid, in muting the alarms of his naval advisers, President Wilson set his face firmly against the preparedness advocates in his annual message to Congress in December, 1914. The president reminded the Congress that the United States was "at peace with all the nations of the world" and that there was no reason to fear a breach with any of the belligerents in the current conflict. "The gravest threats against our national peace and safety," he asserted, "have been uttered within our own borders."[23]

Fiske and his supporters saw another opportunity to publicize their views in the hearings on appropriations before the House Naval Affairs Committee. In his testimony, Fiske declared that "political influences" had so far prevented the navy from reaching maximum efficiency. He blamed the situation on the navy's lack of a general staff and asserted that even if one were established tomorrow, the navy would still need at least five years to become "effective against an effective enemy."[24]

In his own testimony, Dewey was quick to minimize Fiske's charges which, by implication, called into question his own leadership of the navy. In an open letter to Representative Lemuel Padgett, the chairman of the House Naval Affairs Committee, Dewey asserted that "statements that our present fleet is not up to the mark and is being neglected are not true or are greatly exaggerated." American vessels "are as good as any in the world," the admiral observed, but the total fleet was "too small."[25]

Dewey was even less enthusiastic about Fiske's call for a naval

22. *Ibid.*
23. Millis, *Arms and Men,* 215.
24. Fiske, *From Midshipman to Rear Admiral,* 564–65.
25. Dewey to Lemuel Padgett, December 18, 1914, in Dewey Papers.

general staff. This took the form of a bill introduced by Representative Richmond P. Hobson, acting on the advice of Fiske and other insurgents like Dudley W. Knox, Harry S. Knapp, William P. Cronan, and James H. Oliver. Early in January, 1915, these officers met with Hobson to draw up a bill providing for the creation of a chief of naval operations "who, under the secretary of the Navy, shall be responsible for the readiness of the Navy for war and be charged with its general direction."[26] Hobson shepherded the bill through the House Naval Affairs Committee which incorporated it into the Naval Appropriations Bill.

Daniels was furious when he saw the bill, regarding it, not altogether incorrectly, as an attempt to place the direction of the navy in the hands of the professional naval officers. Dewey was even more suspicious of the bill. He feared that the new agency might render the General Board superfluous, and Daniels skillfully channeled the admiral's doubts into public statements against the bill. After Dewey, in direct contradiction to Fiske, had assured Representative Lemuel Padgett that all the navy's war plans could be adequately prepared by the General Board, Fiske and Hobson hurriedly called on the Deweys at home to try and convince the admiral that "this bill will not affect the General Board." Nevertheless, Dewey continued to believe that the General Board might be "pushed out" by the new office.

In the end, Daniels kept the chief of naval operations but got rid of Fiske. The Hobson bill, with important modifications designed to ensure continued control by the civilian secretary, passed the Senate in March, 1915. The following month Fiske resigned as the aide for operations, complaining that the secretary had "treated him with great injustice."[27] Fiske later claimed that Dewey had urged him to stay, but there is no supporting evidence for this in the papers of the protagonists.[28] For the post of chief of naval operations, Daniels chose the affable and unassuming Captain

---

26. For a detailed discussion of the origins of the Office of the Chief of Naval Operations, see Henry P. Beers, "The Development of the Office of Chief of Naval Operations," *Military Affairs* (Spring, 1946), 10–17.

27. Fiske, *From Midshipman to Rear Admiral*, 581.

28. Fiske Diary, April 24, 1915, in Fiske Papers.

William S. Benson, the commandant of the Philadelphia Navy Yard.

In the midst of the internal battles in the Navy Department, Dewey continued to follow the European war with great interest. The sinking of the *Lusitania* and other unarmed vessels by German submarines shocked and angered him. "Germany is behaving outrageously!" he expostulated to George Goodwin. "This comes from her Kaiser, I suppose."[29]

Britain's disregard of traditional maritime international law also aroused his ire. "I hope now the President will call England down on her Orders in Council," he wrote to George Goodwin after Germany, under American pressure, had temporarily called off her submarine campaign. "[They] are nothing more than a paper blockade."[30]

While the German submarine campaign angered Dewey, it failed to impress him with the need to make any changes in American naval plans and preparations. In an article which appeared in the *Scientific American* in July, 1916, Dewey observed that the course of the war had "justified the position of the General Board in continuing to place its chief reliance on big ships." The public, Dewey explained, had "a constant tendency to go off on a tangent in its enthusiasm for that class of ship which at a given time is attracting public attention. Last fall, for instance, the public clamored for many submarines and favored disregarding battleships." The admiral did speak highly of destroyers but discussed them mainly as an offensive weapon to be used against the enemy's battle fleet.[31]

Dewey's views were faithfully reflected by the General Board, which concluded in the fall of 1915 that "undue weight has been given to the submarine as a weapon. . . . At the present time, when the allies have learned in great measure to protect their commerce, as they learnt a few months earlier to protect their cruisers . . . it

29. Dewey to George Goodwin Dewey, July 15, 1915, in George Goodwin Dewey Papers.
30. Dewey to George Goodwin Dewey, September 6, 1915, *ibid.*
31. George Dewey, "Lessons of the Battle of the Skaggerack," *Scientific American*, CXV (July 1, 1916), 10.

is apparent that the submarine is not an instrument fitted to dominate naval warfare."[32]

With relations with Germany strained almost to the breaking point, relations with Britain steadily deteriorating because of the British disregard of neutral rights, and a mounting domestic clamour for "adequate" defenses, President Wilson suddenly reversed himself on the preparedness issue. On July 21, 1915, he ordered his service secretaries to set their military advisers to work on a comprehensive plan for "adequate national defense."[33] The General Board responded three months later with a five-year building program for ten battleships, six battle cruisers, and fifty destroyers at a cost of $100 million.[34] Although he signed the plan, Dewey played almost no part in the drafting of the board's recommendations. The bulk of this work was done by younger activists like Austin M. Knight, William L. Rodgers, and Harry S. Knapp. Nevertheless, the admiral enthusiastically endorsed the plan as "a splendid bill for the Navy."[35]

Small-navy members of the House and Senate were not so enthusiastic. They were deeply troubled by what they viewed as the administration's sudden espousal of rampant navalism. Extremists among the preparedness advocates, like Lodge, Theodore Roosevelt, and Wood, were also dissatisfied. They castigated Wilson's measure as too little and too late. As the criticism of the administration and particularly of Daniels' management of the navy mounted, the secretary called upon Dewey to help in his defense.

It was agreed that the admiral would give an exclusive interview on the state of the navy to George Creel, a prominent journalist friendly to the administration. After extensive backstage preparations, Creel and Dewey met for their three-hour discussion on August 12, 1916, while the House of Representatives was still debating the administration's $100 million naval bill.

The interview, which appeared in six columns on the pages of

32. Grenville and Young, *Politics, Strategy, and American Diplomacy*, 333–34.
33. Link, *Wilson: The New Freedom*, 587–98, and *passim*.
34. For a discussion of the 1916 naval bill, see Braisted, *The United States Navy in the Pacific*, 188–201.
35. Dewey to George Goodwin Dewey, August 22, 1916, in George Goodwin Dewey Papers.

most of the nation's Sunday newspapers on August 20, was an impressive performance. Under a striking picture of the admiral, a large headline read: "DEWEY VIGOROUSLY DEFENDS THE NAVY." Declaring that "the Navy today is more efficient than ever before," Dewey placed the blame for its inadequate size squarely upon the Congress which, over the years, had disregarded the General Board's recommendations. He then proceeded to defend each of Secretary Daniels' innovations. Yes, he favored opening the Naval Academy to enlisted men. Yes, he was in favor of shipboard schools. No, Daniels had not demoralized the navy. That was "Bosh!" "What is all this clamor about a General Staff?" the admiral was asked. "I don't know," replied the old hero. "I've tried to pin them down but no one has been able to make it clear. . . . I suppose down in their hearts they want a small select body to have entire charge of the Navy. . . . I can think of no greater madness.

"I want the people of the United States to know it is all right with the Navy," Dewey finally said at the end of his chat with Creel. "There is no demoralization, no lack of discipline, no absence of enthusiasm. . . . The Navy is more efficient today than ever before."[36]

It was a magnificent performance, albeit one that owed much to Creel's journalistic skill. Although Congress had by this time passed the Naval Appropriations Bill, Dewey's interview was still extremely helpful to Daniels. In effect, the admiral of the navy had placed his immense prestige as a naval authority squarely behind the administration's naval program. "Your fine interview will effectively silence the gossips who have sought to undermine the confidence of the people in their Navy,"[37] wrote Daniels in a grateful letter to Dewey.

Despite his vigorous defense of the secretary and his declaration of Democratic "principles," Dewey strongly favored Charles Evans Hughes for the presidency in 1916 and closely followed the Republican nominee's campaign. "Hughes' speech last night in Chicago was fine," he wrote to George Goodwin. "Believe me he is a fine man." In late October, he predicted that "the West" would be

36. New York *World*, August 20, 1916.
37. Daniels to Dewey, August 20, 1916, in Dewey Papers.

solidly behind the Republican candidate.[38] His political judgment, as usual, was thoroughly faulty. Hughes's failure to carry California proved his undoing, and Dewey glumly contemplated four more years of Wilson in the White House.

On December 26, 1916, the admiral celebrated his seventy-ninth birthday with a small group of naval officers and Secretary Daniels. "I am in fine shape," quipped Dewey, "only suffering from Anno Domini."[39] Two weeks later, on January 11, 1917, he was confined to his bed complaining of severe pains in his back and chest. When he failed to improve, his son was summoned from Chicago. The newspapers were informed on Tuesday, the sixteenth, that the end was near. At 5:56 that afternoon, he was dead.

The body lay in state under the great dome of the Capitol rotunda as congressmen and senators, diplomats and cabinet members filed by. "Many went forward to bow over the calm face of Dewey; generals and admirals with medals dangling from their chests as they bent down, but on Dewey's breast . . . there was but one medal . . . which Dewey wore in reverse to show a gunner stripped for action and the inscription: 'IN MEMORY OF THE VICTORY OF MANILA BAY.' "[40]

"It is pleasant to recall," noted President Wilson in a memorial message to Congress, "the qualities which gave him his well-deserved fame: his practical directness, his courage . . . his readiness to fight without asking any questions or hesitancy about details."[41] Dewey possessed all of these qualities and more, but none of them were adequate for the role of public figure, celebrity, and national monument that he was called upon to play after 1898.

As commander of the Asiatic Squadron Dewey had utilized intelligence and the overwhelming firepower of his fleet to win a dramatic victory in the Philippines. Having routed the Spanish, however, he soon found himself in a delicate political situation which he was ill-equipped to handle. At Manila his impulsive be-

---

38. Dewey to George Goodwin Dewey, August 16, 1916, October 19, 1916, in George Goodwin Dewey Papers.
39. Ellicott, "Contacts with the Hero of Manila Bay," 72.
40. *Ibid.*
41. *Ibid.*

havior toward the Germans and his failure to keep his government advised of the situation nearly resulted in an international crisis. In his dealings with the insurgents Dewey failed at first to understand the aims and nature of the Filipino independence movement. Later, when it became clear to him that the Filipinos were determined to have independence and would fight for it, Dewey wobbled badly on the question of annexation. As he would do in other controversies, the admiral refused to endanger his prestige by taking a public stand on the issue.

During his seventeen years as admiral of the navy Dewey continued the pattern of refusing to wholeheartedly commit himself to controversial issues. He attempted to steer a middle course between the navy's reformers like Sims and Fiske and the conservative bureau chiefs. On issues such as the all-big-gun battleship, the improvement of gunnery in the navy, and Secretary Meyer's reorganization of the Navy Department, Dewey supported the insurgents. On other issues, such as the Newport Conference of 1908 and the general staff, he supported the conservatives. In all of these questions the admiral sought compromise and avoided public controversy. Only on a few issues like the base at Subig Bay and the survival of the General Board, issues with which he felt his prestige to be directly involved, did Dewey commit himself unreservedly.

As a strategist and war planner, Dewey generally embraced a narrow, deterministic view of international politics, typical of the naval officers of his day. This, together with a decided aversion to Germany, prevented him from seeing the shortcomings in the General Board's war plans. With his distaste for controversy, his utterly conventional outlook, and his complete political innocence, Dewey was simply not suited to the role of naval statesman in a world where the simple verities of nineteenth-century Vermont and Annapolis no longer applied.

Bibliography

PRIMARY SOURCES

Private Papers

The most important collections of private papers for purposes of this study are the George Dewey Papers in the Manuscript Division of the Library of Congress, the Diary of Mildred McLean Hazen Dewey, to be found in the same collection, and the Papers of George Goodwin Dewey in the Operational Archives Branch of the Navy Department Naval Historical Center, Washington, D.C. I have noted some of the strengths and shortcomings of these collections in the preface. The modest collection of Dewey Family Correspondence in the Vermont Historical Society contains a small number of very interesting letters from Dewey, most of them written when he was a young officer on the European station in the late 1850s and in the Union Navy during the Civil War. Although few in number, these letters are more personal and revealing than anything in Dewey's later correspondence. The Papers of Nathan Sargent, Dewey's trusted assistant, also contain a few important letters from the admiral, as do the Papers of Henry C. Taylor; both of these rather thin collections are in the Library of Congress.

The voluminous and well-indexed Papers of Theodore Roosevelt and William Howard Taft are also useful, especially concerning the Philippine base controversy. Views of Dewey's contemporaries in the service about the admiral and his policies may be found in the Papers of Stephen B. Luce and Alfred T. Mahan; both are very rich and both are in the Library of Congress. The views about Dewey held by the younger navy reformers may be found in the Papers of William S. Sims and the very candid Diaries of Bradley A. Fiske, also in the Library of Congress. The Papers of Josephus Daniels contain a few items which illuminate the relationship between Dewey and his admiring chief. The Papers of Charles G. Bonaparte, William H. Moody, George von L. Meyer, and Woodrow Wilson were of very limited value. They, too, are in the Library of Congress.

205

Official Records

The voluminous Records of the General Board of the Navy in the Naval Historical Center are, of course, the single most important source for this study. They are complete and tolerably well indexed but still have their drawbacks, as I have indicated in the preface. The most important file areas for the purposes of this study were: File 401.1 General Correspondence; 420.1 Distribution of the Fleet; 420.2 Building Programs; 420.3 Armaments; 420.4 Armor; and 434 Maneuvers. File 425 contains the General Board's "war portfolios," which generally antedate the Black and Orange plans; the color plans themselves are filed separately. Other important collections include the General Records of the Office of Naval Intelligence (National Archives, Record Group 38), particularly the collection of "Cable Correspondence with U.S. Naval Attachés During the Spanish American War, January 20, 1898–November 1, 1899"; the Records of the Office of Naval Records and Library (National Archives, Record Group 45), particularly the Area 10 file, a special collection of documents relating to United States naval activities in the Far East and Pacific; and the Records of the Office of the Secretary of the Navy (National Archives, Record Group 80). The Records of the Joint Army-Navy Board (National Archives, Record Group 225) are, unfortunately, quite thin for this period. The Records of the U.S. Naval War College (National Archives, Record Group 181), in the War College's United States Naval History Research Collection at Newport, Rhode Island, are not, at present, fully organized or indexed; but they are nevertheless an extremely valuable source on the development of strategic thought in Dewey's time.

The Records of the Adjutant General of the Army (National Archives, Record Group 94) shed light on the navy's planning for war with Japan and on the state of interservice cooperation in Dewey's day. Also useful in this regard are the Records of the Army General Staff (National Archives, Record Group 165).

The General Records of the Department of State (National Archives, Record Group 59) contain the consular dispatches from Oscar F. Williams and other American consuls in the Far East and the rather disappointing Records of the U.S. Commission to the Philippine Islands, which shed surprisingly little light on Dewey's role in the commission.

Another important source for the history of the American conquest of the Philippines is Captain John R. M. Taylor's massive compilation of Philippine Insurgent Records (National Archives, Record Group 126), which, however, has only a small number of items directly relating to Dewey.

The U.S.S. Olympia Collection in the United States Army Military History Research Collection, Carlisle, Pennsylvania, is the product of a new and promising program to assemble the memoirs, diaries, photos, and reminiscences of all living Spanish-American War era veterans.

Government Publications

The annual reports of the Navy Department, 1889–1917, are an extremely rich source for all aspects of naval policy during this period. Often running to hundreds of pages, they include transcripts of reports, investigations, and statistics. Of particular usefulness for this study were the Supplement to the Report of the Chief of the Bureau of Navigation, 1899 (Washington, 1899), which contains extensive material relating to operations in the Spanish-American War, and the Report of the Bureau of Equipment and Recruiting, 1889–1893, which describes Dewey's activities as head of the bureau.

   Record of Proceedings of a Court of Inquiry into the Case of Rear Admiral Winfield Scott Schley, USN (2 vols.; Washington, 1902) gives an exhaustive (and exhausting) account of the entire Santiago campaign in the Spanish-American War but conveys little of the atmosphere of the hearings which is more easily obtained from contemporary newspaper accounts. Dewey's account of the Spanish capitulation in the Philippines may be found in "Capture of Manila: A Letter of Admiral Dewey Dated March 31, 1898," *Senate Documents*, 56th Cong., 1st Sess., No. 73, while his confused and sometimes contradictory account of his relations with the insurgents may be found in "Hearings Before the Committee on the Philippines," *Senate Documents*, 57th Cong., 1st Sess., No. 331, Pt. 3. The reaction of the Germans and other foreign powers to Dewey's activities in the Philippines may be found in *Die Grosse Politik der europaischen Kabinette, 1871–1914: Sammlung der diplomatischen Akten des Answartigen Amtes* (40 vols.; Berlin, 1922–1927), XV and XX (cited in the notes as *Die Grosse Politik*).

   Dewey's testimony before Congress was usually even more cryptic and evasive than his published reports, but the *Hearings before the Committee on Naval Affairs, House of Representatives, on Appropriations for 1905 and on H.R. 15403* (Washington, 1904) is useful for Dewey's views on naval administration.

   Documents relating to Dewey's Civil War adventures may be found in the *Official Records of the Union and Confederate Navies in the War of the Rebellion* (30 vols.; Washington, 1894–1927).

Newspapers

The Washington *Post*, New York *Herald*, and New York *Times* were the most reliable barometers of Dewey's popularity during his "Hero of Manila" days (ca. 1898–1900). Other papers consulted were the Columbus *Press Post*, Pittsburgh *Post*, New York *Evening Post*, London *Daily News*, and the New York *World.* Summaries of editorial comment on such episodes as Dewey's abortive campaign for the presidency and his unpopular deeding of his house to his son may be found in the *Literary Digest.*

Letters, Diaries, and Reminiscences

Dewey's own effort, *The Autobiography of George Dewey* (New York, 1913), ghosted by Frederick Palmer, must be used with extreme caution. The admiral could, of course, say little of his service with the General Board since most of that work was still highly confidential. Some brief observations of Dewey in his pre-Manila days may be found in John M. Ellicott, "Contacts with the Hero of Manila Bay," United States Naval Institute *Proceedings* (January, 1950); in Theodore Roosevelt's *Theodore Roosevelt: An Autobiography* (New York, 1915); and in Elting E. Morison (ed.), *The Letters of Theodore Roosevelt* (8 vols.; Cambridge, 1951–54), I.

Memoirs by Dewey's contemporaries that shed light on life in the post-Civil War navy include Alfred T. Mahan, *From Sail to Steam: Recollections of Naval Life* (New York, 1968); Winfield Scott Schley, *Forty-five Years Under the Flag* (New York, 1904); and Caspar F. Goodrich, *Rope Yarns from the Old Navy* (New York, 1931). Two unusually revealing memoirs by Dewey's younger contemporaries are Bradley A. Fiske, *From Midshipman to Rear Admiral* (New York, 1919), and Yates Sterling, *Sea Duty: The Memoirs of a Fighting Admiral* (New York, 1939).

John D. Long's *The New American Navy* (2 vols.; New York, 1903) gives Long's version of how Dewey came to be appointed to the Asiatic Squadron. It should be supplemented by the more candid documents in Gardner W. Allen (ed.), *The Papers of John D. Long* (Boston, 1939).

Of the numerous reminiscences of Dewey's campaign in the Philippines the most important are Oskar King Davis, *Released for Publication* (New York, 1925); Francis V. Greene, "The Capture of Manila," *Century Magazine,* LVII (March–April, 1899); Bradley A. Fiske, *Wartime in Manila* (Boston, 1913); John M. Ellicott, "The Cold War Between Dewey and Diederichs in Manila Bay," United States Naval Institute *Proceedings,* 81 (November, 1955); Frederick Palmer, *With My Own Eyes* (New York, 1934); and Edwin Wildman "What Dewey Feared in Manila Bay," *Forum,* LIX (May, 1915). Andrew D. White, *The Autobiography of Andrew D. White* (New York, 1905), gives the view from Berlin; and H. Wayne Morgan (ed.), *Making Peace With Spain: The Diary of Whitelaw Reid, September–December, 1898* (Austin, 1965) gives the view from the Paris Peace Conference.

Josephus Daniels, *The Wilson Era: Years of Peace* (New York, 1944); E. David Cronin (ed.), *The Cabinet Diaries of Josephus Daniels* (Lincoln, Nebr., 1963), and David F. Houston, *Eight Years in Wilson's Cabinet* (2 vols.; New York, 1926), throw light on Dewey's relationship with Daniels and on the Wilson administration's reaction to the Far East crisis of 1913.

SECONDARY SOURCES

Only works directly utilized for purposes of this study have been included below. My views on those books and articles I thought most important have been given in the footnotes.

Books

Agoncillo, Theodore A. *Malalos: The Crisis of the Republic.* Quezon City, 1959.
Bailey, Thomas A. *Theodore Roosevelt and the Japanese-American Crises.* Stanford, 1934.
Barrett, John. *Admiral George Dewey: A Sketch of the Man.* New York, 1899.
Beale, Howard K. *Theodore Roosevelt and the Rise of America to World Power.* Baltimore, 1956.
Bennett, Frank M. *The Steam Navy of the United States.* Pittsburgh, 1896.
Blum, John M. *The Republican Roosevelt.* Cambridge, 1954.
Braisted, William R. *The United States Navy in the Pacific, 1897–1909.* Austin, 1958.
————. *The United States Navy in the Pacific, 1909–1922.* Austin, 1971.
Brodie, Bernard. *Seapower in the Machine Age.* Princeton, 1940.
Brown, Charles H. *The Correspondent's War.* New York, 1967.
Chadwick, French E. *The Relations Between the United States and Spain: The Spanish-American War.* 2 vols. New York, 1911.
Challener, Richard. *Admirals, Generals and American Foreign Policy, 1898 –1914.* Princeton, 1973.
Clemens, William M. *The Life of Admiral Dewey.* New York, 1899.
Clinard, Outten, J. *Japan's Influence on American Naval Power, 1897–1917.* Berkeley, 1947.
Coletta, Paolo E. *William Jennings Bryan: Political Evangelist.* Lincoln, Nebr., 1964.
Concas y Palau, D. Victor M. *Causa Intruida por la Destruccion de Escuadra de Filipinas y Entreca del Arsenal de Cavite.* Madrid, 1899.
Cooling, B. F. *Benjamin Franklin Tracy: Father of the Modern American Fighting Navy.* Hamden, 1973.
Cosmas, Graham A. *An Army for Empire: The United States Army in the Spanish-American War.* Columbia, Mo., 1971.
Cummins, Damon E. *Admiral Richard Wainwright and the United States Fleet.* Washington, 1922.
Davis, George T. *A Navy Second to None: The Development of Modern American Naval Policy.* New York, 1940.
Dewey, Adelbert. *The Life and Letters of Admiral Dewey.* New York, 1899.
Dunn, Finley Peter. *Mr. Dooley in Peace and War.* Boston, 1899.
Ellis, Edward S. *The Life Story of Admiral Dewey, Hero of Manila, for Boys and Girls.* Philadelphia, 1899.

Friedel, Frank. *Franklin D. Roosevelt: The Apprenticeship.* Boston, 1952.
Gates, John M. *Schoolbooks and Krags: The United States Army in the Philippines.* Westport, Conn., 1973.
Grenville, John A., and George B. Young. *Politics, Strategy, and American Diplomacy: Studies in Foreign Policy.* New Haven, 1966.
Hagan, Kenneth M. *American Gunboat Diplomacy and the Old Navy, 1877–1889.* Westport, Conn., 1973.
Hagedorn, Hermann. *Leonard Wood: A Biography.* New York, 1931.
Halstead, Murat. *Life and Achievements of Admiral Dewey: From Montpelier to Manila.* Chicago, 1899.
Hamm, Margherita A. *Dewey, the Defender: A Life Sketch of America's Great Admiral.* New York, 1899.
Hammond, Paul Y. *Organizing for Defense.* Princeton, 1961.
Hart, Robert A. *The Great White Fleet.* Boston, 1965.
Healy, Laurin Hall, and Luis S. Kutner. *The Admiral.* Chicago, 1944.
Herrick, Walter R., Jr. *The American Naval Revolution.* Baton Rouge, 1966.
Hofstadter, Richard. *Social Darwinism in American Thought.* Rev. ed. New York, 1955.
Hollingsworth, J. Rogers. *The Whirligig of Politics.* Chicago, 1963.
Huntington, Samuel P. *The Soldier and the State: The Theory and Politics of Civil-Military Relations.* Cambridge, 1957.
Janowitz, Morris. *The Professional Soldier.* New York, 1964.
Karsten, Peter. *The Naval Aristocracy: The Golden Age of Annapolis and the Emergence of Modern American Navalism.* New York, 1972.
Knox, Dudley W. *A History of the United States Navy.* New York, 1948.
Lafeber, Walter. *The New Empire: An Interpretation of American Expansion, 1860–1898.* Ithaca, N.Y., 1963.
Langer, William L. *The Diplomacy of Imperialism.* 2nd ed. New York, 1951.
Leech, Margaret. *In the Days of McKinley.* New York, 1959.
Lindley, Ernest K. *Franklin D. Roosevelt.* Indianapolis, 1931.
Link, Arthur S. *Wilson: The New Freedom.* Princeton, 1956.
Mahan, Alfred T. *The Influence of Seapower Upon History, 1660–1783.* 2 vols. Boston, 1894.
———. *Lessons of the War with Spain.* Boston, 1899.
———. *Naval Strategy Compared and Contrasted with the Principles of Military Operations on Land.* London, 1911.
———. *Armaments and Arbitration.* New York, 1912.
Marder, Arthur. *The Anatomy of British Seapower.* Hamden, 1964.
———. *From the Dreadnought to Scapa Flow.* London, 1961.
Marshall, Edward C. *History of the United States Naval Academy.* New York, 1862.

May, Ernest R. *Imperial Democracy*. New York, 1961.

————. *American Imperialism: A Speculative Essay*. New York, 1968.

McCormick, Thomas J. *The China Market: America's Quest for Informal Empire, 1893–1901*. Chicago, 1967.

Millis, Walter. *Arms and Men*. New York, 1956.

————. *The Martial Spirit*. New York, 1931.

Morgan, H. Wayne. *William McKinley and His America*. Syracuse, 1963.

Morison, Elting. *Admiral Sims and the Modern American Navy*. Boston, 1942.

Olcott, Charles S. *The Life of William McKinley*. 2 vols. Boston, 1916.

Palmer, Frederick. *George Dewey, USN*. New York, 1900.

Paullin, Charles O. *Paullin's History of Naval Administration, 1775–1911*. Annapolis, 1968.

Perkins, Dexter. *The Monroe Doctrine, 1867–1907*. Baltimore, 1937.

Pratt, Julius W. *Expansionists of 1898*. Baltimore, 1937.

Puleston, William D. *Mahan: The Life and Work of Captain Alfred Thayer Mahan*. New Haven, 1939.

Root, Elihu. *Military and Colonial Policy of the United States*. Cambridge, 1916.

Schirmer, Daniel B. *Republic or Empire: American Resistance to the Philippine War*. Morristown, 1972.

Spielman, William C. *William McKinley*. New York, 1954.

Sprout, Harold M. and Margaret. *The Rise of American Naval Power*. Princeton, 1939.

Sullivan, Mark. *Our Times*. 4 vols. New York, 1927.

Thayer, William R. *Life and Letters of John Hay*. 2 vols. Boston, 1916.

Thompkins, E. Berkeley. *Anti-Imperialism in the United States*. Philadelphia, 1970.

Vagts, Alfred. *Deutschland und die Vereinigten Staaten in der Welt-Politik*. New York, 1935.

————. *A History of Militarism*. Rev. ed. New York, 1959.

Vivian, Thomas J. *With Dewey at Manila*. New York, 1899.

Weigley, Russell F. *The American Way of War: A History of American Strategy and Military Policy*. New York, 1973.

West, Richard S., Jr. *The Second Admiral: A Life of David Dixon Porter*. New York, 1937.

————. *Admirals of American Empire*. Indianapolis, 1948.

Wolfe, Leon. *Little Brown Brother*. New York, 1961.

Young, Louis S. *Life and Heroic Deeds of Admiral Dewey*. Springfield, Mass., 1899.

Articles

Anderson, Thomas. "Our Role in the Philippines." *North American Review*, CLXX (February, 1900).

Bailey, Thomas A. "Dewey and the Germans at Manila Bay." *American Historical Review*, XLV (October, 1939).

Barrett, John. "Admiral George Dewey." *Harpers New Monthly Magazine*, XCIV (October, 1899).

Beers, Henry P. "The Development of the Office of Chief of Naval Operations." *Military Affairs* (Spring, 1946).

Calkins, Carlos G. "Historical and Professional Notes on the Naval Campaign of Manila Bay." United States Naval Institute *Proceedings*, XXV (June, 1899).

Clifford, John Gary. "Admiral Dewey Visits Chicago." *Journal of the Illinois State Historical Society*, LX (Autumn, 1967).

———. "Admiral Dewey and the Germans: A New Perspective." *Mid-America*, XLIX (July, 1967).

Cooke, A. P. "Naval Reorganization." United States Naval Institute *Proceedings*, XII (October, 1886).

Crosley, Walter S. "The Naval War College, the General Board and the Office of Naval Intelligence." United States Naval Institute *Proceedings*, XXXIX (September, 1913).

Davis, Oskar King. "Dewey's Capture of Manila." *McClure's*, XIII (June, 1899).

Dewey, George. "Lessons of the Battle of the Skaggerack." *Scientific American*, CXV (July 1, 1916).

Ellicott, John M. "The Defenses of Manila Bay." United States Naval Institute *Proceedings*, XXVI (March, 1900).

———. "Effect of Gun-Fire, Battle of Manila Bay." United States Naval Institute *Proceedings*, XXV (June, 1899).

———. "The Naval Battle of Manila." United States Naval Institute *Proceedings*, XXVI (September, 1900).

Eyre, J. K. "Japan and the American Annexation of the Philippines." *Pacific Historical Review*, XI (March, 1942).

Gould, Lewis. "New Perspectives on the Republican Party, 1877–1913." *American Historical Review*, LXXVII (October, 1972).

Greene, Fred M. "The Military View of American National Policy, 1904–1940." *American Historical Review*, LXVI (January, 1961).

Grenville, J. A. S. "Diplomacy and War Plans in the United States,

1890–1917." *Transactions of the Royal Historical Society*, Fifth Series, II (1961).

———. "American Naval Preparations for War With Spain, 1896–1898." *Journal of American Studies*, II (April, 1968).

Heffron, Paul T. "Secretary Moody and Naval Administrative Reform, 1902–1904." *American Neptune*, XXXIX (October, 1969).

Herwig, Holger H., and David Trask. "Naval Operations Plans Between Germany and the United States of America, 1898–1913." *Militargeschichtliche Mitteilungen* (1970).

Holbo, Paul S. "Perilous Obscurity: Public Opinion and Press in the Venezeulan Crisis, 1902–1903." *Historian*, XXXII, 3 (May, 1970).

Livermore, Seward. "American Naval Base Policy in the Pacific." *Pacific Historical Review*, XIII (June, 1944).

———. "Theodore Roosevelt, the American Navy and the Venezuelan Crisis of 1902–1903." *American Historical Review*, LII (April, 1946).

Mahan, Alfred T. "Germany's Naval Ambitions." *Colliers*, XLII, 5 (April 24, 1909).

May, Ernest R. "The Development of Political-Military Consultation in the United States." *Political Science Quarterly*, LXX (June, 1955).

McNair, Frank V. "Our Fleet Maneuvers in the Bay of Florida and the Navy of the Future." United States Naval Institute *Proceedings*, I (1874).

Morton, Louis. "Military and Naval Preparations for the Defense of the Philippines during the War Scare of 1907." *Military Affairs*, XII (Summer, 1949).

———. "War Plan Orange: A Study in Military Strategy." *World Politics*, XI (January, 1959).

Palmer, Frederick. "The Nation's Welcome to Admiral Dewey." *Collier's Weekly*, XXIV (October, 1899).

Sachse, William L. "Our Naval Attaché System: Its Origins and Development to 1917." United States Naval Institute *Proceedings*, LXXII (May, 1946).

Schieber, Clara E. "The Transformation of American Sentiment toward Germany." *Journal of International Relations*, XII (July, 1921).

Seager, Robert II. "Ten Years Before Mahan: The Unofficial Case for the New Navy." *Mississippi Valley Historical Review*, XL (December, 1953).

Shippee, Lester B. "Germany and the Spanish-American War." *American Historical Review*, XXX (July, 1925).

Sims, William S. "The Inherent Tactical Qualities of the All-Big-Gun, Large Calibre Battleship of High Speed, Large Displacement and Gun Power." United States Naval Institute *Proceedings*, XXXII (December, 1906).

Spector, Ronald. "Who Planned the Attack on Manila Bay?" *Mid-America*, LIII (April, 1971).

――――. "Roosevelt, the Navy, and the Venezuelan Controversy, 1902–1903." *American Neptune*, XXXII (October, 1972).

Stickney, Joseph L. "With Dewey at Manila." *Harpers*, XLCII (February, 1899).

Vagts, Alfred. "Hopes and Fears of an American-German War, 1870–1915." *Political Science Quarterly*, LI (March, 1940).

Wainwright, Richard. "The General Board." United States Naval Institute *Proceedings*, XLVIII (February, 1922).

Dissertations

Costello, Daniel J. "Planning for War: A History of the General Board of the Navy, 1900–1914." Ph. D. dissertation, Fletcher School of Law and Diplomacy, 1968.

Nicholson, Philip Y. "George Dewey and the Transformation of American Foreign Policy." Ph. D. dissertation, University of New Mexico, 1971.

Schilling, Warner R. "Admirals and Foreign Policy, 1913–1919." Ph. D. dissertation, Yale, 1954.

Small, Melvin. "The American Image of Germany, 1906–1914." Ph. D. dissertation, University of Michigan, 1965.

Spector, Ronald. "Professors of War: The Naval War College and the Modern American Navy, 1884–1917." Ph. D. dissertation, Yale, 1967.

Index

Adams, Brooks, 133–35
Adams, Charles Francis, 121
Aguinaldo, Emiliano, 44–45, 85–88, 90, 92–94, 97, 102
Alabama, 19
Albatross, 18
Alejandrino, Jose, 88
Almirante Oquendo, 69
Anderson, Thomas M., 71, 90, 91
Andre, Edouard, 84, 90, 92–96, 99
Andrews, Philip, 156
Atlanta, 27
Atlanta *Constitution*, 115
Augustin, Basilio, 53, 55, 56, 62, 64, 93–96

Badger, Charles J., 195–96
Baltimore, 42, 44, 48–50, 58–62, 76, 101, 104
Bancroft, George, 5
Banks, Nathaniel, 15
Barber, Francis M., 80
Barnard, J. O., 12
Barnette, William J., 156–57
Benham, Arthur E. K., 119
Benson, William S., 200
Black, Wilson, 49
Blue, Victor, 197
Blythe, Samuel C., 113
Bonaparte, Charles J., 158–59
Boston, 27, 40, 44, 50, 56, 57
Boston *Herald*, 114
Boyland, Dr., 103
Braisted, William R., 72*n*
Brisbane, Arthur, 114
Brook (mining engineer), 25
Brooklyn, 12, 116, 120
Brownson, Admiral, 163
Bruix, 74
Brumby, J. M., 96

Bryan, William Jennings, 1, 111, 114–16, 137, 191–95
Buck, Solon J., 48
Bülow, Bernhard von, 73, 74
Butler, Ben, 15

Caldwell, H. H., 45, 46 and *n*, 107
Calkins, Carlos G., 56, 58
Camara, Manuel de la, 69–72, 74, 76, 94, 173
Canandaigua, 19
Carlos V, 69
Castilla, 50, 54, 59–60, 62
Castro, Cipriano, 139
Cayuga, 13
Cervera, Pasqual, 69–71, 94, 117, 119
Chadwick, French E., 55, 132
Chambers, Washington Irving, 152*n*
Chandler, William E., 28, 37
Charleston, 42, 81
Chicago, 27
Chicago *Daily Tribune*, 143
Chichester, Edward, 72*n*, 75, 76, 79
Cleveland, Grover, 28, 111
Coghlan, Joseph B., 76, 77*n*, 95–96, 104
Cole, O. H., 65–66
Colon, 69, 120
Colorado, 10
Columbus *Press Post*, 115
Colwell, John C., 69, 80
Concord, 42–44, 56, 57, 77, 104
Connecticut, 171–72
Converse, George E., 157
Cooke, A. P., 124
Cormoran, 74
Cowles, William S., 145
Cox, George, 30, 31
Creel, George, 201–202
Cronan, William P., 199

215

218   *Index*

McClure, S. S., 115
McCulloch, 47, 50, 55–56, 64, 78, 88
Machias, 41
McKinley, William, 1, 2, 35–38, 43, 67, 99, 106, 110–12, 118, 137, 139
Maclay, Edgar Stanton, 117
McLean, John R. (brother-in-law), 111, 115, 116
McLean, Washington, 107
McNair, Frank G., 22
McNair, Frederick G., 38, 41–43
Mahan, Alfred T., 21–22, 39, 125, 129, 148–49, 176–77, 184
Maine, 1, 40, 43, 53
Manassas, 14–15
Manila, 54
Mantey, Edward von, 147*n*
Marble, Frank, 161
Maria Teresa, 69
Marques del Duero, 54
Massachusetts, 29, 105
Merritt, Wesley, 92–95
Metcalf, Victor I., 160
Meyer, George von Lengerke, 180–83, 185–86, 188, 204
Michigan, 175
Miles, Nelson A., 104, 137, 164
Millis, Walter, 179
Milwaukee Journal, 115
Mississippi, 10–18, 27
Mocke, Horace J., 113
Mohican, 42
Monadnock, 70, 71, 82
Monocacy, 40, 41, 43–44, 47, 48
Monongahela, 16–18
Monterey, 69–71, 81, 82, 94
Montojo, Patricio, 50, 54, 55, 59
Moody, William H., 138, 140, 146, 154–55, 158, 164
Morgan, Casey, 96
Morris, Henry W., 13
Morton, Paul, 158
Moseley, R. A., 111

Nanshan, 47
Narragansett, 20
National Life Insurance Company, 4, 24
Newark Evening News, 145
Newberry, Truman H., 158, 161
New York, 105
New York Evening Post, 86
New York Herald, 64, 103, 108, 173, 176
New York Journal, 64, 114

New York *Times*, 103, 104, 109, 114, 115, 146
New York *Tribune*, 141
New York *World*, 1, 110, 113, 115
Noriel, Mariano, 93
North Dakota, 177

Obenheimer, Captain, 76–77
Oliver, James H., 199
Oliver, Robert Shaw, 162
Olympia, 40, 42–44, 50–51, 56–61, 78, 87–88, 95–96, 100–102, 104–105
Oregon, 28, 72, 173
Otis, Ewell S., 99

Padgett, Lemuel, 198–99
Palmer, Frederick, 89, 103, 109, 190
Parker, James, 118
Patriota, 69
Pelayo, 69
Pensacola, 13, 14, 22 and *n*, 27
Petrel, 40, 58, 62, 86, 87, 95
Philadelphia, 30
Philadelphia *Times*, 114
Philippines: planning for and capture of Manila, 2, 33, 35, 36, 52, 62, 68, 72*n*, 89, 91–97, 99–100; Spanish fleet in, 43, 45, 49–55, 58–62, 64, 68–72, 74, 76; insurgent actions in, 44–47, 68, 76, 80, 83–99, 102, 104; U.S. intelligence operations in, 44–47, 51–52, 84–85, 90, 98; and Manila defenses, 46, 49–54, 55, 57–58, 62, 68*n*; and Battle of Manila Bay, 53–63, 72, 203; as territory coveted by foreign powers, 68, 72–74, 79–82; and Spanish reaction to Manila disaster, 69–72; and annexation question, 83, 85–92, 98–100, 111, 204; Philippine Commission appointed, 98–100 and *n*, 112; and Manila versus Subig Bay as base, 165–69, 182
Pillsbury, John E., 140
Pillsbury, Samuel, 150–51
Pinola, 13
Porter, David Dixon, 20, 22, 122
Pratt, Spencer, 88, 102
Prinzess Wilhelm, 74
Proctor, Redfield, 1, 27, 28, 37, 38, 39, 66, 83, 98, 104, 111
Pulitzer, Joseph, 110

Quadt, Wilhelm von, 143

Raleigh, 41, 44, 57, 59, 77 and *n*, 95, 105
Raleigh *News and Observer*, 192